WITHDRAWN

Social Work with Older People

Social Work in Theory and Practice

Ann McDonald, *Social Work with Older People*
Roger Smith, *Social Work with Young People*

Social Work with Older People

ANN McDONALD

polity

First published in 2010 by Polity Press

Polity Press
65 Bridge Street
Cambridge CB2 1UR, UK

Polity Press
350 Main Street
Malden, MA 02148, USA

ISBN-13: 978-0-7456-3955-0
ISBN-13: 978-0-7456-3956-7 (paperback)

A catalogue record for this book is available from the
British Library.

Typeset in 9.5 on 12 pt Utopia
by Servis Filmsetting Ltd, Stockport, Cheshire
Printed and bound in Great Britain by
MPG Books Limited, Bodmin, Cornwall

The publisher has used its best endeavours to ensure that
the URLs for external websites referred to in this book are
correct and active at the time of going to press. However,
the publisher has no responsibility for the websites and can
make no guarantee that a site will remain live or that the
content is or will remain appropriate.

Every effort has been made to trace all copyright holders,
but if any have been inadvertently overlooked the
publisher will be pleased to include any necessary credits
in any subsequent reprint or edition.

For further information on Polity, visit our website:
www.politybooks.com

Contents

Introduction

Social work with older people is a complex enterprise. The legal framework within which decisions are made is less coherent and more diverse than that for working with children or with other adults – for example, those with mental health problems, or those who are described as 'disabled' for the purpose of service provision. This means also that the value base of working with older people has been less explicit, and principles of decision-making have been less prescribed by formal procedures and policy statements. Historically, this has meant that the social work task has had the potential to be creative and imaginative in a way in which it perceives situations, and proposes responses to them. There is considerable scope here for the practitioner to compensate for formal service neglect by finding ordinary-life solutions to the isolation, distress or aspirations of older people – an approach which is very congruent with contemporary notions of the personalization of services in the context of individual choice and empowerment. Because 'older people' are a diverse group of services users, with different accumulations of experience over a lifetime, social work with older people must necessarily be based on an understanding of biography, past and present strengths and established personal and social networks. So, all the diversity of social work practice is brought together in work with older people – and this is a professional strength when agency practice tends increasingly towards a narrow specification of outcomes, and a managerialist approach to processing workloads.

The book is divided into three parts. Part I, 'The Context of Social Work Practice with Older People', covers chapters 1–3. It examines the demographic position of older people, and the significance of different approaches to ageing. Older people's views on the process of ageing are, of course, the most potent, and are expressed through literature as well as through research and political activity. Social work is also a changing profession, and its definition is contested, as the roles and tasks of social work are to a large extent shaped by the policy context in which they operate. Movement from a welfare state model of service provision, where services are directly provided by the state, to an enabling model, where a multiplicity of providers are commissioned to provide a service, has been the key feature of the era of community care. Social workers in this era have become service brokers in a mixed economy of care. The emphasis currently is on partnership between organizations and between service sectors, and on opportunities for the personalization of care through greater use of individual budgets. This means that at all levels social work with older people is in a state of flux, and major issues of principle remain to be settled.

The social work process is the focus of Part II, 'Social Work Processes', which is contained within chapters 4–6. The processes of assessment, care planning and monitoring and review are described in an examination of key concepts of risk, protection and capacity. *The National Service Framework for Older People* (DH, 2001) has given greater prominence to intergenerational equity, focused service provision and holistic assessment, stylized within the Single Assessment Process for Older People. Subsequent care planning requires careful matching of needs and resources, but must also be about desired outcomes and the quality of services. Monitoring and review are particularly important stages in care management for older people whose situation and needs can fluctuate considerably within short periods of time.

Individual, group and community issues are the subject-matter of Part III, 'Social Work Methods and Interventions', chapters 7–9. All social workers have to demonstrate competence in the key roles of social work during qualifying training (TOPSS, 2002). Working with individuals, groups and communities are ways in which essential skills within the key roles for qualifying social workers can be evidenced, but as sites for the development of competence they are not mutually exclusive. Similarly, post-qualifying training, though based on specialisms, enables competence to be consolidated and then enhanced in a range of settings, utilizing workplace learning, but allowing links to be made between individual, group and community interests and concerns. In work with individuals, particular attention is given to therapeutic interventions, an often-neglected opportunity in work with older people. Similarly, work with families may be particularly appropriate as existing relationships are challenged by ill health, or by the reconstitution of families in older age. When the social group is a residential setting, relationships between staff and residents need to be carefully balanced alongside relationships between residents and significant others. Diverse communities pose different challenges for older people – for example, in urban or rural settings – and also provide qualitatively different opportunities for change on a scale that cannot be achieved by individual action alone. With evidence that the well-being of older people is dependent upon social engagement, community support is an important skill for social workers to develop.

This book is intended for use both by qualifying students who are looking at the application of social work theory in relation to work with older people, in a generic course, and by post-qualifying students undertaking specialist training who are consolidating their knowledge of social work with adults, and specifically with older people at a specialist level and beyond. Though the focus is on social work practice and values, a range of other professional groups working with older people may find the knowledge base contained in this book helpful in understanding concepts with which they work and the context in which change for older people takes place.

PART I

THE CONTEXT OF SOCIAL WORK PRACTICE
WITH OLDER PEOPLE

1 The Demographic and Theoretical Framework

Issues considered in this chapter:

- theories of ageing and their implications;
- the demographic profile of older people in the UK;
- the importance of knowledge about disability and mental health for work with older people;
- the context within which social work with older people takes place.

The practice of social work with older people requires an understanding both of the experience of ageing and of the particular skills and knowledge needed to evaluate and respond to the needs of older people. A key foundation for work with older people is an understanding of gerontology (Phillips et al., 2006). Gerontology describes the process of ageing from a number of perspectives: biological, psychological, social and cultural. Each perspective informs, whether consciously or unconsciously, our own experience of ageing and our sense of the status and needs of older people. Thus the 'meaning' of the ageing process is a contested concept, with the consequence that a social work perspective on individual 'cases' or services or organizations may be informed by a variety of different perspectives. Conflicting images, both public and private, are generated of older people: some are constructed through the use of language, some emanate from the views of older people themselves and some are given credence by the way in which the natural sciences and social sciences have dealt with old age (Victor, 2005). So the context within which social work with older people takes place is in itself a source of debate. In addition, social work with older people takes place in a range of locations: in the community, in hospitals and hospices, in residential and day-care settings, and within statutory, voluntary and private sector organizations. The key issues of citizenship, well-being, care and protection which resonate with older people are also the topics which are most susceptible to changes in social theory and social policy. Social work with older people is therefore likely to be both a highly politicized activity and one which requires a personal, reflective approach to individual biography.

Theories of ageing: their source and impact

Theories of ageing have themselves developed within the broader context of political ideologies and theories for understanding social phenomena such as the family, employment and healthcare systems (Thane, 2000). Differential experiences relating to gender, race and disability mean that the assumption of homogeneity amongst older people is a false premise. The strengths and deficits of older people currently are also shaped by past opportunities and losses across the lifecourse, leading to inequalities in older age. Demographic changes due to increasing longevity also raise issues of intergenerational equity, in the meaning of citizenship and in the distribution of resources. The challenge of understanding ageing requires consideration of the 60-year-old black urban gay man recently retired from a managerial position, and the 90-year-old widowed white woman who lives in an isolated rural community (see the case profiles for details). These cases will be referred to throughout this chapter. Adam Broad and Carrie Davies represent different generations of older people, and also different life histories and future challenges. Both are 'older people', but while Adam is considering an active role in the community, Carrie is ostensibly cast in the role solely of a recipient of care from others.

Case profile

Adam Broad is 60 years old. He was born in Trinidad, the oldest of three children. When he was 10 years old his parents moved to the UK to work, leaving Adam and his sisters with their grandparents. Five years later, Adam and his two sisters joined them in London. Adam went to college and qualified as an accountant, a job from which he has recently retired. Adam's mother (now aged 90) lives with one of his sisters; the other sister has returned to Trinidad. Adam is gay and has had a number of short-term relationships, but is currently single. He lives alone in a flat which he owns. He considers himself to be reasonably well-off and he has a wide circle of friends. He is involved in a number of community groups and he is also considering part-time employment, not necessarily in a paid capacity, but possibly working with older people.

The social worker who works alongside either of the individuals described in the two case studies presented here will need an understanding not only of theories about the client's world, but also of theories for practice – theories which support decision-making and effect change. Such theories exist on a spectrum from individual/therapeutic, through reformist/liberal to collectivist/social justice (Payne, 2005). The target for intervention may be the individual, the group, the community or the wider socioeconomic or political structure. The type of knowledge most valued by the worker may be technical/rational or

Case profile

Carrie Davies is 90 years old; she had one daughter who died in childhood. Carrie's husband was a farm labourer. Carrie also worked on the land when work was available. When her husband was evicted from their tied cottage, the family went to the workhouse for six months until he could find work and new accommodation. Carrie currently lives in a council bungalow in a small village five miles from the nearest town. She has rheumatoid arthritis and walks with a frame. She has daily homecare visits, but the carers are concerned that Carrie is increasingly forgetful, is refusing meals and will not let them help with personal hygiene.

constructivist. Taking the former position, the social worker would look to an evidence-base located in law and in formal policy documents, with a focus on problem-solving outcomes. A constructivist approach seeks to understand and work from the inner world of the individual, and here social workers may draw more obviously on their own experience, working reflexively, to apply learning from this case to future cases, building up a body of 'practice knowledge'. Transformationist approaches, on the other hand, look beyond individual experience and are radical in their use of collective strengths to bring about social change. A focus on older peoples' own understanding of their situation shifts power from the social worker as professional, to that of the service user as expert, or the collectivity of older people as effective social actors in their own right.

Processes, as well as outcomes, need to be considered in social work with older people. As well as achieving a desired 'final' outcome, such as sustaining an individual within the community, the process by which this is accomplished – being sensitive to particular cultural needs, or appropriately supporting carers – may be the focus of concern. But from a radical perspective, simply sustaining an individual within the community may be too conservative an outcome; involving that individual, or group, in strategic planning to have direct control over resources may be the desired measure of success. The social worker's role as agent of change may thus be interpreted and operationalized in different ways according to the orientation of the worker and the opportunities available within the organization within which they are located.

This chapter looks at demographic changes and theories of ageing. It looks at different images of older people and how, and by whom, they are constructed. A developmental lifecourse approach to ageing examines cultural, economic and psychosocial changes which impact on older people. Opportunities and diversity in old age describe in positive terms the ways in which change can be channelled to enhance the experience of ageing. The form and context of anti-oppressive practice with older people is explored in order to describe the potential of the professional agenda to enhance the status of older people.

Demographic changes

Demographic changes internationally as well as nationally show that populations are ageing. The UK 2001 Census of Population (ONS, 2003) showed that there were more than 11 million people in the UK aged 65 and over, and that 18.6 per cent of the population was over pensionable age. If we take into account the planned equalization of retirement ages, the number of people over pensionable age will be about 15.2 million by 2031. Living alone is a feature of older age, and, in 2001, 29 per cent of men and 60 per cent of women aged 75 and over were living on their own. The economic position of older people shows considerable diversity. Pensioners living alone who are dependent on state pensions spend 41.9 per cent of their income on housing, fuel and food. At the same time, 56 per cent of owner-occupiers without a mortgage are 65 and over, and people over the age of 65 own 80 per cent of the nation's wealth in savings and pensions. Older people are major users of health and social care services and dominate statistics for GP consultations, inpatients and residential care costs. They are also more likely to vote in elections than younger people in the UK (82 per cent of those aged 65 and over voted at the 2001 general election compared to 43 per cent of those aged 18–24), but in other respects they may be excluded from participation in public life. Therefore, it is true to say that older people occupy a strategic civil, economic and political position, the ramifications of which will pose major issues for policy-makers and service providers. It also means that debates about the 'meaning' of old age in terms of citizenship, rights and individual well-being are ripe for debate.

The ageing population is without cultural precedent. The growth in numbers of very old people is striking: in 2005, there were 410,700 UK residents aged 90 or over – an increase of 22 per cent over 2002. In the 1960s, there were fewer than 300 centenarians; in 2004, there were more than 6,000 people over the age of 100. Although the UK has a lower proportion of its population aged 65 and over (one in six) than many other European nations, it has a higher proportion aged 85 and over than, for example, France, Germany and Portugal (Grundy, 2006). In 2003–5, a man of 65 could expect to live for a further 16.5 years, and a woman of the same age for a further 19.4 years. The category of older age thus covers a wide age span, and increased longevity means that the years beyond 65 will be a time of development and change. In 1916, there were 28 per cent more women than men aged 50 and over in the UK; in 2005, there were only 16 per cent more women than men, and the gap is closing. The feminization of old age will therefore become less relevant. Minority ethnic groups, however, have a younger age structure compared to the white population. One in three of the white British population is aged 50 or over, while just one in ten of the Asian and black or black British populations fit this profile. However, former patterns of immigration mean that one in four of the black Caribbean population is now aged 50 or over.

Geographically, the older population is unevenly dispersed, with a higher proportion above state pension age in Cornwall and Wales and along coasts, and a lower than average concentration of older people in London and in Northern Ireland. Planning services for these groups will provide different challenges and possibly different outcomes, reflecting the diversity of past lives and future prospects. So Adam Broad's current situation locates him culturally within a cohort of people on the threshold of older age, who provide significant support for those who are the 'fourth age' (Laslett, 1972). Gender and ethnicity will also impact upon the experience of older age. Carrie Davies, one of our case studies, will face poverty, isolation and the likelihood of mental disorders that affect people in old age. The Audit Commission (2008) gives guidance to local authorities on preparing for an ageing population through increased awareness of such issues and better engagement with older people to shape both universal and targeted services.

Understanding ageing in social theory

Lymbery (2005) uses a framework developed by Beattie (1994) to categorize different ways of understanding ageing as structural/organizational, professional/cultural, and interpersonal. These categories will be used here to explore different ways of thinking about the significance of age, or, more precisely, the way in which social science has dealt with old age, politics and power (Vincent, 1999). It must however be recognized that theory development is itself a social enterprise (Kuhn, 1962) shaped by historical, institutional and professional contexts. The ascendancy or demise of different theories of ageing thus will be influenced by changes in the age structures of nations, changes in governmental expectations and responsibilities, the extension of the lifecourse, and changes in family structures and relationships (Marmot, 2004). There is a broad distinction between consensus theories of social functioning and conflict theories.

The consensus theory of social functioning is represented by functionalism (Parsons, 1991). From a functionalist perspective, the maintenance and integration of social networks for the preservation of consensus is the primary goal. Within this perspective, the transition of power from older people to a younger generation necessitates a social and personal adjustment to changes and losses in social roles. So, Cumming and Henry's (1961) 'disengagement theory' describes the seemingly inevitable, but also desirable, withdrawal of older people from public and social life. As such, functionalism provides a justification for age-segregated policies such as retirement, and the rationing of health and social care services to older people. Structural factors such as income and accrued health status differentially affect the experience of old age as a continuation of earlier life choices. 'Successful ageing' within the functionalist paradigm is best represented by Havighurst's (1963) activity theory, which places a premium on continuity and preservation of the attitudes and activities of middle age in order to keep physically and mentally healthy. So Adam Broad, by remaining socially if not economically active in older age, consolidates his acquired social standing, while contributing to the economically useful function of freeing up employment opportunities for younger people.

Economic theories potently impact upon the experience of older people, so political economy perspectives examine the relationship between economic and political forces in determining how resources are allocated and 'deserved', with less productive older people relegated to a marginalized position. In social policy terms, the democratic state will compensate for the negative outcomes of ageing within capitalist societies by providing pensions, social housing and residual social care services, but only to the extent that is necessary to preserve minimal social cohesion. The individual is seen as a unit of consumption within a political economy perspective. Such marginalization creates a structured dependency for older people (Townsend, 1981) who have to accept the state's retirement policies, income inequalities and the passivity of state community care policies. At the same time, economically stronger older people are also consumers of service goods. Hence the development of private markets in care has been a feature of political economy-driven responses to growing numbers of older people with more spending power of their own.

The growth of consumerism within a neo-liberal political agenda, supported by both the New Right of the 1980s and the New Labour government that came to power in 1997, is seen as disempowering older people who may lack the resources or the ability to exercise choice (Vincent, 1999; Higgs, 1997). The social and medical needs of older people are, through consumerism, transformed into commodities for specific markets such as private provision of health and social care services (Estes, 1979). The focus on the individual or family unit displaces collective obligations to older people. Carrie Davies, who has no family, is likely therefore to experience a residual welfare provision in her older age which is governed by economic imperatives.

Conflict theories expose class and gender divisions in society by focusing on the continuation into old age of earlier inequalities. Older people form an undervalued and marginalized group chiefly because they are no longer economically active, and so receive a more meagre allocation of society's goods. Estes (2001) critiques the social construction of old age as the product of economic, social, political and cultural forces, operating at a structural and organizational level. For women like Carrie Davies, widowhood is, in addition, likely to lead to economic loss – her status as a single person is different in quality from that of the planned retirement of Adam Broad. Notions of 'hierarchy' and 'duty' serve to perpetuate age-based social structures, within which the interests of older people are not only not recognized, but in some instances are actively suppressed. Individual experience is to be understood by the way in which the lifecourse is structured: the identity of someone with a full-time job at 70 is coloured by the fact that others of that age do not have such jobs.

This devaluation of advanced age will also affect organizations working for and with older people as part of an 'ageing enterprise' which sets apart older people from other groups in society. The status of social work with older people will be dependent upon the status that its users have in society, as the identity of associated groups is linked with those seen as less integrated into the mainstream. Social workers with older people may therefore be structurally disadvantaged within their own organizations in terms of esteem and resources because of the social and economic status of those with whom they work.

This focus on the structured dependency of older people as a class has been criticized by Gilleard and Higgs (2006) for ignoring the differential experience of individuals, and particularly the intersectionality of gender, race and class. The concept of critical gerontology (Phillipson, 1998) brings together the political economy perspective and a recognition of the importance of these other sources of oppression. Critical gerontology enables us to differentiate the experiences of Adam Broad and Carrie Davies. Such an approach acknowledges the potency of individual biography in locating sources of disadvantage in structural factors, while acknowledging individual resilience and strengths. Gubrium (1993) thus advocates the use of narrative in understanding the experiences of individual ageing as influenced by social definitions and societal structures within an interpretive paradigm. 'Labelling' Carrie Davies as a person in the early stages of dementia objectifies her situation, and obscures the personal experiences of loss, poverty and hardship with which she is overwhelmed in older age, which themselves may be the focus of social work intervention.

Biological ageing and body politics

Vincent discusses the importance of body politics, professional politics and party politics for older people in the UK: old age is 'political' because 'old age has been used in all societies as a way of differentiating people, in modern Britain it forms part of the power structure by which collective life is ordered' (1999: 7). Biological ageing itself is subdivided into a number of different theories which seek to explain physical changes over time. Cellular ageing focuses on the curtailment of DNA replication in explaining physical decline in old age. Developmental theories of ageing see this decline as pre-programmed either by genetics or by evolutionary senescence – the process of natural selection which accelerates in the period post-reproduction. Stochastic theories of ageing attribute causation to an accumulation of insults from the environment, leading to failure of basic functions. Therein lies the possibility of delaying the loss of function by adapting the environment, by taking exercise, by appropriate nutrition or by avoiding harmful substances. In this way, biological ageing may have a social component, and could therefore be a matter for public as well as private concern. Much of the current focus on well-being reflects a concern to delay the biological ageing process – publicity for cosmetic treatment reflects a desire to disguise that process.

Though biological ageing may be medicalized as an involuntary phase, distinguished by disease and decline (Victor, 2005), the ageing body is seen also as something on which culture can be inscribed. Control over the body and maintenance of a youthful appearance are seen as key cultural attributes of adulthood (Featherstone and Hepworth, 1989). In a similar way, mental impairment which leads to inability to communicate in a manner that is seen as fully adult infantilizes older people and threatens their identity. This decline of the body and mind gives power to professionals, and in addition acts as a barrier to adult discourses on difficult topics such as death and dying (Hockey and James, 1993).

Psychosocial theories of ageing

Psychological theories of ageing may focus either on cognitive abilities, personality development; or psychological interactions. Though there is evidence that fluid abilities such as learning, memory and spatial ability decline with old age, 'crystallised' abilities are stronger (Coleman and O'Hanlon, 2004). So although it may be more difficult to learn 'new tricks', the strengths and resiliencies built up over a lifetime pay dividends in old age. Personality traits (neuroticism, extroversion, openness to experience, agreeableness and conscientiousness) become more pronounced in old age as we become 'more ourselves'. It is the development of personality through relationships with others which here defines the psychosocial.

Social exchanges, within which individuals weigh up the balance between personal gains and losses in relationships, change and may become less frequent as people grow older. Social circles may narrow, but emotional closeness often grows between those who remain within a relationship. So, couples and families may become closer as members age. Carstensen's socioemotional selectivity theory (1992) explains how older people focus on fewer, but stronger, emotional attachments. Managing the dynamics between gains and losses is a major challenge for older age. Focusing on positive achievements, 'making the best of what one has left', and compensating for lost functions or declining strengths, has been theorized by Baltes and Carstensen (1996) as 'selective optimization with compensation', protecting and developing the self at a time of adversity. Selective optimization has become a key theoretical construct for understanding the ways in which older people are able to adapt to physical impairment or cognitive decline, and is the basis for much social work intervention. So utilization of the theory of selective optimization would support the development of assistive technology to enable older people to continue to carry out activities of daily living and to maintain some independence. Enabling older people to focus on existing strengths such as musical ability or creative writing may also be harnessed with the benefit of maintaining ties with the wider community.

The lifecourse

As well as chronological ageing, the idea of the lifecourse covers all of historical, biological and social time (Laslett, 1972). So instead of taking a staged lifespan approach based around psychosocial tasks such as that described by Erikson (1980) and Levinson (1986), lifecourse approaches recognize that roles such as parent, student and worker may happen in a different order for different people, or may not happen at all. Utilizing the idea of lifecourse, rather than lifespan, frees individuals from a deterministic view of what are appropriate actions and feelings at different ages. Nevertheless, there are key ways in which we can describe experiences within the lifecourse. One is by the use of the word 'generation' to describe a position within the family that is linked to a particular role such as being a grandparent; another is by reference to 'age cohorts', or groups of people assumed to have a common identity because they have lived through the same period of history (Evandrou and Falkingham, 2000). Within the lifecourse, significant transitions may occur which require adaptation, such as bereavement, illness and retirement. In this way, individuals' assessment of their own well-being is not only related to the here-and-now, but to an evaluation of this event in the context of their opportunities and achievements over the lifecourse (Godfrey et al., 2004)

The way in which the past contributes to our sense of ageing is expressed through biography. Victor has described this interpretivist view of old age as 'an understanding of the meaning and interpretation of the events which accompany old age and which are articulated and defined by older people' (2005: 35). Yet older people do not approach this task in a vacuum. Like all social actors, they construct meaning by a process of social interaction. Thus, symbolic interactionism (Mead, 1934) attributes roles such as 'carer' and 'cared for' to a set of interactions between individuals in a specific social and cultural context. Social networks similarly contribute to the development of the self through a process of exchange, involving family and wider networks (Godfrey et al., 2004).

Such social roles may be comfortably assumed, and individuals may readily adopt the designation of either 'carer' or 'older citizen', or these labels may be rejected. Gender differences may be relevant to the ease with which new social roles are developed in older age. There is evidence that women needing assistance in older age may be more skilled than men in eliciting social support in a way which supports autonomy rather than creates dependence (Ogg, 2003). Gender as a major organizing principle across the lifecourse makes the accumulated experience of women in older age fundamentally different from that of older men. Similarly, different cultural traditions will prepare people for older age in different ways, reflecting different family forms and individual expectations. So Adam Broad's sister's return to Trinidad reflects a desire to reconnect with early sources of identity, while another sister has assumed the role of carer for an ageing parent.

Adaptation in older age

Ogg's (2003) research into role adaptation in old age has also shown the relationship between psychological and social factors; so, loneliness is mediated both by earlier life experiences in the psychological management of living alone and by the frequency of social contacts. By adapting to transitions in this way, Giddens sees older people as achieving 'reflexivity', which he defines as 'a project of the self, which consists of the sustaining of coherent, yet continuously revised, biographical narratives' (1991: 5). Protection of the self against public negative images of ageing is achieved, it is suggested, by the construction of a 'mask' or 'disguise' to establish the distance between the personal experience of ageing and the stereotype of old age (Featherstone and Hepworth, 1989). This may be achieved through the use of cosmetics or surgery, to disguise the physical effects of the ageing process. The medicalization of the ageing process may itself be a form of denial by the transformation of images of decay into images of disease (ibid.: 317) and the search either for cure, or for containment of older people whose physical or mental decline cannot be denied.

How do people understand the experiences of older age? Research by Townsend et al. (2006) explored the views of older people themselves. Contrasting images were observed between 'those like us' – the heroines of old age – and the 'others', seen as the 'villains' who refused to be helped or who took without giving back. The 'victims' of old age were primarily people with dementia, who were seen as objects of pity and concern. Thus we see how older people incorporate societal stereotypes of ageing into their own self-management of the ageing process as they describe how private and public images of living a dignified old age are linked. As a consequence, the personal and the public status of older people are not separate, but related issues.

Successful ageing

Health inequalities, poverty and social isolation are structural factors that will affect the life chances of older people. Grundy (2006) describes the ability to cope with life chances in old age in terms both of a threshold of 'reserve capacity' acquired through the lifecourse, and compensatory interventions in times of crisis and in the longer term. Hence the importance both of universal preventative services and of targeted and timely health and social care interventions. Past deprivations, inequalities and relationship difficulties will continue to have an impact in older age and will therefore be an important part of the assessment of needs and resilience.

There is increasing interest in how to age 'successfully' and in reaching consensus over its definition (Bowling and Iliffe, 2006). There are a number of different models. Biomedical models focus on the ageing body and count the number of diagnosed chronic medical conditions, the absence of psychiatric morbidity and the degree of difficulty in carrying out activities of daily living to determine 'quality-adjusted life years' (QALYs). The social functioning model looks at the frequency and diversity of social activities engaged in, the frequency of social contacts and the amount of support received from others. The psychological resources model combines self-efficacy with measures of optimism and self-esteem. In their longitudinal survey of ageing, Bowling and Iliffe (2006) combined the above measures with 'lay' indicators of well-being comprising annual gross income, perceived quality of the environment and feelings of personal safety. Though each model was able independently to predict 'quality of life', or well-being, the lay model was the strongest; within this model, those who were classified as successfully aged, compared with those classified as not, were five times more likely to rate their quality of life as good rather than not good. The conclusion is that multidimensional interventions and measures all contribute to successful ageing, rather than medical, psychological or social factors separately, and there are trade-offs between these different measures. Living in a good environment was especially highly rated by older people themselves; having low levels of health and physical functioning did not prevent most people from being in good psychological health; requiring assistance from others in daily activities or socializing was a feature of 75 per cent of older people's lives and not an extraordinary need. Autonomy and independence therefore are not necessary components of well-being, though environmental factors are potent indicators of perceived quality of life.

Social comparisons and expectations (being in better health or in better circumstances than other people, or exceeding one's own expectations for old age) appear to contribute to quality of life (Bowling et al., 2002). Giving equal opportunities to all groups of older people to maintain good health will be an important element in the promotion of well-being. Research on inequalities among older people from different ethnic groups (Moriarty and Butt, 2004) shows that there is a need to examine the effects of ill health and material disadvantage and the cumulative effects of the experience of racism between different racial groups, and within those groups themselves. This is particularly important given the demographic profile of the UK, where there is an opportunity for positive preventative work before people reach older age.

Such findings are consonant with current public health agendas, and with multi-agency and multi-professional approaches to working with older people. They have implications for the ways in which social workers assess the needs of older people, for the provision of services, and for the evaluation of the outcomes of intervention. The importance of what may be called social capital (Putnam, 2000) – being actively involved in society and being valued for that contribution – supports a proactive role for social work in ensuring that older people are involved in the creation of social policy as well as being beneficiaries of its development.

Strategies for living well in later life

Between 2000 and 2004, the Joseph Rowntree Foundation developed a programme of research by and with older people to examine the priorities which they themselves defined as 'living well into later life'. Its first finding was that strategies should start with older people's own definitions of 'a life worth living' (Joseph Rowntree Foundation, 2004). Rather than seeing older people as the passive recipients of policy initiatives, the key message from the programme was that if older people are not actively involved in research and service evaluation, then the knowledge thus gained was unlikely to be enduring. Although Adam Broad is more likely to be directly involved in policy formulation than Carrie Davis, it is important that her voice is also heard and that her particular understanding of growing older – informed by experience of a less benign view of the state, of economic and gender inequalities and of social isolation – is also taken into account.

Crucial is recognition of the diversity of older people's lives, strengths associated with growing older, continuation of the ordinary things of life and involvement in service planning. Particular barriers to well-being in later life include age discrimination, a 'deficit' model of ageing within which older people are seen as a burden and a lack of flexible person-centred services which are responsive and adaptable to older people's needs. Dignity in the provision of care thus relates not only to sensitively provided services, but also to an acknowledgement of diversity and choice as an attribute of citizenship.

Despite greater social mobility, and a marked trend towards living alone, research into the family and community life of older people has confirmed the important role of extended family ties in the lives of older people, and the significance of social and friendship networks (Phillipson et al., 1998). This will not, however, be the experience of all older people; nor can it be assumed that living in proximity to family is unproblematic. Multigeneration households were found to be significant amongst Indian and Bangladeshi families in two of the areas studied by Phillipson et al. – Wolverhampton and Bethnal Green – though poor-quality housing and overcrowding were also found to be prevalent in these locations (ibid.). Not all older people will have access to such support (for example, only 20 per cent of Afro-Caribbean older people have a child living in the UK), and it cannot be assumed that communities will necessarily provide care without structural support being in place (ODPM, 2006). Understanding and working with changing families and communities is thus an important part of contemporary social work practice with older people.

Disability and older age

Building bridges, theoretically and in terms of policy development between older people and disability commentators, has been an important recent issue. The focus has been on exploring through research studies the similarities and differences between these two groups in making claims for social inclusion (Priestley and Rabiee, 2002). However, although policy agendas such as health, housing, social care and employment might be shared, organizations of older people surveyed in this research did not perceive older people with impairments as being disabled by social barriers in the same way that the disability movement has conceptualized the social model of disability. Groups that were already politicized in relation to issues of racism/ethnicity or gender equality were more open, however, to a similarly politicized view of disability rights. Significantly, the onset of old age was often associated with the onset of impairment and functional inability to live independently. Yet organizations of older people had different expectations of adaptation to the onset of impairment in later life (e.g. deafness) than they would have in relation to younger people and were less demanding of service providers as a result. Sharing perceptions may, therefore, be fruitful for older people's groups in supporting them to challenge social barriers to participation that disability groups more readily identify.

Key issues that the disability movement has promoted have been:

- the championing of independent living in the context of civil rights;
- involvement in service design as a matter of citizenship;
- rights to support, rather than segregated and commodified 'care';
- the removal of disabling barriers to employment and community participation.

Each of these agendas resonates also with older people. The increased longevity of people with learning difficulties, and the large number of older people with physical impairments and mental health problems, mean that, conceptually, more attention needs to be drawn to similarities between groups of people who traditionally have been supported by different agency specialisms. Bigby (2004) discusses the challenges presented by increasing life expectancy for people with intellectual disabilities who may be 'retired' from programmes for younger people and placed in inappropriate accommodation as a result of families becoming unable to continue to provide support. Conversely, earlier quality of life and adequacy of social networks will impact on later experiences of ageing. Disability services must also work with service users and carers to prepare for transitions as parents age, in the context of greater emphasis on choice and community presence than may have been anticipated when the disabled person entered services some 20 or 30 years previously.

Mental health and older age

Mental health in old age is a key concern of social policy. There are a number of issues to be considered:

- the prevalence and causes of different types of mental disorder in older age;
- the experiences of older people in understanding the impact of mental disorders;
- the configuration of services in different settings; and
- good practice in social work intervention.

Recent developments in mental health services for older people have recognized both structural and ethical issues. There are key concepts in any discussion of mental health services for older people: discrimination, providing person-centred care, integrating services, and timely access to assessment. The updated *Practice Guide 3: Assessing the Mental Health Needs of Older People* (SCIE, 2006a) emphasizes the importance of understanding the complex interaction between specific medical conditions and social circumstances. The promotion of well-being in older age also prioritizes emotional support, social contact, participation, learning new skills and sustaining a sense of purpose for positive mental health. Current research is correctly described by Moriarty and Butt (2004) as focusing on the ways in which mental health is influenced by gender, socioeconomic status and ethnicity. Compulsory intervention from mental health services also needs to be sensitive to the particular needs of older people in the context of their life history, as well as the progressive nature of disorders such as dementia and the differential diagnosis of depression in older people.

Understanding depression

Though dementia is seen as the 'classic' mental disorder in old age, it is in fact depression that is the most common. Social factors are significant. According to Harris et al. (2006), independent predictors of the onset of depression in a longitudinal study of older people were:

- high baseline depression score;
- increase in disability;
- poor general health;
- dissatisfaction with support; and
- loneliness.

Depression persistence is a major public health issue, with 61.2 per cent of people in this study remaining depressed after two years. Yet there is a lack of responsiveness on the part of formal service providers to the prevalence of depression amongst users of social care services. Recognition of depression by care home staff is low (Godlove et al., 2004) and depression amongst users of domiciliary services is double that of the general older community (Banerjee and Macdonald, 1996). Institutionalization and the perceived lack of a role in life are possible explanations. Research by McCrae et al. (2005) looked at social workers' experience of working with depressed older people. Participants reported very high levels of established indicators for depression, such as problems in sleeping and eating and a decline in physical and mental activity. The reticence of older people in discussing emotional problems (especially with much younger people) was a barrier to seeking help. Access to earlier clinical diagnosis, and more resources for social interventions, were seen as necessary. Counselling interventions available to younger people were rarely offered to older adults, and GPs were seen as difficult to engage in securing access to appropriate secondary services.

The profile of depression amongst BME (black and minority ethnic) older people is largely unknown (SCIE, 2006a).Government policy for this group has focused on physical illnesses – the meaning that is given culturally to symptoms of depression – and the range and effectiveness of service provision is in need of further research. The impact of discrimination and exclusion across the lifecourse will be seen in older age. An ecological model best describes the context within which particular older people from minority ethnic groups will experience personal, relational and cultural change in older age. Norman (1985) has described the 'triple jeopardy' experienced by older women who are living in a second homeland, facing discrimination because of their gender and receiving inadequate assessment of their mental health needs.

Dementia

The incidence of dementia rises with age: one in five people aged over 85 will have dementia. The Alzheimer's Society has produced the most detailed and robust picture to date of the prevalence and economic impact of dementia in the UK (Alzheimer's Society, 2007a). The report concludes (p. 57) that dementia has the 'potential to overwhelm' health and social care services and is 'one of the main causes of disability in later life' (p. 23): the financial cost of dementia to the UK is over £17 billion a year. Key issues include:

- improving diagnosis;
- identifying people (under 65 years) with early onset dementia;
- meeting the needs of people from minority ethnic groups;
- supporting family carers; and
- providing support in accordance with the wishes of users and family carers.

Though the availability of social support is a protective factor against the development of mental disorder for older people in the community, there is also evidence that the loss of autonomy associated with the receipt of long-term care, both in the community and in residential settings, has an impact on older people's mental health (Boyle, 2005). Boyle's study, carried out in Northern Ireland, compared the quality of life, autonomy and mental health of people living in nursing and residential homes with those receiving domiciliary care. The key factor in sustaining good mental health was not the setting of the care, or the degree of impairment, but the ability to make decisions about care. A study of people with dementia being cared for by relatives at home (Askham et al., 2007) similarly concluded that the routinization of daily life had a negative impact on the mental health of the person cared for, notwithstanding the homely environment. In some of the observations, the social identity of the person with dementia as home-maker or car driver was denied as a result of the inability to sustain an intimate relationship alongside the routinization of care tasks. Social work practice thus needs to focus on the quality of individual interventions, and not simply the setting, when assessing where an individual's mental health needs can best be met. Providing support to carers to enable them to recognize the older person's need for autonomy will be critical, as will the provision of respite care for carers who lack the time or the energy to allow the older person to continue to participate in domestic tasks or familiar roles, as their capacity is impaired.

We also have a poor understanding of how cultural beliefs and values influence the presentation, help-seeking behaviour and referral processes for people with dementia and their families (Lawrence et al., 2008). Research into the attitudes of white British, South Asian and black Caribbean older people with dementia revealed differences in their understanding of their situation and of their willingness to seek different types of support. The findings show different attitudes to stigma, family support and the normalization of memory loss in older age. White British respondents were most likely to deny memory problems and to withdraw from social activities. They were the only group to talk about the impact of memory problems on their marriage; a major concern was being a burden to others, and entry to residential care was seen in terms of relieving the burden. Black Caribbean older people were more open and likely to seek help; this was attributed in many cases to employment or family links that they had with NHS services. However, they tended to conceptualize dementia in physical terms as an organic disorder. They had a very negative view of residential care, but valued greatly the support of their peer group – for example, in day services. South Asians were less conscious of the progressive nature of their condition, and confident of family support; they also felt able to continue to reciprocate within the marital relationship. Responses to services therefore will need to be monitored in terms of their acceptability and meaning as physical or mental frailty grows.

Emphasizing the importance of a whole systems approach, in 2009 the government published a *National Dementia Strategy* (DH, 2009c), as a first attempt to focus specifically on strategic issues across services. The report calls for:

- dementia to be made a national priority;
- a substantial increase in publicly funded dementia research;
- an improvement in dementia care skills;
- more low-level community support;
- a guarantee of carer support packages;
- a national debate on who pays for care; and
- the development of comprehensive integrated dementia care models.

In many ways, then, dementia care is a microcosm for a whole range of issues facing health and social care in meeting the needs of older people. Internationally, most other countries are moving to a system of community care, but face common difficulties with stigmatizing attitudes about mental health and ageing. To this might be added a failure to develop the concept of a 'right' to care, insufficient preventative resources, an approach to practice which routinizes care at the expense of individuality and a focused holistic approach to the needs of this group of older people.

Setting the agenda for social work

Demographic and social changes thus provide the context within which social work with older people will take place. An ageing population will 'normalize' the position of older people and challenge traditional views of their role in society. At the same time, issues of particular relevance to an ageing population will have to be addressed, such as policies on employment and retirement, income generation and pensions, the allocation of health and social care services, community involvement, appropriate housing and support for family life for carers and supporters of older people. Older people as a group, and individually, will bring with them into older age experiences from earlier life stages. This will include the legacy of earlier social and health inequalities, greater or lesser opportunities to save for old age and different expectations of state and family support. As Evandrou (1997) points out, the baby-boomers of the immediate post-war years will bring with them into older age experiences of the welfare state and a history of relatively stable employment and opportunities for home ownership. Those born later are likely to have experienced a more fragmented working life, the impact of divorce and more expensive property ownership. Men and women of different generations will have experienced different life choices, and the impact of discrimination will continue into older age. Some of the oldest people in contact with social workers will, like Carrie Davies, remember the days before the welfare state, and will fear the 'workhouse' and the 'poor law' not as historical remnants, but as real lived experience.

Concern about changes in the 'dependency ratio' of working to non-economically active members of the population has influenced views about the retirement age, the affordability of pension provision and paying for long-term care, subjecting older people to the harsh effects of economic change. The provision of family care for older people has involved increasing numbers of people in 'caring' tasks, such that, in the 2001 census, 10 per cent of the population were able to describe themselves as a 'carer' (ONS, 2003). Whether such an undertaking has truly created a 'sandwich' generation of middle-aged women (mostly) with responsibility both for older family members and for children is an emergent question; nevertheless, the definition and meaning of 'caring' has become a focus of debate (Stalker, 2003) and for older people has created the potential for a socially defined relationship of dependency.

Anti-oppressive practice with older people can thus operate at an individual level, acknowledging the legacy of past disadvantages and strengths; at the level of the family or group within which there will be continuities, but also the possibility of new roles; and at a political and organizational level, where views about the value of older people's contributions to service development will need to be interrogated and at times challenged. Centrally important are understanding and attitudes underpinning social work interventions with older people. Involving service users in constructing their own narratives is critical to acknowledging the diversity of knowledge and experience that has to be understood.

Conclusion

Demographic changes provide an opportunity for older people's voices to be heard. The way in which older age is structured and perceived reflects the political, economic and social context in which older people live their lives. But approaches which acknowledge that older people individually and collectively are experts on their own lives seek to redress the power of social workers and social work agencies to define the agendas of older age and older people. The history of service development for older people is the theme of the next chapter, which also examines the impact of policy changes on the practice of social work.

Chapter summary

1 Gerontology describes the process of ageing from biological, psychological, social and cultural perspectives: theories of ageing are also developed within political and economic contexts.

2 Older people's experience of life is diverse and is influenced by past as well as present relationships and opportunities and is structured by gender, race and disability. Understanding the impact of disability and mental disorder in older age is particularly important.

3 Increasing longevity means that 18.6 per cent of the population of the UK is over pensionable age; demographic change leads to unprecedented challenges for health and social care services, and an interest in 'successful ageing', and well-being.
4 Extended family ties and social and friendship networks remain significant sources of support for older people, alongside formal services.
5 Older people should be actively engaged in research and service evaluation, rather than being seen as passive recipients of welfare.

Key lessons

1 Social work perspectives on working with older people are influenced by social, organizational and individual difference.
2 Theory for practice may focus on individual need, social change, group processes or citizenship rights; social work may be informed by any or all of these perspectives.
3 The complexities of older people's situations call for multi-agency and multi-professional responses.
4 Anti-oppressive practice recognizes both the structural factors that affect older people, and the importance of respect for individual differences.
5 Professionals should be aware of the power that they may have when older people are physically and mentally incapacitated; older people themselves emphasize control rather than independence as a factor in self-esteem and well-being.

Activity

Alice, Brenda and Charlotte are three generations of women within the same family.

Alice was born in 1915. She was the youngest of nine children, and left school at the age of 14 to go into service. In 1946 she married Ronald and had one daughter, Brenda. Alice was a housewife throughout her married life, and was widowed in 1985. She now lives in a local authority owned bungalow in the town in which she was born.

Brenda was born in 1950. She is divorced from her husband John, by whom she had three children, including Charlotte. She works part time as a secretary and shares a house with her partner, Frank; they both contribute to the mortgage. Brenda lives in a city 20 miles away from Alice, whom she visits every week-end.

Charlotte was born in 1972. She attended university and qualified as an accountant. She lives alone in London in a privately rented flat. Charlotte visits her mother and grandmother at holiday times.

Consider the impact of the different life experiences of Alice, Brenda and Charlotte upon their expectations of ageing.

Further reading

M. Forster, *Have the Men Had Enough?* London: Penguin, 1989.

This novel depicts the different responses of family members to a grandmother who develops dementia. There is black comedy and pathos, but also an examination of gender expectations and the rights of older woman through the medium of literature.

P. Thane, *Old Age in English History: Past Experiences, Present Issues.* Oxford: Oxford University Press, 2000.

This key text argues that, historically, the benefits of an ageing society have outweighed the costs, and that older people have always made important contributions to their families and to society.

2 The History of Service Development for Older People

Issues considered in this chapter:

- the development of community care policy in respect of older people;
- the impact of care management processes on social work practice;
- the modernizing of health and social care and the impact of the personalization agenda;
- the importance of a rights-based framework for the citizenship of older people.

This chapter will explore the history of social work provision for older people in the changing policy context since 1948. The welfare state, based on cradle-to-grave provision by statutory services, has given way to a mixed economy of care in the community within which scarce resources are targeted on the most needy. More recently, the personalization agenda has enabled individuals to have access to money, or money's worth (i.e. the estimated value of directly provided services), to purchase a wider range of services than traditionally was provided through commissioned services. Each phase in the historical development of services for older people has been based on a different conception of the status of older people as variously welfare beneficiaries, consumers or proactive citizens.

Responding to the diversity of older age

In surveying the history of service development, it is important to consider the impact on older people of the ways in which knowledge is constructed within cultural, historical and local contexts. Also significant is the language used to interpret social experiences (Payne, 2005: 58). In this way, as we have seen in chapter 1, the knowledge base of social work with people with mental health problems, and potential alliances between the disability movement and older people's interests, will create new understandings of older people's experiences. There is great diversity in old age, reflecting previous life choices, present living arrangements and self and societal perceptions of older people. How these differences are to be understood, and their consequences for social work practice, are key themes of this book. Evidence from research illustrates the divergence between what is provided and the support that older people say they want and the services they need (Manthorpe et al., 2008). Tensions between providing universally accessible, preventative and closely targeted services have provided the background to recent developments in social policy. The solution currently proposed is the introduction of personalized budgets enabling older people to make their own choices about the things that will improve their quality of life. In this context, we might then look at one example of 'traditional' service provision, and the way in which it absorbs, or obscures, a diversity of need amongst older people.

Case profile

The following people are all regular attenders at a luncheon club for older people organized by their local Volunteer Bureau:

- Greta Harries likes to recount how people are surprised to hear that she is over 80, and tell her that she 'wonderful for her age'. She always uses make-up, and wears fashionable clothing. Her favourite activity is dancing.
- Ivor Jenkins's wife died six months ago. He says that he has 'no idea' about cooking, or looking after the house. He sits on his own, and declines to join in with group activities.
- Kathleen Lewis is married to Malcolm who is several years younger than her. Malcolm has served a number of prison sentences for fraud and assault – a fact which is well known in the local community. Frequently, there are signs of bruising on her arms and face, and sometimes Kathleen appears reluctant to go home.
- Martin Newell has a diagnosis of dementia. Recently, he has became agitated when his wife leaves him to go shopping, and the luncheon club helpers feel that they will have to tell his wife that they cannot take responsibility for him anymore, even though they know that this is the only opportunity that she has to leave him.

Greta, Ivor, Kathleen and Martin are all provided with the same service; a luncheon club for older people (see the case profile above). The service defines them by age and by a very broad-brush definition of social need. The service itself fulfils a statutory obligation to promote the welfare of older people, but in a mixed economy of care it is commissioned from a voluntary organization, and may be run by paid staff or by volunteers. It may be held in a designated building or a community centre, but not a restaurant or a pub, so that, although it is within the community, those who use its services are differentiated from other groups of people who meet together for a weekly meal. There are eligibility criteria to receive this service: Martin is in danger of being no longer 'eligible' because of the deterioration in his mental health. There is also an inherent monitoring function, to which Kathleen is subject.

Ivor and Martin are probably outnumbered by the women in the group. The nature of the group activities is not specified; who chooses them, and their relevance to Ivor's difficulties both personal and domestic, are not explored. Greta's self-esteem is strongly linked to differentiating herself from other older people in the group: the identity of 'older person' is not one that she has accepted.

The day-care scenario reflects traditional service provision for older people and access to it is mediated through professional assessment of need. Those who attend may now be called people who use services rather than clients, but it is not identified as a service user-led organization. The function that it performs is one of providing monitoring and respite as well as social activities. There is likely to be a charge for the service, which may be means-tested. Its existence presumes a community of interest among older people and a belief in the virtue or economy of collective provision. If Greta, Ivor, Kathleen and Martin had access to personal budgets, would they choose to buy in to such a service? Does association with an older person's luncheon club define their status in a way that is acceptable to them? What will become of the luncheon club if fewer people seek to make use of it in the future?

A history of service neglect

Means and Smith (1994) have described the history of service neglect, the emphasis on stigmatized institutional provision and negative stereotypes of old age, all of which have historically informed the provision of services for older people. The legal framework for providing services to older people continues to incorporate the 'poor law' values, thresholds and definitions of the 1948 National Assistance Act. An unsympathetic legislative framework has inhibited the development of anti-discriminatory practice by focusing on individual deficit and the provision of care as a commodity (McDonald, 2006). Older age is presented not as a developmental stage, but as a 'problem' for policy-makers to address.

The social democratic, functionalist view of service provision for older people was the dominant post-war model. Presenting change as incremental, based on consensus and a humanitarian reaction to objectively verifiable 'facts' such as demographic change or increased prosperity, pension provision increased in line with the growth in wages, and domiciliary or residential services were provided directly by the state operating through large unified social services authorities. Social work in this area was predominantly generic, rooted in casework as a method of intervention, and unconcerned with economics (ibid.). Much social work with older people was carried out by unqualified staff, and the dominant model was the medical model of diagnosis, prescription and warehousing of those assessed as being in need of longer-term care, usually in residential settings.

The development of community care

In the 1980s a number of changes happened which lead ultimately to the development of 'community care' as the predominant model of service delivery. Concern, even then, about growing numbers of older people within the population was expressed as a 'demographic time bomb'; unrestricted access to an emerging private residential care market was also identified as an expensive 'perverse incentive' for older people to enter residential care by the direct payment of fees from the social security budget without a proper assessment of need (Audit Commission, 1986). But, most significantly, a new Conservative government challenged the ideological basis upon which state-funded care was to be provided. Direct provision was superseded by the vision of the 'enabling state' contracting with independent providers to produce a range of service options. This 'New Right' philosophy of care was endorsed by the entrepreneurial report of Sir Roy Griffiths (Griffiths, 1988) and the subsequent White Paper, *Caring for People: Community Care in the next Decade and Beyond* (DH, 1989), the six objectives of which were stated to be:

- to promote the development of domiciliary, day and respite services to enable people to live in their own homes wherever feasible and sensible;
- to ensure that service providers make practical support for carers a high priority;
- to make proper assessment of need and good care management the cornerstone of high-quality care;
- to promote the development of a flourishing independent sector alongside good-quality public services;
- to clarify the responsibilities of agencies and so make it easier to hold them to account for their performance;
- to secure better value for taxpayers' money by introducing a new funding structure for social care.

Although debates have changed about the way in which care is provided, and by what combination of organizations, to some extent these agendas are still being played out in contemporary debates concerning the effectiveness of different types of service in enabling people to be:

- well supported in the community;
- in receipt of the support that carers need in order to continue to provide care;
- efficiently prioritized for services through new models of assessment;
- appropriately signposted to the separate and shared responsibilities of health and social care agencies; and
- economically dealt with in 'value-for-money' debates around outcomes, and charging policies.

So, supporting people in the community is recognized to be a choice of location preferred by older people themselves, and also congruent with values of citizenship and inclusion. Yet, if the cost of community care is greater than the cost of residential care, and a sufficient volume of support is not available, then individuals will still be directed to residential care, even if this is not their first choice. Support for carers has been strengthened by the legal framework of the Carers and Disabled Children Act 2000 and the Carers (Equal Opportunities) Act 2004 (McDonald and Taylor, 2006), but carers are nevertheless poorly remunerated for the value of the service that they provide, and are seen as a resource rather than as a partner in care provision. Using assessment to prioritize individuals for services is also explicitly a rationing device, and the structuring of assessment and care management processes has led to further bureaucratization of the social worker's role. The boundaries between health and social care continue to be problematic, particularly in terms of eligibility for NHS-funded care and at the point of hospital discharge. The fairness of funding policies and means-tested assessment remains contentious, particularly as privately accrued pensions and the value of people's homes continue to be taken into account when calculating charges for state-provided services.

More contemporary debates about social policy and older people have thus still seen older people to a large extent as a demographic problem to be solved, rather than as citizens who have the right, individually and collectively, to a guaranteed amount of service provided by the state, designed in accordance with their wishes and with respect to core values of dignity and autonomy and the protection of fundamental rights.

The development of care management

The advent of community care in the 1990s also had a major impact on the social work role. Research published by the Personal Social Services Research Unit at the University of Kent and commissioned by the Department of Health (Davies and Challis, 1986) also appeared to confirm the value of targeting scarce resources on those most vulnerable to admission to expensive residential care, by means of a 'production of welfare' approach, balancing the cost of inputs against outputs. The method by which the process of assessment, planning and review implicit within this model was to be developed was that of care management. Department of Health Guidance (DH, 1991) described in detail how agencies were to set up systems and how individual care managers (from a range of professional groups, not just social workers) were to identify and allocate resources within 'a package of care'. A number of models of care management are potentially available (Pilling, 1992), but the one most common in practice has been that of 'social entrepreneurship' by which the care manager effectively contracts on behalf of the individual for a range of services. Direct control and ultimate choice thereby rest with the professional rather than with the older person. During this period, the language of service provision underwent significant change. 'Clients' (on the professional model) became 'service users' or even 'customers', reflecting a more consumer-orientated focus, paving the way for later debates on the importance of choice as an aid to self-sufficiency. Social workers in some locations were redesignated as care managers, a task which was shared with other occupational groups such as nurses and occupational therapists.

Managerialism, in the sense of proceduralized control of working practices (Clarke et al, 2000; Harris, 2003) has been an essential corollary to the development of a regulated market economy. Professional discretion has to a large extent been replaced by formulaic approaches to assessment and service eligibility. There has been an emphasis on efficiency and productivity, supported by the application of technology and budgetary procedures. Social work managers, under this model, are less valued as expert practitioners and more likely to be chosen for their generic management skills. The effect of this is that managers become monitors of workloads, rather than sources of professional supervision. Routinized practice is introduced, which ill equips practitioners to understand and respond to the real complexities of people's lives. The nature of relationships between social workers and clients then changes from the interpersonal to the economic, from therapeutic to transactional, from being nurturing and supportive to being contractual and service-orientated (Howe, 1996). So, social workers in adult care teams have increasingly found that the rhetoric of community care does not match the reality of their everyday work (Gorman and Postle, 2003).

Modernizing the social services

A change of government in 1997 set the modernizing agenda of New Labour (DH, 1998). The emphasis on competition changed to that of partnerships, and market forces were supplemented with arm's-length processes of regulation and inspection (McDonald, 2006). The dominant model was a neo-liberal emphasis on the individual and personal responsibility for change, and it paralleled the retreat from universal welfare provision by other European states. Outcomes for individuals became the significant measure of success (Henwood and Waddington, 2002) and there was an increasing emphasis on well-being and social inclusion. The White Paper, *Our Health, Our Care, Our Say* (DH, 2006c), focused on prevention, community development and the personalization of care tailored more closely to individual preferences. Direct payments, enabling individuals to receive cash instead of care, and individual budgets, where different types of funding are brought together to purchase a varied package of care, are seen as a means to enable older people to be self-directing within available resources.

For older people, key policy landmarks have reflected the modernizing tendency to set standards centrally for local performance:

1 *The National Service Framework for Older People* (DH, 2001) was based on equitable treatment for older people, led by the NHS, comprising eight key standards:
   i rooting out age discrimination by basing services on clinical need, but also preventing social services authorities from using age within their eligibility criteria to limit access to services;
   ii person-centred care, through what was to become the Single Assessment Process, and through integrated commissioning arrangements;
   iii access to intermediate care services at home or in designated care settings;
   iv general hospital care which is appropriate and specialist and which respects privacy and dignity;
   v progress in reducing the incidence of stroke in the population, and to ensure prompt access to integrated stroke care services;
   vi a reduction in the number of falls that result in serious injury, and the development of effective treatment and rehabilitation;
   vii access to integrated mental health services, with a particular focus on depression and dementia;
   viii the promotion of health and active life expectancy in older people.
2 *A New Ambition for Old Age* (DH, 2006a) raised debates about dignity in care, joined-up care and healthy ageing following the implementation of the National Service Framework. The care of frail older people is described in this document as the 'core business' of the Department of Health.
3 *A New Deal for Welfare* (DWP, 2005) encouraged the continuation of economic and social involvement in older age by focusing on work opportunities beyond the age of 50 and a reform of pensions provision to support savers and compensate carers.
4 *A Sure Start to Later Life* (ODPM, 2006) modelled preventative services for older people on those for children in communities experiencing deprivation.

Many of these initiatives have been paralleled with changes for other user groups within adult services, the focus in this period being on the targeting of socially excluded groups with high service costs.

The impact of rationing

Despite the agenda of social inclusion and prevention, more recently concern has been expressed about the number of older people who are effectively excluded from receiving a social work service either because of increasingly high eligibility criteria, or through their status as 'self-funders'. The CSCI report, *The State of Social Care* (2008c), surveyed the years 2005–7, mapping trends in provision. It found that, compared to 2003, fewer older people were receiving care in the community, and that many who were turned down for services experienced the assessment process as 'frustrating and disappointing'. Despite a 3 per cent rise between 2003 and 2006 in the population of those aged 75 plus, the number of service users declined from 867,000 to 840,000. Nevertheless, 61 per cent of councils' expenditure on social services was directed at older people. The trend towards using voluntary and private sector providers continues; from 59 per cent of gross expenditure in 2001/2, to 72 per cent of gross expenditure in 2005/6; of the expenditure on residential provision, 82 per cent supports independent sector providers. Older people contribute significantly to the cost of their care; in 2005–7, half the total expenditure on social care for older people (£5.9 billion) was provided by self-funders or by assessed care charges. Yet during the same period it was found that one-third of care homes and homecare agencies were performing poorly in relation to care plans. Clearly, important issues remain about state responsibility, rights to receive minimum levels of service and the quality of care being provided, which makes the transformation agenda now being developed the catalyst for fundamental debate about service provision for a diverse range of older people, and not simply the preferred 'solution' to manage demand on formal services.

The transformation agenda – individual and personal budgets

A relocation of responsibility for the planning and management of social care to individuals in the community has resulted from the introduction of individual and personalized budgets. Potentially, this is a major shift, both in the way in which services are provided and in the role of professionals. Individual budgets seek to bring together diverse streams of funding from health and social care: 'supporting people' budgets from housing services and 'independent living fund' monies for younger disabled people. Clearly coordination of such diverse sources with different legislative sources will be complex. Personal budgets are more modest in their scope, being funded solely from social services monies. The rationale for both is that individuals should be able to manage for themselves an amount of money, or money's worth of services, rather than have services commissioned through the care management process. Tanner and Harris (2007) see this as a fundamental shift away from state responsibility for the welfare of older people and a relocation of risks to individuals away from the state. Whereas previous modernizing initiatives have been concerned with fostering social inclusion, responsibility for this now rests with older people themselves. 'Personalization' within the transformation agenda is thus the epitome of a neo-liberal approach within which individuals create and manage their own life chances.

The Local Authority Circular, *Transforming Social Care* (2008), describes how local area agreements are the means by which collaboration between services will happen. Current organizational arrangements are seen as inadequate to support the volume of demand from increasing numbers of older people. Are there concerns for older people here? There may be a number: the focus on individual responsibility could easily lead to blaming of individuals who are unable to manage the complexities of personalization; finding and training sufficient personal assistants is already problematic; quality is harder to track in diversity; safeguarding vulnerable people may be an issue; and established services may decline if a critical level of funding cannot be accessed.

Once again, as with community care in the early 1990s, a new policy is being introduced across the board with limited evidence of its effectiveness. An evaluation of individual budget pilot schemes by Glendinning et al. (2008) found that accountability and risk management processes needed further development; there was also no evidence of cost-effectiveness differences between individual budgets and standard support arrangements. Significantly, older people were less likely than other groups to report having higher aspirations for themselves as a result of having an individual budget, and were also anxious about taking on the 'additional burden' of planning and managing their own support. It was also unclear whether professional time would be saved, given the complexity of setting up new systems. Considerable uncertainty thus exists about the benefits of a policy intended to be mainstream by 2011.

Supporting evidence-based practice

A number of supports have been developed to provide the evidence base and legitimacy for developing change agendas. The Social Care Institute for Excellence (SCIE) has been established to provide practice guidance and policy reviews on a range of subjects. Similarly, the National Institute for Clinical Excellence (NICE) oversees the dissemination of guidance on service development, and the prescribing of medication, as well as good practice for NHS personnel. The merger of the Commission for Social Care Inspection, the Healthcare Commission and the Mental Health Act Commission into a joint Care Quality Commission in 2009 was intended to enable common standards in service provision to be set and to be monitored thematically in a range of different settings.

How have such changes been perceived by older people and their representatives, and what impact has it had on their lives? Reports based on national surveys highlight contradictions inherent within current policies. Banks et al. (2006) used information from the 2001 census to show that, although residential provision for older people had declined overall between 1991 and 2001, this decline was uneven and more marked in deprived areas with higher rates of poor health amongst older people. Also, there was a tendency for local authorities supporting high levels of residential care also to support relatively high levels of homecare services. This suggests (according to the authors) that the substitution of residential care with homecare (as per the 1989 White Paper objectives) has not been large scale. The lack of equity in care home provision also raises concern about the ability of central and local government to successfully conduct needs-based planning when dealing with market forces that are to a large extent out of government control; this lack of planning will then impact on the choice of accommodation that older people have, particularly for those in minority groups. In 2007, the charity Counsel and Care similarly surveyed local authorities' care charging and eligibility criteria policies, and concluded that higher charges and fewer services meant that (to quote the subtitle of the report) 'the squeeze is tightening for older people'. Although there was evidence of a more strategic, partnership-based focus on improved housing, integrated responses, rehabilitation and telecare services, limited funding meant that preventative services were patchy and still largely provided through the voluntary sector. The preventative agenda was thus sidelined by a focus on those with high dependency needs or no family support; charging policies also continued to vary between authorities, but overall charges were increasing.

In Scotland, a major review of social work provision, *The 21st Century Social Work Review*, took place in 2005 to assess the current state of knowledge and thinking about social care. Among the papers produced was one entitled 'Effective Social Work with Older People' (Kerr et al., 2005). A key question was whether and how the need for social work may be heightened by the combination with age (ibid.: 22). Broadly, the conclusion was that older people do not need social workers simply by reason of their age; it is when sudden 'shifts' happen, or recur, or when gradual change becomes apparent that social workers may effectively intervene (ibid.: 29). Reliance is placed on Smale et al.'s (2000) analysis of the social worker's distinctive role:

- where no one knows what the answer is;
- where relationships are complex; and
- where there is a high degree of risk.

Scotland has provided the same level of free personal care for eligible older people in their own homes as is provided in residential care. Yet the proportion of older people in Scotland over the age of 65 who are in residential care is 4 per cent, compared to 2.5 per cent in England. Expenditure per person in residential care in Scotland is almost a third higher than expenditure in England (Alzheimer's Society, 2007a). Curtice and Petch (2002) attribute such divergence to a different value and attitude base in Scotland, with more support for public spending. The 62 per cent increase in the number of people receiving personal care in Scotland between 2002 and 2005 cannot be explained by demographic trends, higher rates of disability or reductions in informal care, but is thought to be due to uncovering unmet need. Thus the experience in Scotland exposes both the demand-led nature of care provision for older people, and the potential of systems change in response to a challenge to the traditional value base of care for older people, based on rationing and paucity of service.

The importance of a rights-based framework

In surveying the current framework for service provision, the Joint Committee on Human Rights (2007) has drawn attention to the dichotomy between the 'duty to provide' and the citizen's 'right to receive'. The legal framework within which community care services are provided is piecemeal and complex (McDonald and Taylor, 2006). From an individual perspective, Ann Stewart (2005) has described the challenges that she faced in supporting her older parents. Professionally, she was a lecturer in law and very aware of the absence of a clear value-based legal framework for providing care to adults, or of an entrenched human rights culture in public care. Her experience was of bureaucratic delays, inadequate welfare benefits, unstable service provision and a culture that was not based on rights for older people. The lack of a contractual relationship between the provider and the service user when care is publicly commissioned means that the individual is at the mercy of market forces and has no effective redress for breach of contractual terms. Even when the author's mother began employing carers directly, the acute shortage of carers in the market meant that she had no choice. Collective challenges to administrative decisions are unlikely, because older people have limited access to advocacy and public law rights. Individual challenges are tempered by a reluctance to risk being further deprived of scarce resources, or an underlying diffidence about entitlement.

The current legal framework for working with older people imposes a duty to assess need (NHS and Community Care Act 1990), but discretion in determining which needs will be met supports the targeting of resources. The model is based on individual deficits, and although it is framed as 'needs-led', it cannot be described as user-led insofar as it is the agency that determines eligible needs. The focus on risk has the effect of prioritizing basic physical needs over social and emotional concerns (McDonald and Taylor, 2006); it is not surprising, therefore, that requests for support in the community may be rejected on financial grounds in favour of admission to institutional care for those with complex needs. Recognizing that the absence of a coherent legal framework for adult social care has compromised access to service, the Law Commission (2008) carried out a mapping exercise of the current deficits within community care law. Its tentative recommendation that a number of guiding principles to do with rights, equality and partnership are built into any new regime would appear to support the modernization of services with clarity and conviction. Until this is done, the extent to which the 1998 Human Rights Act can support the citizenship of older people is in doubt, even though rights to respect for family life, freedom from inhuman and degrading treatment and support for life are clearly of relevance to older people. The effective application of such principles depends not only upon sufficient resources, but also on the willingness of professionals to identify issues as matters of rights, and of the availability of means for challenging decisions (McDonald, 2007). An examination of the functions of social work and of the policy that supports it is the subject of the next chapter.

Conclusion

Focusing on age alone in social work with older people ignores the commonality of interest that older people may have with other users of community care services. The responses that social workers are able to make are shaped by the context in which they work and, historically, social work with older people has been under-resourced and defined in terms of process rather than content. Good practice with older people requires a range of skills in dealing with change, complexity in relationships and the continuing need to protect the status of older people as individuals. Though there have been inconsistencies over time in the stated objectives of social work involvement with older people, a market-led approach to care management, the impact of rationing and the absence of a rights-based framework have created a gap between policy aspirations and actual outcomes for older people.

Chapter summary

1 The theoretical and knowledge base of social work faces a particular challenge in understanding the interaction between organic disorders, social circumstances and individual responses as people age.
2 Social work with older people has been characterized by a history of service neglect and a legislative framework that has been based on a deficit model of agency responsibilities.
3 Community care policy in the 1990s reframed the role of the state as that of 'enabler' rather than 'provider', and gave rise to systems based on managerialist principles rather than professional knowledge and skill.
4 The 'modernizing' agenda in health and social care, and the transformation agenda in the current era, are based on neo-liberal principles of consumer choice, individual responsibility and the personalization of service delivery.
5 The focus has shifted from inputs to process and outcomes, with an

emphasis on meeting targets, promoting well-being and reinforcing individual responsibility.

Key lessons

1 Social work practice with older people has moved forward from a generic to a specialist context, and must be informed by evidence from research of the support that older people want and need.
2 Social work has been remodelled by a changing political and environmental context; the development of care management has opened up roles and tasks to a range of professionals and differently qualified staff.
3 Social work with older people has to respond to the consequences of rationing services, which jeopardizes the development of a preventative agenda and responsive practice.
4 A rights-based approach to services for older people is still at a beginning stage of development, but will require changes in practice and the organization of services as well as legislation and policy.
5 If the transformation agenda in social care is to give people real choice, adequate resources and easy access to support in managing complex packages of care will be needed.

Activity

1 To what extent do services for older people still reflect the priorities and standards of earlier times and how prepared are we for the impact of *Transforming Social Care*?
2 If older people do not need social workers simply by reason of their age, then why is social work with older people required at all as a separate specialism?

Further reading

S. Carr, *Personalization: A Rough Guide*. SCIE report 20. London, 2008.
SCIE sets out 'the story so far' for our understanding of the personalization agenda at this early stage of implementation.
J. Lewis and H. Glennester, *Implementing the New Community Care*. Buckingham: Open University Press, 1996.
This describes the history and origins of the community care reforms of the early 1990s and presents research findings on their impact on organizational and professional practice.

3 Functions of Social Work

Issues considered in this chapter:

- the functions of social work in society and the different tasks social workers may undertake;
- the range of skills and knowledge needed for work with older people;
- the classification of social work theories;
- the difference between qualifying and post-qualifying skills, and the changing roles of social workers.

Social work with older people has no distinct professional identity. At qualifying level, *The National Occupational Standards for Social Work* (TOPSS, 2002) describe generic skills which are applicable to practice with a range of individuals, groups and communities in any setting. Key roles 1–4 cover the practice of social work, and follow the social work processes of:

- assessment, care planning and review (key roles 1 and 2);
- support for individuals to represent their needs, views and circumstances (key role 3);
- the management of risk (key role 4).

Key role 5 describes individual workers' relationships with their employing agency: how to manage and be accountable for, with supervision and support, their own social work practice within their organization. Key role 6 underpins all other roles; it is about the demonstration of professional competence in social work practice. This competence-based framework seeks to preserve a unity within the profession through shared knowledge, skills and values. At post-qualifying levels, the prescribed generic curriculum for social work with adults (GSCC, 2006) has no separate requirements for specialist, higher specialist or advanced work with older people as a separate user group. Common knowledge and skills relate to the policy and legal context of practice, human growth and development and inter-professional working. In addition, at post-qualifying level, there is a requirement to 'enable others': this supports the learning of qualifying-level students in the workplace, and gives a proactive role to qualified social work staff in the learning organization. The protection of the title 'social worker' requires evidence of continuing professional development of 15 days over the three-year registration period.

The functions of social work and the different roles that social workers may undertake in statutory, voluntary and independent organizations are explored in this chapter. There are tensions between supporting individuals and protecting them from harm, and between understandings of the social work role, which differentially emphasize the social worker's legal, agency and professional allegiances. The case profile in this chapter is used to look at social workers' roles in assessment, in finding out more about what is going on in the situation and planning appropriate responses to it, while also reviewing outcomes. At each stage, the way in which the situation is perceived is influenced by different theoretical frameworks which guide understanding and intervention.

Case profile

Winifred Yates lives in a house inherited from her parents. She also inherited a number of valuable antiques and has substantial personal savings in addition to a small pension. Her only living relative is her nephew Gerald, aged 35, who visits her fortnightly. Gerald is unemployed and has three small children. Over the past year Winifred has given Gerald money to buy a new car, money for a deposit on a flat and has paid for holidays for his family. Gerald has now suggested that he take charge of selling some of his aunt's antiques. Zena, Winifred's cleaner, has become concerned about things going missing from the house. Winfred has been recently diagnosed with dementia. After Gerald's visits Winifred is often upset, saying that he has told her that she will have to go 'into a home', and that he will make arrangements to deal with her financial affairs.

Winifred's case highlights different perceptions that may be held of the same situation. When discussing Winifred's case with a group of post-qualifying students, ambivalence was expressed about Gerald. Is he a concerned, but harassed, carer, or is he a self-interested threat to Winifred's autonomy? Is Winifred a victim, or is she a generous benefactor concerned that her family should be protected from a predatory state which had an interest in inheriting her property? Is Zena a neutral informant, or does she have an interest in maintaining Winifred at home to her own advantage? How is power distributed between these three people? Is it with Winifred who has the advantage of wealth, with Gerald in his masculine role of family decision-maker, or with Zena who has the ability to withdraw her labour that maintains the domestic situation? To this might be added the power of the social worker: to define need, to conceptualize the situation as one of support or protection and, ultimately, to make decisions based on Winifred's best interests. These perceptions are, in turn, informed by different discourses: social, psychological, economic and legal.

The knowledge base of the social worker includes an awareness that the onset of dementia may lead Winifred to forget that she has given away her possessions or that she has mislaid them. Further multidisciplinary assessment may be required which may lead to an assessment of Winifred's legal capacity to manage her own affairs. The Mental Capacity Act 2005 tells us that Winifred's capacity to make decisions is specific to the decision under consideration. This may be the decision financially to support Gerald and his family, or the decision to enter residential care. The wisdom or otherwise of this decision from the perspective of other people, including the social worker, is not relevant to her capacity to make it.

Winifred's vulnerability to exploitation, emotional or financial, is, however, something of which the social worker should be aware. Exploring Winifred's past and present relationship with both Gerald and Zena, and discussing choices with her in a variety of ways and in different settings, will inform the assessment of capacity. Winifred may be aware of the extent to which she is being pressured financially to support Gerald, but may be willing to pay this cost to retain her relationship with him and his family, or to prevent her estate from being used to finance her future care or to avoid inheritance tax. Gerald's understanding of dementia may be limited and he may (wrongly) believe that institutional care is inevitable. The social worker's role may then be to advise him of sources of information and advice. The construction of Gerald as a 'carer' for his aunt will give him a statutory right to an assessment of his ability to provide care, taking into account his other family responsibilities and his desire to find paid employment. He too will be required to have regard to the principles of the Mental Capacity Act in respecting and responding to the autonomy of his aunt's decisions. More formally, he may have been given the legal authority to act on behalf of his aunt under a Lasting Power of Attorney for the making of financial or welfare decisions, or both.

The policy framework for inter-agency collaboration to safeguard adults, *No Secrets* (DH and Home Office, 2000), is premised upon definitions of vulnerable adults as those in need of community care services, but this may not reflect Winifred's view of her situation or of her actual needs. In any event, legal remedies are limited if no criminal act has been committed; for the protection of adults there are no statutory powers compulsorily to intervene in situations that might warrant action in relation to children. Without cooperation from Winifred or Gerald, there is no legal mandate even to investigate. The Human Rights Act imposes a protective duty upon the state, but it also imposes a duty to respect privacy and family life. The social worker thus faces a choice of ethical and legal imperatives to guide practice, mediated by their own views about the status of older people, about the integrity of families and about the compatibility of their views with those of the agency within which they work.

Defining standards

The International Association of Schools of Social Work's (2001) definition of social work is:

> a profession, which promotes social change, problem solving in human relationships and the empowerment and liberation of people to enhance well-being. Utilising theories of human behaviour and social systems, social work intervenes at the points where people interact with their environments. Principles of human rights and social justice are fundamental to social work.

This definition places social work practice within systems theory, and assumes a dynamic rather than a reactive stance to social as well as individual factors which affect well-being. Although the GSCC's *Code of Practice for Social Care Workers* (GSCC, 2002) is set out as a necessary standard against which practice is to be judged, it falls short of a statement of values for the profession in the sense of stating universal precepts of moral action. The emphasis within the *Code of Practice* is upon equal opportunities rather than anti-oppressive action (Fook, 2002) and the tradition of reformism rather than radical action (Braye and Preston-Shoot, 1995). The *Code of Practice* states that social workers must:

- protect the rights and promote the interests of service users and carers;
- strive to establish and maintain the confidence of service users and carers;
- promote the independence of service users while protecting them as far as possible from danger and harm;
- respect the rights of service users while seeking to ensure that their behaviour does not harm themselves or others;
- uphold public trust and confidence in social care services;
- be accountable for the quality of their work and take responsibility for monitoring and improving their knowledge and skills.

The rationing and prioritization of needs within current social work practice with older people fits well with this utilitarian view of values. Individuals present risks to be assessed within a legal framework, with due consideration for the claims of others and the limited availability of resources. This is seen as a greater good than self-actualization of the individual (Biestek, 1957). Jordan (1995) argues that different approaches to values, from individualistic, utilitarian and radical perspectives, cannot be reconciled without acknowledging that the achievement of some is dependent upon the destruction of others. Liberal values of choice and privacy are among the strongest intellectual defences of the privilege of wealth, whiteness and masculinity on which standard oppression is based (ibid.). Age might be added to this list of structural oppressions, if presumptions about the role of older people in society limit their freedom in economic and social roles. The formal 'mandate' for social work practice, between the IASSW and GSCC guidelines, thus contains inconsistencies and conflicts. How these are interpreted is critical. As Lymbery states: 'While a social worker can be instrumental in supporting the struggle of others to achieve empowerment, s/he also has the capacity to be obstructive' (2005: 134).

Social work roles

The Quality Assurance Agency benchmark for social work training acknowledges that the social work role itself is a contested one. Though the IASSW definition (p. 39) focuses on radical change, social work may also be perceived to have a maintenance function (Davies, 1994), supporting individuals within their current environment and facilitating adaptation to socially sanctioned roles in older age. Social workers may also work in a variety of settings, from fieldwork, to day services, to residential care, and with older people whose predominant need is attributable to factors other than their age – for example, to learning difficulties or temporary homelessness.

As seen in chapter 2, the *21st Century Social Work Review* in Scotland identified the roles of social workers variously as counsellors, advocates and assessors. Asquith et al. (2005) further identify the key social work roles in contemporary practice as:

- counsellor;
- advocate ;
- assessor of risk and need;
- care manager;
- agent of social control.

The counselling/social care planning divide was described by the Barclay report on the roles and tasks of social workers in 1982 as the most significant differentiation to be drawn between social work roles. Both roles, it may be argued, require a knowledge of loss, change and transition, as well as an ability to understand the complex nature of human relationships. In addition, social workers need the skills to intervene in times of crisis, the ability to assess risk and need, and the competence to intervene compulsorily in situations in accordance with legal requirements. So, in the case of Winifred Yates, the onset of dementia is a challenge to her previous competence in managing her own financial affairs and relationships. She may require external support to deal with the demands that her nephew is making on her, but legal powers to intervene may be limited, particularly if she retains the mental capacity to decide both where to live and with whom to associate, as well as the right to refuse intervention that she may feel will alienate her family. Exploring Winifred's view of the situation, assessing her ability to make decisions, and planning for formal and community support to monitor or alleviate risks will all come within the social work role.

Clarity in respect of the roles that social workers perform may not be as obvious to older people as they are to social work managers. Older people themselves are aware of ambiguity in the tasks that social workers perform in rationing resources alongside person-centred practice; in other words, they are aware that what they will be offered is constrained by resources. On the other hand, they expect 'their' social worker properly to present their case; thus they feel entitled to expect an advocacy approach. Research by Manthorpe et al. (2008) into older people's views about social workers is one of the few sources of information derived directly from interviews with older people themselves about their perceptions of the social work role. Social workers' roles are seen as unclear and variable. Older people look for an approach that is knowledgeable about their needs and an approach that is 'on their side'; criticism is directed at social workers who appear not to understand the needs of older people, and those who are obviously driven by agency agendas. A knowledge of physical, social, psychological and economic issues that older people experience is thus of critical importance to acceptable social work practice. Social workers who are driven solely by an organizational mandate are easily 'rumbled' by older people, and may deliver services that are not wanted and not needed.

Social work tasks

The context within which social work is practised influences the tasks that social workers perform. Though the majority of social workers now work outside the statutory sector, statutory sector commissioning of services can control the content of the task that voluntary and private sector services perform. Managerialist agendas which focus on processes and which reserve decisions with high resource implications to senior managers can have the effect of stifling initiative and making workers feel de-skilled and undervalued (McDonald et al., 2008). The development of care management in the era of community care from 1993 onwards has been pervasive, though it has taken a number of different forms: as a generalized approach to all referrals concerning older people, or as a targeted approach for those with the most complex needs. Research by Challis et al. (2007) found that those authorities with a targeted approach undertook more multidisciplinary assessments and gave more support to people with mental health problems, but spent significantly less time in direct contact with service users and carers. This means that social workers within the context of care management are diverted from direct contact with service users to support complex systems.

Lymbery (2005), commenting on the impact of the Blair government's modernizing agenda, focuses on the importance of organizational context for defining and understanding the tasks that social workers perform. He refers to the 'twin dynamics' of partnership and performance 'which have a major impact on the nature and content of social work practice' (2005: 179). So 'partnership' has forced closer working, particularly between health and social care and the development of multidisciplinary teams, comprising social workers, nurses, occupational therapists and others. Two consequences arise from this: a concern that a medical model of practice may dominate (ibid.) and an increased emphasis on skills-mix rather than on a distinct professional role. Performance measures which focus on quantity rather than quality of service, and which are constructed around stereotypical rather than creative responses to problems such as hospital discharge arrangements, also have a tendency to stifle creativity and submerge individual responsibility. So, paradoxically, the two 'modernizing' issues of partnership and performance are capable of exerting contradictory pressures on social services organizations, when solutions to problems are dependent upon inter-agency cooperation, but each individual organization is constrained in its decision-making by its own performance indicators (ibid.). 'Getting it right' in care management is an economic as well as a professional imperative. Care management costs are rising: in 2005–7 they accounted for £1 out of every £8 spent on social care services (CSCI, 2008c). It is critically important, therefore, that professional decision-making is correctly pitched and effective in delivering the outcomes that will work for older people.

Social work theory

Healy (2005) uses a discourse analysis approach to consider the (competing) ideas that shape the institutional context of social work practice, and which provide the means by which particular social work practices can be justified and evaluated. These discourses are biomedicine, neoclassical economics, law, psychology, social science, consumer rights and spirituality (ibid.: 5). Each of these perspectives offers a framework within which social work with older people can be understood.

Biomedicine	This approach assumes that difficulties lie within the person rather than the environment. The medical model of disease detection and management is based on a biomedical approach, within which diagnostic power is seen to reside in the knowledgeable physician. More recently, 'expert patient' groups and practitioners of complementary medicine have provided alternatives to formal sources of knowledge in the understanding and treatment of illness. The study of health inequalities from a social work perspective (McLeod and Bywaters, 1996) has, however, shown how the enjoyment of good health is not equally available and, to a large extent, is governed by social and economic factors.

Economics	Neo-classical economics is based upon the rationality of allocating scarce resources for maximum benefit. The targeting of resources towards those at the greatest risk of costly admission to residential or hospital care, or breakdown, was a key cornerstone of community care policy. However, services were not free to all those in need; the capacity to pay was (and is) an important mediating factor in determining how much service will actually be provided. Efficiency and effectiveness have thus become key measures of agency performance.
Law	Much of law is presented in positivist terms as objectively setting out rules of conduct for application to standard scenarios, sometimes at odds with the real complexities of people's lives. Critics of the 'neutrality' of law, see it as a system based on class, gender and status inequalities. Some groups, including older people, may have limited formal rights under the law, and may be subject to excessive surveillance on the basis of assumed legal 'duties of care'.
Psychology	Psychological theories explain human motivation and functioning. They may be used to consider sources of continuing disadvantage over the life-course, which become manifest in old age, and the understanding thus gained may be used therapeutically as a basis for intervention. In addition, from the practitioner's perspective, critical practice requires an ability to analyse the impact of personal biases on professional practice.
Social science	Sociology provides an alternative focus for the understanding of concepts that may otherwise be presented as 'psychological' or 'biomedical' in their genesis, So, the 'social construction' of dementia, observed in the departure from accepted norms of behaviour by some older people, acts as an alternative explanation to dementia as a cognitive deficit or as an organic disorder of the brain. The 'problem' is thus located outside the individual, as an outcome of social structures or socially created rules.
Consumer rights	The consumer rights discourse that emerges from neo-classical economics sees older people as 'consumers' of social goods, which, through the operation of the market, will act to assure quality, as only efficient and effective providers

– e.g. of residential care – will survive. An amelioration of this position is the development of the quasi-market (Le Grand and Bartlett, 1993) within which the social worker as care manager is the actual purchaser of the service, and the state, through its regulatory bodies, takes some responsibility for the quality of the product on offer.

Consumer rights *movements* on the other hand, have a social basis. Healy (2005) sees the Independent Living Movement campaigning for the rights of disabled people as a consumer movement based on collective and shared experience. Representative groups of older people may also be developed on consumerist principles to secure a better 'deal' for their members over issues such as work and pensions, or as campaigning groups for better legal protection of disadvantaged individuals.

Spirituality

The history of social work has evolved to a large extent from the work of philanthropic and religious organizations, and this history particularly resonates with the provision of welfare services for older people (Lymbery, 2006). In this context, Holloway (2007) considers that religious organizations can attract support and funding that enables them to offer a more extensive service than secular state-run organizations.

At the individual level, the moral framework of spirituality can challenge the positivist assumptions of law and economics about the proper organization of services, and the ultimate indicators of a successful outcome. The valuing of non-material things may have a particular congruence with older people's lives and priorities.

Such key discourses, which provide for theories of intervention in social work, lead to different, and sometimes conflicting, understanding of the issues that affect older people. 'Choice' of the dominant discourse will depend partly upon the orientation of the practitioner, and to a large measure upon the orientation of the organization or team within which they work. Thus the social worker in a hospital team may experience a predominantly biomedical discourse, while someone working in an advice bureau may have to balance consumer rights and economic models.

Theory, whether explicit or not, exerts a powerful influence over practice, which is cumulative in its impact. Healy (2005: 9) describes how theory shapes the purpose of social work practice by defining the political orientation of the social worker, whether motivated to maintenance, control or change over individuals or their environment. Not only do theories 'map' (Milner and O'Byrne, 2002) the complex world of practice, they also define who or what should be the subject of social work intervention, and the practical approaches that should be taken to achieve defined purposes (Healy, 2005). In the process of knowledge development and knowledge use, a symbiotic relationship exists. The technical-rationalist approach of selecting theory 'off the shelf', as if it had an objective validity, is in itself transformed by its application in practice to a diversity of 'cases' and 'situations'. The reflective practitioner (Schön, 1993) weighs up the utility of particular approaches in different cases, transfers learning from experience to new situations and new environments and adjusts their practice accordingly. Taylor and White (2000) go beyond reflection to set out a view of the 'reflexive' practitioner who not only uses knowledge, but *makes* knowledge, shaping theory through doing. So 'truths' about the social, individual and collective experiences of older people and appropriate social work responses are 'constructed', rather than discovered as learning is transferred to new situations.

The methods that social workers use are derived from different theoretical understandings of the social world. Howe (1987) develops sociological approaches which present and separate ideas about the nature of society, and the understanding that this brings about the needs and motivations of individuals within it. Fundamental debates about whether society is based on order or conflict, and whether individuals are to be understood 'subjectively' or objectively, produce core classifications for development by theorists. These core theories, or 'paradigms', as ways of seeing the world, are presented thus (Howe, 1987: 50):

Functionalists	The fixers
Interpretevists	The seekers after meaning
Radical humanists	The raisers of consciousness
Radical structuralists	The revolutionaries

Within each paradigm, a particular theory for social work practice can be located, which in turn produces methods of intervention. Thus Howe sees 'the fixers' as being represented by social work in the psychoanalytic tradition and by behavioural social work – very different in their practice, but each constituting what Healy (2005) alternatively calls a 'problem-solving' approach. The 'seekers after meaning' are those who will pursue person-centred approaches, with a strong emphasis on 'the art of helping' (Howe, 1987: 111). Radical humanists see society as a problem for the individual, not the individual as a problem for society; so anti-discriminatory practice brings into consciousness for individuals the discrimination, based on gender, race or age, that they suffer through membership of a socially constructed group. Radical structuralists turn awareness into social action. When this idea is translated into social work, it manifests itself as anti-oppressive practice which challenges power relationships and, through conflict, creates change in the social structure. Cultural practices (for example, those which segregate older people into 'care' settings) and social structures (which may exclude them from the workplace) are thus seen as a legitimate site for social work intervention (Healy, 2005).

In addition to these historic categories of social work theory, post-modernism has provided another way of understanding the world, based on four key concepts (ibid.): discourse, subjectivity, power and deconstruction. Discourse 'constructs' knowledge from particular perspectives, such as the medical, legal or social, which in turn shape our response to the problems thus identified. The theory can be applied to social work with older people. For Healy (ibid.: 200) social work agencies will be the site of competing discourses – for example, on public and private responsibilities for care in older age. The subjectivity of experience in postmodern theory enables multiple perspectives to be incorporated as 'worker', 'carer', 'older person', 'disabled woman', rather than one fixed identity predetermining experience. Discourses from the social world themselves shape identity, so the experience of being an older person will shift according to time and place. Similarly, 'power' is seen not as a fixed quantity which operates hierarchically, but as an ever-present feature of social relations, such as the 'power' that a carer (a socially constructed identity) may have over the choices that an older person can make. Deconstruction is the tool which exposes the social construction of societal/organizational and social relationships in postmodernism. Reconstruction is thus the therapeutic means of fitting the life-story, or situation which is presented, into a more positive discourse – not a search for a different 'truth', but as a more positive way of celebrating the enduring strengths of older people.

Qualifying and post-qualifying knowledge and skills

So how prepared are social work students to practise competently and ethically in this context? The expectation that beginning social workers will be able to integrate theory and practice as well as develop good communication skills is a prominent feature of the new social work degree (Ford et al., 2006). Social workers are expected to make connections between critical disciplinary knowledge from the social and human sciences and relevant legislation, within a principled ethical framework. They must also have communication skills sufficient 'to talk to those requiring and using services, and their carers with due respect for their age, ethnicity, culture, understanding and needs' (TOPSS, 2002: 2). Learning these skills is a complex and iterative process, requiring students not only to be self-critical, but also to be constructively critical of their peer group. Mercer (1995, in Ford et al., 2006) stresses the importance of working with, rather than simply being exposed to, information. Practice placements provide such an opportunity, but so also do practical role-play opportunities within the curriculum. In constructing such a curriculum, Ford et al. add 'interprofessional activity' to the defining skills of a professional practitioner, which are otherwise described by Barnett (1997) as:

- the ability to interpret the world through theory;
- a facility in understanding and handling different frameworks in action;
- an ability to work within ethical codes and values;
- a right and a duty to speak out on public controversies relevant to the profession, and their particular knowledge-base;
- a loyalty to the profession, rather than self-interest;
- an ability to deploy professional knowledge beyond their own specialism;
- an ability to engage with multiple and competing discourses around needs, services and resources; and
- personal qualities of fortitude, steadiness and integrity.

These different domains of theory, action and the self are explored within social work education as students acquire skills in communication, but also learn professional identity.

At post-qualifying level, the generic learning of the social work degree is consolidated within a specialist delivery context (GSCC, 2006). Even here, guidance on specialist standards and requirements is based on a common framework of knowledge and skills, relevant to work with all adult service user groups. None is identified specifically for work with older people (though assessment in the workplace will be based on the application of the framework skills to work with the specific user group). The common framework of knowledge and skills for social work with adults comprises:

- legislation, social policy and social welfare;
- adulthood, development and transitions;
- communication and engagement;
- assessment, independence, risk, vulnerability and protection; and
- inter-professional, multi-agency working, networking, community-based services and accountability.

Further links are made to the person-centred values of independence, well-being and choice; and the social model of disability is put forward as the 'appropriate model' for thinking about and engaging with the partnership of expertise with people who use services. Thus, individual and political values are directly incorporated into the assessment of the continuing professional development of social workers.

Post-qualifying education will, in particular, address findings that some practitioners are out of date, unclear how to operate their legal knowledge (Braye et al., 2005), and not necessarily updated on recent research findings relevant to practice. Despite the increased proceduralization of practice, the General Social Care Council acknowledges that social workers must still work in a context of 'ambiguity, uncertainty and risk' (GSCC, 2006: para. 8). Furthermore, employer sponsorship of training is linked to the development of agencies as learning organizations and as facilitators of continuing professional development.

Though Adams (2007) accepts that a hard-and-fast distinction between basic and post-qualifying social work is hard to maintain, his contention is that a distinction does exist in the complexity of the situations presented, and the life-changing significance of the decisions that may have to be made. To illustrate this, Adams gives the case example of Mrs Khan, who makes what is described as a 'simple' request that her husband, who has been discharged from hospital, be admitted to residential care because she cannot cope. Adams (2007: 39) then relates possible responses to this scenario in terms of reflective, critical and transformational practice. Reflective practice in this scenario entails working within the status quo and following procedures, though acting thoughtfully and with self-awareness, probably offering services from a pre-existing list. Critical practice locates current practice within its policy context and, being self-critical, considers how it could have been improved or done differently, by challenging the power of the hospital, or the explicit construction of Mrs Khan as a carer. Transformational practice challenges the status quo, changing the current practice and encouraging collective action with others by challenging agency protocols, or by seeing Mr and Mrs Khan's situation as representative of discrimination at a structural level against older people. Although there is not a hard-and-fast distinction, in terms of level, this analysis illustrates how practice may progress through specialist, higher specialist and advanced levels.

Future roles

Options for Excellence: Building the Social Care Workforce of the Future (DH, 2006b) focuses on the options available over the next 15 years to improve recruitment and retention, to define the role of social workers, to improve the quality of social care practice, and to develop the socio-economic case for investment. Specifically, it is predicted (para. 4.9) that from 2006 to 2020 the number of staff working with older people will need to rise by over 25 per cent to meet demographic pressures. For all workers in all sectors, the emphasis is on the achievement of a positive perception for social work: participation by service users, partnership across agencies and necessary developments in professional training. At the same time, the GSCC in England has been considering a review of the changing roles and tasks of social workers. To inform the review, Blewett et al. (2007) have produced a literature-informed discussion paper which identifies seven core components of the debate about the key roles of tasks and social work. These are:

- an understanding of the dynamic between the individual and the social;

- the relationship between social work and social justice;
- the transformatory significance of the relationship;
- the enabling role of social work;
- the control role of social work;
- the management of risk both to the community and to the individual; and
- the evidence base for social work practice.

Such a distillation of tasks is an attempt to move away from the historic tendency of social workers to be defined by who they work for, rather than what they do. Whether such a review is sufficiently radical in meeting the aspirations of service users depends upon the interpretation given to the service user consultation carried out for the same review (Beresford, 2007). Instead of focusing on present roles, service users challenge social workers to tackle the structural issues of political power, limited resources and the domination of social care provision by large organizations. Problems within contemporary practice are identified as stigma, a lack of preventative services, a loss of continuity and risk aversion. Particularly disliked is the rationing role of care management. A narrow focus on 'specialisms' is also seen as divisive; this includes being required to change services at the age of 65. People who use services would like to see more attention paid to disablism and ageism, with a generic understanding of direct payments, social models of disability and a reconceptualization of the social work role as enablers in a collaborative process.

'Putting People First'

An appetite for change in adult social care culminated in 2007 in a joint statement from government, the GSCC, Skills for Care and representatives of private care providers, entitled 'Putting People First': a shared vision and commitment to the transformation of adult social care. Recognizing that the community care legislation of the 1990s had led to a system which can be over-complex, and which too often fails to respond to people's needs and expectations, 'Putting People First' seeks to promote the personalization of care through organizational change. There is a focus on intergenerational programmes, integrated policy developments across agencies and the opportunity to share funding between the NHS and social care. Key features of the policy are:

- a universal information, advice and advocacy service, as a 'first stop shop';
- a Common Assessment Process of individual social care needs with a greater emphasis on self-assessment – this is intended to free up social work time for support, brokerage and advocacy;
- the mainstreaming of person-centred planning and self-directed support;

- a system of 'champions', promoting dignity in local care services; and
- personal budgets for everyone eligible for publicly funded adult social care.

The ideological basis of these changes, focusing on individualism, choice and self-responsibility, with a strong emphasis on health interventions and support to remain in employment, has not gone unchallenged. Traditional areas of work for social workers and social care workers, supporting people through trauma or tragedy, or physical or mental frailty, homelessness or debt, do not figure in this debate. Jordan (2007) expresses dismay at a shift away from public support by the state for interdependent citizens towards a new contractual relationship between the state and the individual. There are contradictions between the new policy emphasis on individual autonomy and collective solidarity, with the latter providing a more stable context for personal satisfaction through community cohesion. Thus the collective context of practice deserves attention in its own right (ibid.) separately from consumer-orientated individualism. The tasks of social work, as explored in Part III of this book, thus need to range from direct work with individuals, to work with families and groups, to work with communities, whether geographically located or comprising groups of older people with common interests in structural change.

Conclusion

Social work with older people is in a state of flux. Values, roles, tasks and skills are being re-ordered, and the process of debate is redefining the role of the social worker as that of 'enabler' in a process of collaboration with service users to challenge resource-led and bureaucratically defined ways of organizing services and to challenge structural inequalities for older people.

Chapter summary

1 Social work with older people has no separate training agenda within the broad description of social worker roles at qualifying and post-qualifying level.
2 The nature of social work is a contested concept, and definitions at international and national levels raise questions of ideology and values.
3 Social workers work in a variety of settings and in a range of roles; older people themselves are aware of conflicts and ambiguities in the social work role.
4 The role of social work in adult services is currently under review by government and by professional groups; this is a response to policy shifts as a legacy of the community care era, and the modernizing agenda of New Labour.

5 The trend towards individualization is not without its critics, who see strengths in collective support and community responses.

Key lessons

1 Generic competence at qualifying level is consolidated and developed by post-qualifying opportunities, which will enhance the knowledge base and skills base of those who work with older people.
2 The title 'social worker' is now protected by law following registration, but re-registration requires evidence of continuing professional development.
3 The GSCC's *Code of Practice for Social Care Workers* provides a mandate for social work practice, but one based on a utilitarian view of social work values.
4 Social workers are constrained by the context in which they practice; though the emphasis is changing from 'who employs them?' to 'what do they do?' in setting future agendas for acquiring skills, the form that this will take is subject to debate.
5 Demographic changes mean that there will be a greater demand in the future for social work with older people.

Activity

Queenie Rogers is 55 years old and has Down's syndrome. She has recently shown signs of developing Alzheimer's disease. Queenie has always lived with her parents, who are now in their mid-80s. Despite an earlier reluctance to plan for the future, Queenie's parents feel that they should begin to consider different options as Queenie's needs change, and they become less able to support her.

Consider specific methods of intervention, and their appropriateness in this situation; and whether practice with Queenie and her family may in consequence properly be described as reflective, critical or transformational.

You may, for example, consider:

1 Care management approaches – to follow through the process of information, assessment, care planning, monitoring and review to plan for Queenie's future care.
2 Task-centred work – to identify with Queenie and her parents their priorities; to break down into stages tasks to be accomplished; and to build personal strengths in tackling challenges that will arise in the future.
3 Solution-focused approaches – looking prospectively at ways in which Queenie can be supported in separating from her family, and identifying locations in which she can receive appropriate support.

4 Psychosocial approaches – which explore past and present barriers to progress decision-making, and which are emotionally as well as practically acceptable.
5 A radical systems-based approach, which links Queenie with other women with learning difficulties who live in the same community to challenge inequalities.

Howe (1987) provides an excellent account of the link between social work theory and specific methods of intervention proposed here.

Briefly, any assessment of Queenie and her family would look at the extent to which the development of Alzheimer's disease has affected Queenie's behaviour and needs. If providing support to her has become more difficult, can this be addressed by extending existing services, or is some more fundamental change needed as both Queenie and her parents enter different stages in the lifecourse? A strengths-based approach would build upon the adaptations that Queenie and her parents had developed over the past 55 years; for the social worker to assume the role of 'expert' clearly would be inappropriate. On the other hand, linking the social worker's knowledge of the prognosis for this type of dementia, or their ability to liaise with other professionals, can usefully inform planning and decision-making. Identifying and, where necessary, modifying a support network will build upon existing strengths to ameliorate difficulties in transition. For Queenie's parents, there is the prospect of living without the child whom they have supported, and who has supported them throughout most of their adult lives. They will face not only a loss of role, but also the practical and emotional support that Queenie was able to give them. Particularly difficult for parents would be a situation where the child becomes unable, because of the dementia, to recognize and acknowledge the parents, and the history that they have shared. Therapeutic interventions to capture significant memories through life story work and the creation of memory boxes would enable Queenie and her family to link past and present experiences of them as a family. Given the paucity of community and residential resources specifically designed for people with learning difficulties who develop dementia, Queenie and her parents, and associated professionals may wish to lobby for better public acknowledgement and the development of appropriate services. The starting point for such analysis is the assessment of Queenie and her family, and it is to social work skills in assessment that we turn in chapter 4.

Further reading

C. Bigby, *Ageing with a Lifelong Disability: A Guide to Practice, Programme and Policy Issues for Human Services Professionals.* London: Jessica Kingsley, 2004.
Explores the particular experiences of disabled people as they grow older. Includes work with carers and lifestyle planning.

S. Neysmith (ed.), *Critical Issues for Future Social Work Practice with Ageing Persons.* New York: Columbia University Press, 1999.
A critical feminist analysis of the social position of older people and of appropriate social work interventions, drawing from international sources.

PART II

SOCIAL WORK PROCESSES

4 Assessment in Social Work

Issues considered in this chapter:

- different theories and approaches to assessment in social care, and the legal framework for assessment;
- barriers to accessing appropriate assessments;
- the Single Assessment Process as an assessment tool;
- assessment in multi-professional contexts.

Good-quality assessment is the cornerstone of effective social work practice, whatever the setting (McDonald, 2006). It is not a process confined to individuals: a 'unified' assessment (Specht and Vickery, 1977) may be applied to individuals, groups, neighbourhoods, organizations and the wider environment. Assessment is 'a perceptual/analytical process of selecting, categorising, organising and synthesising data' (Coulshed, 1991: 30). The form that an assessment will take and the use to which it is put will depend on the theoretical orientation of the assessor, their professional perspective, their degree of knowledge about this and comparable situations, their value system and the synthesis of the relationship between worker and client (McDonald, 2006). So a psychodynamic approach to assessment will seek to explore the origins of current difficulties through an examination of earlier life stages; a behaviourist view of assessment seeks to describe and measure activity so as to intervene strategically to effect change; and an ecological view of assessment looks at the environment within which people live and with which they interact. The SCIE Knowledge Review of Assessment (Crisp et al., 2005) usefully brings together a range of literature on different types of assessment and on methods which can be used as tools in the assessment process.

For older people, assessment is a focused and, increasingly, task-centred event. Government-initiated performance indicators have meant that eight out of ten new assessments of older people are completed within four weeks, and nine out of ten receive a service within four weeks after completion of the assessment: 67 per cent of those assessed receive some sort of service (CSCI, 2008c). It appears, therefore, that assessment is predominantly seen as a gateway to service provision. Within this chapter, approaches to assessment with particular relevance to older people are highlighted, and implications for social work of the development of self-assessment are discussed.

Assessment of older people cannot, however, operate in isolation from the family and social systems that surround them. In carrying out key roles, social workers with older people must be mindful of cultural and intergenerational issues, and of their statutory duties towards other family members, as the case profile described here illustrates.

Case profile

Imran Nazir is 70 years old; he was born in Pakistan, and at the age of 20 he came to the Midlands to work in the textile industry. His wife's family also came from Pakistan at about the same time. Imran's wife died two years ago, and he lives with his son and daughter-in-law and their two teenage children. Imran is critical of his grandchildren's lack of respect for him (as he sees it), of their tastes in music, and of their friends. There are frequent arguments. Anita, the granddaughter, aged 13, complains to her schoolteacher that her grandfather has hit her, and that she is 'fed up with him being there all the time'.

In the case presented here, three generations are involved. Imran Nazir represents a new generation of those who have 'grown old in a second homeland' (Norman, 1985). Assumptions about what growing old will mean may have to be reassessed in the light of cultural changes and new family dynamics. Imran's life history, his gender and the impact of the death of his wife will all affect his understanding of his current situation. Exploring these issues with him will be an important part of the assessment task. There are, however, other needs in the family. The generic training of social workers and the statutory role of child protection require that the welfare of all members of the family is considered. Within a holistic assessment, not only must the social worker have an understanding of the needs of carers, they should also have an appreciation of child development and the impact of family conflict on children. Although roles in intervention may be taken by others, the social worker working with an older person may be called upon to assess situations in which the wishes of that person are only one of a number of factors to be balanced. So, in this case, the risks to Anita the granddaughter must also be assessed, and any intervention developed holistically.

Types of assessment

Smale and Tuson (1993) describe the interaction between assessors and service users as fitting one of three models: questioning, administrative and exchange, each with a different balance within the relationship between the person assessing and the person being assessed. It is likely that in many encounters, there will be movement between these three models. In the questioning model, the assessor is perceived as the 'expert' and it is he or she who sets the agenda for the assessment. In the administrative model, the use of proformas and checklists is commonly devised by managers to constrain both the worker and the service user. The exchange model, by comparison, is a shared enterprise, and the user is respected as the expert on their own life. Needs-based assessment is often presented as the converse of resource-led assessment: within a needs-led assessment, the focus is on explaining individual difference; within a resource-led assessment, eligibility for a predetermined menu of services is the focus of the intervention.

The legal framework within which assessment takes place is explicitly needs-led. The legal mandate for social work with older people clearly separates assessment from service provision (McDonald, 2006). So, s.47 of the National Health Service and Community Care Act 1990 (which is the statutory duty to assess) talks about an 'assessment of the need for community care services' based on the appearance of need; then, having regard to the results of that assessment, the decision is made as to whether those needs call for the provision of any particular service. Needs-led assessment is not, however, the same as user-led assessment; what people say they want or would like may not be the service that the local authority can provide. So, following assessment, *Fair Access to Care Services* (DH, 2002a) provides guidance for local authorities in targeting resources according to whether the level of need disclosed and the threat to independence associated with it is critical, substantial, moderate or low. Furthermore, the type of service that is provided, whether a 'social work service', domiciliary support or residential care, is largely determined by the resources of the provider, not the choice of the individual. Exploring the ramifications of this position is a key challenge to social work, for the promotion of older people's citizenship (looking at the issue in political and social policy terms), social inclusion (taking a sociological view of the status of older people) and well-being (focusing on health and developmental issues).

The importance of context

To what extent, therefore, do social work assessments reflect those agendas? The context within which social work takes place will influence the experience of individuals. Gorman and Postle (2003) and Richards (2000) describe the conflicts between work which aims to be person-centred, and the resource constraints, reductionist approaches to assessment and pressure for throughput and early closure of cases which exist within agencies. The difference may be a methodological one. Richards (2000) describes the extent to which agency-centred assessments overlook or even ignore the efforts of older people to analyse and manage their situation, expressed in narrative form. She also highlights differences between the observed lack of congruence between the process of assessment and the assessor's reported understanding of the extent to which they were able to maintain the older person's views as central to the assessment process. Even where the older person had a decided view of what was needed, the assessor's emphasis on justifying agency expenditure through the recording process made the service user the passive recipient of an assessment, rather than an active participant.

Denial of a rights-based approach has implications for the citizenship of older people. In a study of practice in two local authorities, covering specialist, generic and hospital teams, Rummery (2002) found that access to assessment was treated as a privilege rather than a right. Ellis (2004) similarly found that social workers did not explicitly take a human rights perspective in their work with vulnerable people. Entitlement to services was linked to a willingness to take personal responsibility for one's health or well-being, rather than being seen as an attribute of citizenship. Some groups of older people may be more excluded than others from citizenship. Older people who are resident in care homes are no less entitled to be involved in community and political debates that concern them, and to have effective advocacy for their personal concerns, than those who live in their own homes (Scourfield, 2006). Older people from minority ethnic groups may be reluctant to access services that they see as not relevant to their cultural needs. A forensic view of assessment, focusing on present difficulties instead of past strengths, denigrates the value of skills learned over a lifetime. A focus on social work as 'rescuing' individual casualties also detracts from preventative work in which collective and community interests provide vital support for older people within their own neighbourhoods (Ogg, 2003). Older people like Imran Nazir and his family, in our case profile above, therefore may face particular barriers to accessing appropriate assessment of their complex situation in a context that is respectful of their family history and culture.

Access to assessment

Increasingly, access to social work is negotiated through the use of telephone screening within call centres – a development which replaces face-to-face encounters with technological mediation (Coleman and Harris, 2008). The use of call centres in social services is seen to bring together four aspects of the modernization agenda: learning from the private sector, cutting costs, technology and consumerism (ibid.). Greater proceduralization increases control over professional discretion, and creates a task-centred approach to delivering services. The role of the 'customer' is held at arm's length and is disembodied. The diffidence of older people in approaching a formal organization for help, their reluctance to use technology, previous poor experiences of commercial call centres and the effects of sensory impairment all combine to make call centres an obstacle rather than an aid. Professional discretion in determining who and what should be assessed was shaped by call centre technology which determined both workflow and the bounded nature of contact with callers.

Channelling professional discretion into a predetermined question-naire format is assumed to be antithetical to a negotiated dialogue between social workers and potential customers about the outcomes that they would prioritize. This assumes that, given a freer opportu-nity to negotiate services, a wider range of results should be achieved. Research by Foster at al. (2008) into practitioners' documentation of assessment in social care, however, showed that professionals selected services from a relatively narrow and traditional list. The range of serv-ice user outcomes thus met were broadly clustered into categories: access in and around the home, personal care and comfort, inde-pendence, social activities, activities of daily living and finance. Five categories of assistance accounted for 70.3 per cent of all documented service recommendations; these were: equipment/aids, help with housing, financial help, professional support and domiciliary support. As Foster et al. (ibid.: 556) conclude, this focus on self-care and physi-cal access, rather than the broader policy outcomes of independence and inclusion, militate against individualization of services. The link between service outcomes and professional role, or role within the agency, confirms earlier research by Chevannes (2002), which showed the limited framework within which assessments of older people can take place. Nurses within this framework will pursue medical solu-tions, occupational therapists will focus on equipment and activities for daily living and social workers will look at personal care and social activities. The challenge then is to review traditional service assump-tions in order more flexibly to meet user-identified outcomes. This is a challenge for the agency to devise means of access which are inclusive and supportive, but also to individual practitioners to move away from stereotypical assumptions about older people's priorities for service.

Components of assessments of older people

What then should be the key components in assessments of older people as part of a negotiated process, and as a means of enabling a less restricted range of outcomes to be considered? Learning from research, we might identify the following as components of good-quality assess-ment of older people:

1   *A strengths perspective.* This involves focusing on the older person's continuing ability to perceive and analyse problems and to iden-tify solutions. Selective optimization, whereby the individual can focus on what they do well, as compensation for a decline in other areas of ability is essential for coping and resilience in older age. Assessments should therefore focus on abilities rather than follow a deficit model. So, older women in particular may wish to retain responsibility for directing the way in which household tasks are

prioritized, rather than being told that vacuuming and window-cleaning are low priority. Assistance in continuing to prepare food may also be preferred to having ready-made meals delivered.

2 *Citizenship.* Having one's views respected is an important barometer by which to monitor whether one retains membership of a socially valued group. Participation in decision-making is a key attribute of citizenship. In particular, social workers have a role to play in ensuring that older people placed in care homes have advocacy built into care plans so that they can continue to make their views known on matters of importance within the home and in the community (Scourfield, 2006). Arranging for older people to attend political meetings and to vote is a significant recognition of their citizenship in the wider community.

3 *Autonomy.* Older people are autonomous individuals whose capacity for decision-making is assumed by reference to their adult status. Assessors need to be aware that referrals from relatives and others may prioritize their own concerns over the older person's wishes (Richards, 2000). Families may be unhappy about the personal, and financial decisions that older people make, but the converse may be true: older people may not wish to support their adult children through emotional and financial difficulties, or may be particularly troubled by family break-up and estrangement.

4 *Information.* Information is often difficult to access and not well coordinated across agencies. Older people often know little about the assessment process that they have been through, but welcome clarity about its purpose, format and outcomes (Baldock and Ungerson, 1994; Richards, 2000).

5 *Personal development.* Assessment brings with it an opportunity for personal development and growth. Restrictive agency agendas undermine the narrative processes by which people develop understanding of their situation and communicate it to others (Blaug, 1995). So the very fact of being able to tell one's story to a concerned individual is intrinsically of value.

The Single Assessment Process

Formal assessment documentation is commonly used by statutory agencies to structure assessments. The *National Service Framework [NSF] for Older People* (DH, 2001) introduced the Single Assessment Process (SAP), which 'aims to make sure older people's needs are assessed thoroughly and accurately, but without procedures being needlessly duplicated by different agencies' (DH, 2002b).

A number of models are available, but the key intention is to enable different assessors to share information so that the older person does not constantly have to repeat personal information. If more specialized or complex assessments are needed, then these can be built onto the core information already provided. Guidance is available at HSC

2002/001, and the Centre for Policy on Ageing is collating examples of assessment tools, protocols and training materials. There are three broad levels of assessment within SAP: contact assessment, overview (or multi-dimensional) assessment and specialist assessment. These are differentiated in the following way:

- contact assessment should screen in people who may require support from a number of different services;
- overview assessment should support multidisciplinary working by considering mental, physical, social and environmental needs; in addition, the impact of a person's needs on their family and any carer should be considered;
- specialist assessment should be undertaken when there is a need for more information about the cause or nature of a presenting need or about ways of meeting that need, such as through the provision of specialist therapeutic intervention;
- supported assessment may be offered by any of a range of professionals to the individual as part of the process of self-directed support.

Within the SAP, a review of needs is seen proactively as part of the continuing process of assessment.

The SAP has been implemented incrementally, but there has been considerable slippage from its anticipated final implementation date of April 2004. Early outcomes of research into the working of the SAP have focused on both professional and service user experiences. Issues arising include:

- the ability of agencies to work together to implement SAP;
- differences in perception between different professional groups;
- older people's satisfaction with the process;
- evidence of improved outcomes from the use of the SAP.

The PSSRU study (Challis et al., 2004) conducted a literature review, surveys of managers in health and social care, data from psychiatrists working with old age and from specialists in geriatric medicine, as well as from older people themselves. It found that there was a lack of coherence and trust between agencies in implementing the SAP. Incompatible IT systems are a major barrier. A sample of an assessment schedule for an overview (basic, generic) assessment is given in the box below. As can be seen, the assessment is structured around a number of 'domains', some of which may require more detailed assessments by specialist professionals. The model of assessment within which the format is designed is clearly an administrative model, with pre-coded answers being anticipated in response to 'expert' questioning.

The SAP has potential for use as a preventative tool and to support self-management of chronic conditions, not only to facilitate inter-agency work. But how well designed is it as a tool for self-management? The feasibility of using such a 'case finding' assessment tool within primary care was evaluated by Roberts et al. (2006). The process highlighted the time-consuming nature of assessment, with the research nurse spending half an hour with the patient for an overview assessment, one and three quarter hours for a comprehensive assessment, with an additional one and a quarter hours of preparation and recoding time. The most frequent trigger issues for assessment were immunization and screening, medication management, communication disorders and pain. There were no triggers for alcohol misuse or abuse of older people. There was a high refusal rate both for assessment (54 per cent) and for services. Interviews with participants suggested the importance of timing in acceptance of new services or referrals; the authors also consider (p. 397) whether the concepts of self-care and self-management, which are central to chronic disease management, may be more difficult to achieve with frail older people than with people with specific conditions such as diabetes. The majority of older people favoured the idea of a regular check-up, through continuing contact with the primary care team, rather than a 'case finding' approach. Seeing assessment as an event rather than a process which is integral to continuing contact with primary care professionals may therefore not be as acceptable to older people as policy suggests, particularly if its use requires complex personal circumstances to be condensed into pre-coded categories of need.

The core assessment and outcomes package for single assessment

FACE Overview Assessment Version 5
Key/Annotation method for completing the assessment items
- problem / need
? possible problem / need
no no need / problem
n/k not known
n/a not applicable
u not assessed

1. Brief description of person's presenting problems or needs.
2. Relevant personal history.
3. Cultural / spiritual / personal issues relevant to assessment.
4. Formal care / support currently received.
5. Domains of assessment.
   a. physical well-being
   b. psychological well-being
   c. activities of daily living
   d. social circumstances
   e. family and carers
   f. carer's needs and concerns
6. Assessment summary: strengths and weaknesses and protective factors / risks.
7. Health and social care needs + FACs banding and justification.

Research into older people's perceptions of assessment by social workers have similarly shown that the opportunity for unhurried discussion in the context of a relationship was particularly valued (Powell et al., 2007), with the sensitivity and interpersonal skills of the assessor making it a memorable event, echoing findings from Richards (2000). One difficulty was raising expectations of service that cannot be satisfied (Powell et al., 2007). Linking domains of social circumstances, family and carers and carers' needs is critical in order to obtain a rounded picture of the strengths within the environment surrounding the older person. Importantly, for the older people in this survey, the blending of formal support from health and social care services, with ongoing informal support from friends and family, was an equilibrium that the domains of 'relationships' and 'immediate environment' within the SAP could investigate if sensitively used. Similarly, the acknowledgement that community-based support for older people remains critically important within the assessment process for locating assessments of individuals within their social setting. However, understanding culture, life history and older people's sense of their place within the community is unlikely to be capable of being condensed into a checklist, and needs a narrative approach properly to analyse within a theoretical framework the accumulated wisdom of older people.

Counsel and Care's (2006) research into the working of the SAP in 33 London boroughs was a response to their finding that many older people and carers in contact with the Counsel and Care Advice Service experienced poor-quality needs assessment and duplication of information. Survey results from professionals and from service users were analysed under five themes: information sharing, consultation and involvement, joint working, monitoring and review. While professionals viewed information provided within the SAP as adequate, or better, 33 per cent of older people or their carers viewed the standard of information provided to them as less than adequate, or viewed it negatively. Their responses (ibid.: 10) showed how a lack of information can lead to feelings of erosion of power and increased anxiety and frustration. The lack of provision of any written details of the assessment and care planning process also undermined the positive experience of the assessment itself. Though staff consultation appeared to have been effective in embedding ownership of the process in the working practices of professionals, for users and carers the most positive feedback was provided when it was felt that a person-centred assessment had been carried out. For health and social services professionals, the key SAP principle of joint working was identified as difficult where more joint working meant having to change the culture of the organization. Not many of the agencies had themselves taken steps to audit the impact of the SAP by asking for feedback from service users or collecting data from reviews.

Making older people more aware of the existence of assessment criteria and explaining the process clearly appear to be key. Also important is the proactive involvement of the social worker. Independent advice and information are particularly valuable in helping people to navigate their way through systems and, more importantly, to emphasize citizenship.

Self-assessment

Why should professional gate-keeping of assessments be seen as the norm? Self-assessment, completed without the immediate involvement of professionals, has been reviewed by Griffiths (2005). 'Self-assessment' itself is a contested term, but Griffiths views the following as essential components: self-report, self-completion/direction and self as beneficiary. Self-assessment thus lends itself to various, sometimes complex, combinations of elements (ibid.), not all of which are necessarily 'client-centred'. The SAP itself may be presented as a key tool in self-assessment (DH, 2002b), utilizing models which normally involve the user in completing short scales and questionnaires, sometimes internet-based.

Most studies of self assessment, however, are of general health-related assessments used as screening tools. These are seen to work most effectively (Griffiths, 2005) where the reference standard is well developed, for example in mental health, osteoporosis and for mobility problems. Though self-assessment can enhance user involvement, there is little evidence of how older people feel about self-assessment. If a self-assessment opportunity comes from a reliable source, such as a GP, it is more likely to result in participation rates. Where self-assessment is targeted at those over 75, non-responses are more likely than not to suggest unmet needs and unidentified problems, rather than a general absence of reportable problems (ibid.). It cannot be assumed, therefore, that a refusal of assessment is indicative of an absence of need.

"Supported" self-assessment, on the other hand, is seen as a positive experience for older people (ibid.), although lay or professional input is still valued as a facilitator in interpreting the results. An example of an effective self-assessment tool is the HOOP (Housing Options for Older People) assessment (available at www.housingcare.org), which enables older people to make their own decisions about whether or not to move home, based on their own perceptions of need. This has proved particularly useful for older people who were feeling pressured into making a decision by family or friends. In the health field, more evidence is needed of how self-assessment can lead to behavioural change. Having resources available to meet identified need is also crucial. Evidence from systems-based research into assessment processes for older people thus appears to favour its use in situations where needs are clearly identifiable and resolvable. When issues are complex, direct professional skills are still needed to tease out difficulties and to provide continuing support and monitoring. Such support needs to be available within a relationship of trust, which signifies that evolving individual needs and structural barriers to their realization will be addressed. Understanding the source and complexity of such needs in a theoretical context is thus a major component of the social work task.

Social workers as assessors in multi-professional contexts

Increasingly, social workers work in multi-agency and multi-professional contexts. A number of agencies – social care, health, social security and environmental services – may be involved jointly or separately in the assessment process. In a community care assessment, there is a legal duty (s.47(3) of the National Health Service and Community Care Act 1990) to invite health and housing agencies to participate in the assessment. The use of Health Act flexibilities for pooled budgets and the development of Care Trusts and Practice-Based commissioning have broken down some of the structural barriers between health and social care to the extent that roles in commissioning services following assessment are interchangeable. At the individual practitioner level, multidisciplinary working, where each profession contributes its unique knowledge and skills to the assessment, may exist alongside interdisciplinary working, where focus is on outcomes to be achieved – 'what needs to be done', rather than 'who does what' (Øvretveit, 1997). The attribution of improved outcomes to new partnership arrangements is not straightforward or necessarily generalizable; they are complex social interventions requiring individuals to act in different ways within specific service contexts (Freeman and Peck, 2006). Coordination between services may thus be a more measurable gain than advantages to individual service users (Lymbery, 1998).

Nevertheless, different professions will have different approaches to assessment and priorities in service provision. For example, while social workers and occupational therapists share a focus on keeping older people in the community, their choice of resources usually has different emphases. Occupational therapists seek to optimize independence by the adaptation of the environment or provision of equipment, whereas social workers are more likely to recommend personal care assistance. The CAMELOT trial, a randomized control test (Stewart et al., 2005) found that there was no significant difference on a range of clinical outcomes between occupational therapy and social work-led assessments for frail older people and their carers. The study did, however, find that social workers as a group were less likely to respond to articulated healthcare needs by referring onward to a wider range of community healthcare professionals such as psychotherapy, speech therapy and community nursing. This was so even though such interventions led to a better self-assessment of well-being for carers.

There is a lesson here for social workers in being alert to healthcare needs. The provision of a social work service is no substitute for appropriate healthcare. The same point is also made from a research study into the placement of social workers in acute hospital settings. While the provision of a social work service in A&E departments can support older people in a confusing situation, it can only operate to prevent admission to hospital if adequate healthcare as well as social care resources are in place (McLeod et al., 2003).

Assessments often take place under pressure, where time, resources and skill are limited. The process of discharging patients from hospital provides a clinical indicator of the state of partnership working between health and social care agencies (Henwood, 2006). Expectations of professional roles have been attenuated by changes in the legislative framework with the introduction of the Community Care (Delayed Discharges) Act 2003. This established a system of reimbursement for delays caused by a shortfall in the provision of community care services, and older people were the primary group to which this legislation applied. This legislation has had an impact upon professional practice, and upon the experience of older people at the point of discharge from hospital and beyond. Research by the Commission for Social Care Inspection (CSCI) in 2004 and 2005 found that there was a significant reduction in delayed discharges, though experiences of rehabilitation were mixed and there was evidence of inadequate post-discharge support, increased admissions directly to residential care (in some areas) and an under-investment in services that prevented admission (ibid.).

The 2005 CSCI report focused on the long-term consequences for older people of rushed decision-making. Though the report noted (para. 2.3) that efforts to maximize independent living in old age are likely to be thwarted without a fuller debate and agreement about responsible, positive risk-taking, fewer than half the case records examined contained thorough risk assessments and robust crisis plans. A key finding was the value that older people placed on a named person from social services overseeing their care, not only in terms of the cumulative knowledge that they had of the person's needs and preferences, but in the continuity of relationship that they offered. Actively addressing the anxieties of family members and engaging them in risk assessment and contingency planning was also seen as assisting crisis management in the future. So in the case of older people from minority ethnic groups, a worker able to communicate in their own language and with an understanding of specific care needs as well as the family's changing ability to offer accommodation and an awareness of alternative resources will counteract stereotypical responses attributable to a lack of confidence in the worker concerning their assessment skills.

Older people excluded from assessment

Yet before social work involvement is even considered, there are two groups of people who are particularly vulnerable to being excluded from such sources of support as may be available: those who do not meet eligibility criteria and those who are self-funding. Exclusion from assessment requires older people to fall back upon their own resources, even in situations which display the range of complexities discussed in this chapter. For these two groups, disadvantage can operate either at an organizational or at an individual level.

In a background paper for the CSCI report on the State of Social Care, Henwood and Hudson (2008) produced an analysis of those 'lost to the system'. They found that older people were vulnerable within the assessment process to both cultural and institutional ageism (ibid.: para. 25), which failed to recognize the value of participation and social inclusion (ibid.: para. 3.86). There was a reluctance to acknowledge low-level need, and (particularly amongst non-professionally qualified staff) a continuation of service-led approaches to care. For professional staff, discretion was limited by organizational directives, and reinforced in training programmes, peer-review arrangements and in supervision and management. Self-funders fared badly under such a system; they tended to be diverted away from the assessment process, relying heavily on word of mouth or 'feel' for services rather than on independent advice or research (ibid.: para. 3.64).

Such self-funders may of course be hostile to social work involvement, but they are seen as preferred residents for care homes, as they are less debilitated and pay higher fees. This means that they are taking the momentous decision to move into residential care in haste, and before other options have been explored (ibid.: para. 14). Cumulatively, the effect of excluding self-funders from assessment at lower levels of need means that care 'tariffs' will rise, and that in the longer term pressure on scarce and expensive resources will increase. The number of crisis situations thus created is likely to rise. As councils raise their eligibility criteria to meet only critical and substantial need, the consequence is predicted to be a significant drop in the take-up of care support. Such rationing of preventative services will in some time period lead to an increase in the supported population who are resident in care homes. For self-funders, the effect is likely to be a delay in accessing care support, as pensioner wealth increases (Wanless, 2006). More people proportionately will fall into the self-funding bracket; reaching such people with timely assistance and advice becomes more critical. The people who will do such reaching out may not be social workers, but they will need similar knowledge and skills.

The outcome of assessment decisions is the making of a care plan, and it is the process of care planning which is the subject of the next chapter. Within the process of care management, service provision must meet the challenge of locating resources that are sufficient to meet assessed needs at a level which anticipates a degree of flexibility, while preserving the privilege of reassessment when progression to more expensive levels of service is anticipated. Within the experience of the user of services, assessment will be tolerable only if it is a negotiated process, supported by accessible information leading to the offer of appropriate services.

Conclusion

Though assessment is a key skill for social workers, it is not their exclusive domain. Other professional groups contribute to the assessment process, and a common use of paperwork may disguise an absence of shared values and the potency of contextual factors. Self-assessment is put forward as an opportunity for older people to prioritize their needs; however, resources must be available to support the choices that older people themselves wish to make.

Chapter summary

1 Assessment may be applied to individuals, groups, neighbourhoods, organizations and the wider environment.
2 The legal framework for assessment is needs-led, but eligibility criteria target resources on those in greater need.
3 The Single Assessment Process for Older People seeks to prevent duplication of procedures by different agencies; research shows that older people value continuity, a person-centred approach and a blending of formal and informal support.
4 Self-assessment is in need of further evaluation in terms of its acceptability to older people, but is reliant upon having resources available to meet identified need.
5 Discharge from hospital is a critical time to test the robustness of assessment processes and congruence between professionals and older people in evaluating risk.

Key lessons

1 Assessments based on an 'exchange' model acknowledge older people as experts on their own lives, but administrative models may prescribe the agenda for assessment in a managerialist context.
2 Social workers and other professionals may not explicitly adopt a rights-based approach to the assessment of older people, but not to do so is a denial of citizenship.
3 Social workers who place older people in care homes have a continuing responsibility to assess their needs; building advocacy into care plans enables older people to express their opinions through formal processes.
4 Different professionals approach assessment in different ways; the institutional context may prioritize rapid throughput over considered decision-making.
5 Social workers need to be aware of discrepancies between their everyday practice, their professional values and contextual pressures.

Though self-assessment may be empowering for older people, those who have needs that are not eligible for service, or who have self-funding may be effectively disenfranchised from receiving support, guidance and protection.

Activity

Bowes and Dar (2000) have conducted research into reasons for the non-use or problematic use of social care services by older Pakistani people and their families. While emphasizing the importance of hearing users' voices, the theoretical and practical difficulties involved when working with relatively powerless groups, and the obstacles of linguistic and cultural communication, are also discussed as methodological issues. Information about cultural practices is seen as increasing confidence in social work staff, but, conversely, staff of the same ethnicity as service users should not be assumed to have competence in professional areas.

How then might you design a culturally sensitive service for older people from a minority ethnic group?

Further reading

J. Butt and A. O'Neil, *Black and Minority Ethnic Older People's Views on Research Funding*. York: Joseph Rowntree Foundation, 2004.
Contains a review of the literature and findings from direct consultations with older people to try to determine new research priorities that would have a direct impact on the availability of appropriate services for people from diverse communities.

J. Milner and P. O'Byrne, *Assessment in Social Work*, 2nd edn. Basingstoke: Palgrave, 2002.
This is a classic text on different 'maps' of assessment in social work, linked to methods of intervention ranging from the therapeutic to the solution-focused. It is recommended for the clarity of its exposition and the quality of its guidance to practitioners through dilemmas of choice of method.

5 Care Planning

Issues considered in this chapter:

- the focus on outcomes within care planning;
- the range of care providers and the operation of the market in care;
- domiciliary services, assistive technology, day-care services and residential services in community care planning;
- understanding the needs of carers;
- user-directed care planning.

The process of care planning identifies the most appropriate ways of achieving the objectives set out in the assessment of need. Care planning involves the identification of service providers, the commissioning of resources and the consideration of outcomes. Reconfiguring specialist services to bring care closer to home is a key policy aim for older people (DH, 2006c). Key elements of such care are identified as:

- early intervention and assessment;
- management in the community of long-term conditions;
- early supported discharge from hospital;
- fast access to acute hospital care; and
- partnership's built around the needs and wishes of older people and their families.

The NHS and social care agencies have a clear interest in ensuring that older people receive the right kind of services. People over the age of 65 account for 43 per cent of the NHS total budget, 58 per cent of the social services budget and 71 per cent of social care packages (ibid.). Care planning for older people is therefore a key issue for each service.

There is an increasing emphasis on outcomes, rather than the provision of standard services. An outcomes focus means simply that services should be fine-tuned and evaluated for the difference that they can make to people's lives. For example, the outcome that involves extending leisure opportunities may be met by providing transport to enable people to attend adult education classes or sports centres, rather than by the provision of a day centre place, which is a more traditional model for service provision. Further emphasis is placed on the experience of using social care, as a 'process' outcome, promoted particularly through the 'Dignity in Care campaign' (DH, 2008b). Dignity here is seen as having many overlapping aspects, involving respect, privacy, autonomy and self-worth.

The personalization of care – tailoring it to individuals – is increasingly seen as the key aim of service provision to meet the aspirations of older people. The input of family carers remains central to care planning; designing services that meet their needs as well as the needs of those for whom they provide care is important for the achievement of both process and final outcomes. In this chapter, we can consider the case of Una and Alf Vernon (see the case profile).

Case profile

Una Vernon and her husband Alf are both aged 68. Three years ago Alf retired from his job as manager of a large retail store. Since then, Una and Alf have been on a number of foreign holidays and Alf has joined the local golf club. He had always worked long hours, and they had moved around the country a lot with his job. Una found it difficult to make friends and relied on Alf to make major decisions. Six months ago, Alf had a stroke. After a short period in hospital he returned home, and has just completed a course of physiotherapy at the local day hospital. Una has told staff that Alf will not let her leave the house without him, and that he is constantly requiring attention from her. Una says that she 'does not feel cut out to a carer', but doesn't know how Alf would manage without her.

Following a stroke, Alf has followed a pathway involving admission to acute hospital care and early supported discharge from hospital. As a person with a long-term condition, he will require advice and monitoring to enable him to manage his condition in the community. Una, his wife, has also become his carer – a change of role for her. Alf has been socially defined as a 'disabled person'. He may face barriers to resuming his former hobbies and interests and his involvement with the community in which he lives. Care planning will involve building a partnership around the needs and wishes of Alf and Una, which addresses not only service provision, but also their response to change in their personal relationship and social identity.

What outcomes are valued by older people?

If services do not meet the needs of people such as Alf and Una, they will either not be taken up, or will fail to be experienced as helpful and supportive. The 'Outcomes in Social Care for Adults' (OSCA) initiative (Henwood and Waddington, 2002) moves the focus away from a crude purchaser/provider split, which concentrates on who provides the care, and instead places it firmly on the quality of services experienced by, and outcomes achieved for, individuals and their families and carers. Outcomes are also disaggregated into maintenance outcomes based on quality-of-life measures such as cleanliness and security, but also social participation and control; change outcomes, tackling barriers to achieving quality of life or reducing risks – for example, improving relationships, assisting recovery and rehabilitation; process outcomes, looking at the impact of the way in which services are delivered against measures such as cultural sensitivity, choice and respect (Henwood and Waddington, 2002).

Glendinning et al. (2007) present a review of research evidence on the outcomes valued by older people and the factors that facilitate and inhibit achieving those outcomes. They found that older people valued the same broad range of outcomes as service providers, although the priority given to them could vary according to age, living circumstances and type of impairment. Valued outcomes were:

Change outcomes:

- improvements in physical symptoms and behaviour;
- improvements in physical functioning and mobility;
- improvements in morale.

Maintenance or prevention outcomes:

- meeting basic physical needs;
- ensuring personal safety;
- having a clean and tidy home environment;
- keeping alert and active;
- having social contact and company, including opportunities to contribute as well as receive help;
- having control over daily routines.

Service process outcomes:

- feeling valued and respected;
- being treated as an individual;
- having a say and control over services;
- value for money;
- a good 'fit' with other sources of support;
- a compatibility with, and respect for, cultural and religious preferences.

(ibid.: vi)

Factors relating to the operation of social care quasi-markets, part of the legacy of community care in the 1990s, are seen as affecting the delivery of outcomes-focused services. These include service-led assessments, irregular reviews, purchasing by time or task rather than outcomes, rigid commissioning practices and difficulty in recruiting and retaining staff. More recently developed services such as intermediate care and reablement services have a stronger outcomes focus. Nevertheless, even such services as these may be experienced as unhelpful if they do not acknowledge difficulties that older people have in accepting support in the context of physical and psychological changes brought about by critical events.

Organizational barriers may also militate against an outcomes focus. Domiciliary care provided by private agencies faces particular difficulties in developing an outcomes-focused approach where care is allocated according to inflexible time slots or tasks. The role of the assessor is critical; older people's ability to identify outcomes for themselves may be restricted by their perceptions of social services' responsibilities, of the help that they think it is legitimate to ask for and of the services that they think are available (ibid.). It should not be assumed therefore that potential service users will be aware of the possibility of help within the home from social care, unless this is explicitly raised with them. Understanding the meanings that older people give to their experiences is also critical. Having control over one's life appears to underpin all other outcomes. Older people are likely to reject service outcomes that they perceive as incompatible with their concept of independence, with their self-image or which emphasize dependency.

Exploring the perceptions of Una and Alf about the type and frequency of service that might be acceptable to them is critical. So, in a study of the meanings that older people give to their experience of inpatient rehabilitation, mismatches between the offered programme and what older people felt that they needed affected individuals' subsequent ability to live at home (Wallin et al., 2006). Not only was there a need to individualize the rehabilitation regimen, there was also a need to involve older people to a greater extent in the planning of the service. The message is that involving older people in the identification of outcomes, and tailoring services to maximize independence and control, are not desirable just in terms of respect for older people; they are also critical to the achievement of successful outcomes.

The range of care providers

Taking into account process outcomes as well as final outcomes, assessments should specify not only what services will be delivered, but also the manner in which they are to be delivered. Commissioners of service exert a major influence over whether outcome-focused services are delivered. Bamford (2001) describes how the replacement of compulsory competitive tendering with 'best value' regimes means not selecting the cheapest service, but balancing cost against the quality of service provided. Local authorities employ three main types of contract:

- block contracts, where the purchaser buys access to whole or part of a service or facility, such as a certain number of beds in a care home, for a specified price;
- cost and volume contracts, where a volume of service and a total cost is agreed, and any additional service is provided on an individual price basis;

- individual or spot contracts, where the purchaser contracts for a service for an individual user for a specified time at an agreed price.

The commissioning role of the agency is put into operation at practitioner level by the process of purchasing services within an individual package of care – Bamford (2001) calls this 'micro commissioning'. An inevitable tension is created between the economic and social objectives of care management – managing the budget – versus advocacy for the best interests of the service user (McDonald, 2006). The social work task is extended beyond a traditional coordinating role to that of actively seeking out new services and providers, with attendant complexities of transaction costs. Nevertheless, for many older people the creative use of commissioning may enable services such as transport or 'sitting' services to be provided to enable elements of their former lifestyle to be maintained.

The market in care

The management of the social care market has become increasingly complex. Since the beginnings of community care in 1993, the proportion of residential care places provided directly by the statutory sector has declined, such that the voluntary and private sectors are now the major providers of care. The proportion of domiciliary care provided by private agencies has also increased. Growth however has been uneven. There have been particular issues highlighted both in London and in rural areas. In London, the King's Fund inquiry (2005) found that, as a result of above-average care home fees, staff shortages and higher rates of social problems, the capital's care system is underfunded and understaffed and offers little in the way of choice and quality. Older people therefore had restricted access to care and practical support, and were being put at risk from untrained and unqualified staff. Older people were vulnerable consumers in a poorly developed care market, as they lacked knowledge of what was available, opportunities to influence the quality of care on offer, and money to purchase what they needed. People with mental health problems and those from black and minority ethnic communities were particularly affected. Patchy coverage by private domiciliary agencies, and high transport costs also restrict choice in rural areas (Glendinning et al., 2007). It is questionable, therefore, whether a market approach to care does provide choice. For the individual older person such choice is mediated through the decisions made by the care manager in choosing which resources to access, and at what cost. Greater emphasis upon personal choice has seen a challenge to professionally led models of care planning through a number of recent initiatives: direct payments, individual budgets and practice-based commissioning, which in turn will both extend the range of possible services available, but also destabilize care markets as systems of cost and volume and block contracting become less viable.

Domiciliary services

The move from home help to homecare, moving away from low-level practical assistance to personal care, has targeted service provision on a smaller group of eligible users. Though the number of individuals in the UK in receipt of homecare services went down from 500,000 in 1991 to 384,000 in 2006 (CSCI, 2006b), the average number of hours received by each individual increased. Local authorities were given targets to work towards this increase. One effect has been that low-level services – 'that bit of help' (Clark et al., 1998) – have decreased. Domiciliary agencies were brought within established inspection regimes in recognition of the state's interest in regulating the quality of care provided. CSCI's first inspection report (2006b) focused to a large extent on process issues, and found that the allocation of time to domiciliary visits was often inadequate, leading not only to a lack of control for older people, but also to a threat to their dignity in having intimate care provided by people with whom it was difficult to establish a trusting relationship. Older people may find it difficult to accept assistance with intimate matters such as bathing and toileting from people they do not know, and this may contribute to the refusal of services assessed as needed.

Demand for domiciliary services exceeds supply. In Scotland, the introduction of free personal care has led to a 62 per cent increase in demand for services. Research by Bell et al. (2008) showed that this was not necessarily offset by a fall in informal care-giving: friends and family were now equally involved, but gave social and emotional support, rather than the direct provision of 'care'. The research also found that there were wide differences in the amount of care that authorities were able to provide for a given cost. Yet for someone who finds 'hands on' care difficult, the provision of practical assistance may enable Una, in our example, to concentrate on the social and emotional aspects of her relationship with Alf, while delegating 'hands on' care to others.

Finding an appropriate balance between targeting resources on those most in need and providing an accessible service has proved complex. Concern to 'invert the triangle of care' and to provide more low-level preventative services was seen in a report from the Association of Directors of Social Services and Local Government Association (2003); it was also the focus of the White Paper on health and social care (DH, 2006c). Services have, however, to be acceptable to older people. A balance has to be found between supportive and intrusive intervention. De-skilling by the use of domiciliary services for people who took pride in their own housekeeping abilities may precipitate depression (Banerjee and Macdonald, 1996). Care managers need to be aware of gender bias in the services that are provided: older men living alone may be seen as less capable domestically, and both men and women may wish to express an opinion about having care provided by a person of the opposite sex, or the exposure of the body to scrutiny by others.

Social connection through care workers is highly valued by older people. The qualities that are particularly valued are consistency, time-liness, thoroughness and efficiency (Godfrey et al., 2004) Older people themselves may experience conflict between the tasks which can be given over to others and those which are central to identity or well-being and will not be given up without a struggle (ibid.). Exploring this through the care planning process is therefore critical. In fact, purchasers have a critical role to play throughout the commissioning process in affecting all types of outcome, even when supply chains appear to distance responsibility for outcomes from the commissioning process. In a study of homecare providers, Patmore (2004) found that purchasers affected service quality through the amounts of time which they commissioned, and through their willingness to purchase help for quality of life as well as for physical needs. However, providers differed amongst themselves as to the amount of flexible additional help they were willing to allow staff to give. There were also differences in the extent to which small changes in routine, or additional time, needed to be approved by care managers as purchasers before a provider could go ahead. Different organizational arrangements may thus lead to differential experiences for older people in the provision of domiciliary care. Specialist homecare for people with dementia is, however, beneficial in ensuring that fluctuating needs are understood and responded to consistently (Chilvers, 2003).

Assistive technology

After homecare services, the next most frequent service to be provided to older people is assistive technology (McCreadie et al. 2007), and the chief functional problems that it addresses are walking and climbing stairs. The term 'assistive technology' covers the range of aids and adaptations provided to assist people in activities of daily living, but increasingly the term is used to include the application of technology such as sensor mats and tracking devices. Technology may be fixed, for example grab rails and stair lifts; it may be portable, such as walking sticks; or it may be electronic, providing community alarms or 'Smart House' technology to alert carers to difficulties in daily routines. The majority of these devices are manufactured by the private sector, but are recommended by occupational therapists employed in care management roles. McCreadie's research found that information about such devices was given reactively and that this was seen as a rationing device; their link to disability services made them less appealing to older people than a more neutral concept such as the 'functioning home'. Rules and procedures were also complex, and means testing and long waiting times were disincentives. Useful though such aids may be technically, how they are designed for the domestic environment, and how they are presented to older people, need further study. Home-owners may have mixed feelings about the installation of equipment such as stair lifts and hoists in a home which has been a place for relaxation and entertaining, particularly if such aids recall a hospital environment. More fundamentally, the surveillance of older people that such technology can provide raises ethical issues about intrusion on privacy and consent, particularly if applied to people with dementia to constrain their freedom of movement.

Reablement

'Reablement' is a social care-focused approach which seeks to ensure that 'the lowest appropriate level of intervention is provided set within an active and ongoing process to balance risk against "quality of life" for adults who need care' (DH, 2009a). In effect, this means a short-term task-based approach which diverts individuals from long-term care or support by the provision of a time-limited service such as homecare or physiotherapy. Such services are likely to become more widespread, as they are financially supported under the 'Putting People First' concordat. The Department of Health's Care Services Efficiency Delivery Network has purchased customized functional assessment tools and satisfaction surveys and is engaged in a longitudinal study of the effectiveness of 'homecare reablement' in improving choice and quality of life, making best use of limited resources. 'Home' in this context can mean an individual's residence or sheltered or extra care housing. The emphasis is on preventing hospital admission or post-hospital transfer to long-term care. Another objective is to reduce long-term reliance on domiciliary care by providing intensive but short-term periods of support to deal with sudden deterioration in health. Alternatively, homecare reablement will be targeted at those people on 'maintenance' packages of homecare who could recover some use of function if supported to do so. Older people will account for almost half the increase in the total number of households in the UK by 2026 (DH and DWP, 2008). New housing will have to meet lifetime home standards by 2011; a target set to seek to ensure that appropriately designed houses are available to meet changing needs as people age or are affected by an impairment.

Day services

In order to provide services to older people as a group, and respite for individuals, day services would conventionally be considered as a service within a care plan. A number of models of day services exist, ranging from education to reablement to social care (Seed, 1988). In addition, day services may provide valuable respite to carers, and support in short- and long-term planning by enabling needs to be monitored (Clark, 2001). Moriarty and Webb (2000), looking at the effectiveness of services for people with dementia, found that older people who attended day care were more likely to have remained in the community by the time of the six-month and twelve-month follow-ups than those

who did not. Day care therefore can perform an important maintenance function. In order for outcomes to be assessed, care plans need
to be explicit about the function of the service, and the criteria against
which it is to be evaluated. This is particularly so, given that there has
been a move from the provision of day 'centres' to the commissioning
of a range of day services, more clearly based in the community and
more time-limited in their provision. Clark (2001) suggests that day
services need to be flexible, responsive to individual needs, culturally
and ethnically sensitive, adaptable to variable and complex needs and
supportive of wider social integration.

Referral for day services needs to take into account people's previous strengths and interests. For example, the Forum lunch club at
Fulbourn Hospital, Cambridge, runs an art group for people with
dementia who have an interest in creative projects. Community-based
organizations also run luncheon clubs or special interest groups for
older people, based upon open access. The model is that of active older
age and continuity of interests. Former professional roles, and interests
in sport or domestic skills, may provide a focus for discussing what type
of occupation, if any, older people would like to consider.

The significance of place

Generally, older people are satisfied with their housing and neighbourhood and prefer to stay put, if possible (Oldman, 2000). However, a
crisis such as bereavement or illness can quickly change the situation.
Research by the Department of Health (1995) found that fear was a
key factor in influencing whether to move: fear of falling in particular,
but also fear of isolation and of crime. Tackling these fears will be key
in supporting older people in the community. 'Home' has connota-
tions of stability and belonging which go beyond bricks and mortar
(Heywood et al., 2002). Poor design can be disabling to older people
who wish to pursue home-based activities; yet most specialist housing
for older people tends to be small, and without space for family to stay.
Statistically, older people are more likely to live in poor housing, which
makes no allowance in its design for poor mobility, frailty or sensory
loss. It is rare for older people to be involved in the design of the buildings that they will live in, yet design is important in preserving homely
features. So the design of a building may indicate whether it is intended
to be for care management and protection, or for independence and
connectivity.

Retirement villages have developed to provide purpose-built accommodation and services on the model of extra care housing where care
staff are available to provide assistance on a 24-hour basis. The desire
to maximize security and independence are important motivations in
moving to retirement villages; there is an assumption also that progression to a higher level of care facility, particularly if co-located, will
be seamless. Certainly, couples requiring minimal services might well

be seen as potential 'customers' for retirement village development, with the expectation that additional care might be available on site for either partner should needs change. Cheek et al. (2006), however, found that such transitions were not always available, and there was a need for support in navigating a way through the information available. 'Opportunistic' movers who had taken up a residential place when one became available compared favourably with those whose move was precipitated by a health crisis and who had difficulty in securing a seamless transition. Negative views of residential care are widely held by older people (Davies and Nolan, 2003), and, on the one hand, may act as a barrier to preparatory planning; on the other hand, complex terms and conditions of residence need to be clearly understood by older consumers before irrevocable decisions are made.

Family placement and respite

In children's services, family placements rather than residential services are the norm. For adults, there have been some examples of adult placements on the same model, and the SCIE *Practice Guide* (2006) in this field aims to help local authorities to meet the aims of the White Paper (DH, 2006c) by encouraging commissioning of such services and making placements. Services on a small scale, such as adult placements, can extend the range of person-centred services available, but require proper planning and support. Arksey et al. (2004) found that adult placement schemes were particularly valued within the spectrum of respite services for their flexibility and responsiveness to individual need.

Respite care is also seen as valuable to carers, and may be so if arranged explicitly to give them a break (Arksey and Glendinning, 2007) though there is evidence (Levin et al., 1989) that by the time it is presented as a service, many carers have resolved that they are no longer able to carry on caring – in other words, it is presented too late. Planned respite may also be used to orientate the older person to the idea of permanent residential care. Certainly, clarity about the purposes and intended outcomes of respite care is required to prevent older people from being cajoled into situations which may have adverse longer-term consequences for them. Exploring the expectations of family members is particularly important where relationship issues are as yet unresolved. Arksey et al. (2004), similarly, could find no evidence that respite care (whether in a domestic or residential setting) for people with dementia had any significant impact on the progression to permanent care so as to be cost-effective from an economic perspective.

Residential services

Seeing residential services as a resource, rather than beginning from a model of residential care as a home for life, widens the opportunity for using residential resources for assessment and respite as well as for 'care'. The dichotomy between care at home and 'institutional' care attributed to residential settings has continued to be questioned. Morris (1993) has constructed debates around the custodial nature of both formal and informal care in the community for people with considerable support needs. Gubrium and Holstein (1999) see institutionalization as a descriptive phenomenon for ideas about and practices towards the ageing body, as much as a location of care. Bland (1999) has also examined structural and individual factors which differentiate between a 'service' and a 'social care' approach to residential care in enabling older people to preserve autonomy and privacy, contrasting favourably the hotel environment of some private care provision with the institutional practices of state-funded care. Seeing residential care as inherently less desirable than care services in the community is therefore open to challenge.

An analysis of past trends and of current and future demands for residential care has shown that demand is likely to continue to outstrip supply. The residential market has come to be dominated by large organizations as small providers have found it more difficult to survive financially. Factors which impact upon the demand for residential care are, at a structural level:

- the availability of continuing care support from the NHS for older people;
- the availability of intermediate care;
- commissioning and contracting strategies; and
- market forces.

At an individual level, key issues are:

- choice;
- paying for care; and
- emotional as well as social aspects of the transition to care.

The fact that there are increasing numbers of older people who do not qualify for state-funded care has raised concerns that they are also effectively excluded from professional advice about the appropriateness of particular forms of care in meeting their needs, and of quality issues when making choices. Given the enormity of the decisions to be made, most older people would benefit from focused advice when planning for future care. As self-directed care becomes more widely available, systems will need to reconsider the dichotomy that past welfare systems have created between state-provided care and private initiative.

Moving into residential care

There is considerable evidence that older people are not sufficiently involved in decision-making about the move into residential care: carers, medical professionals and care managers are primary decision-makers.

Understanding social and professional relationships is therefore critical. Cheek et al. (2006) found that relatives recognized the declining health of the older person more clearly than the older person themselves, who was more likely to speak of a sudden decline. Ware et al. (2003) found evidence of poor professional practice and a lack of consultation with older people or carers, with organizational demands taking precedence when allocating placements. Challis and Hughes's (2002) survey of older people admitted to care in a single local authority found that almost one quarter could have been supported at home. What then is going wrong in decision-making about the appropriate location of care? There appear to be a number of factors: poor preparatory work, a lack of clarity about objectives, limited choice in a market economy and rationing through panel systems as arbiters of need. Those who are dependent upon state funding in the move to residential care therefore face considerable barriers to choice. But those who are self-funding face their own difficulties arising from a lack of advice and forward planning.

Decision-making about long-term care

Professional perspectives on decision-making about long-term were were explored by Taylor and Donnelly (2006). They found that 'thresholds' for admission to residential care were affected by service availability and workload pressures on primary care services. These factors, as well as individual fears and motivation and family support, needed to be acknowledged in assessments alongside assessment of functional and medical needs. The crisis context for decision-making created conflict for a range of professionals who required time for assessment, particularly the use of 'time as a diagnostic tool' (ibid.: 813) for judging the impact of medication or changed living arrangements. Open and honest communication essential for effective care planning was easier at later interviews, when older people were less defensive and more willing to accept help. Practitioners from the range of professions – medicine, social work, nursing, occupational therapy and homecare management – identified factors (also described in the earlier literature) as 'reasons for admission' to institutional care. These were:

- mental impairment, including dementia;
- falls and fractures;
- physical limitations in activities of daily living;
- inability to manage medication;
- incontinence;
- health-related needs;
- sleep problems;
- nutrition.

However, the perspective of patients varied greatly regarding similar physical needs, showing the importance of looking beyond conventional measures of activity. Family provision of health and welfare

monitoring was an important element of the physical care they provided. Applying such assessments to the situation of older people on
the threshold of residential care, it appears that, even when the ability
to remain in one's own home is compromised by physical frailty, the
most important factor is the individual's perspective on the situation.
With no evidence that mental capacity is affected, the issue of relocation is for older people themselves to decide, taking into account
their family's anxieties. Support may be needed to challenge others'
perspectives on the priority to be given to declining physical health
compared to continuity and familiarity of location.

Multidisciplinary assessment may also reduce precipitate entry into
residential care before other options have been considered. Challis et
al. (2004) have researched the value of specialist clinical assessment of
older people prior to entry to care homes. Assessment by a geriatrician
or old-age psychiatrist uncovered conditions previously unknown to
care managers, particularly cognitive impairment. Those receiving
the clinical assessment experienced less deterioration in their physical
functioning, and had a reduced need for emergency intervention or
care home admissions; carers also reported an improvement in their
own well-being. The study supports the role of community geriatri-
cians as part of a multidisciplinary team to improve decision-making at
a critical point and adds to the literature which cautions against precipitate decision-making when critical life changes are under discussion.

The CSCI (2005) research on entry to residential care at the point of
hospital discharge revealed the fact that large numbers of people move
straight into residential care following an acute admission. Many older
people admitted for physical conditions will also have mental health
problems. Anderson (2001) found that the prevalence of dementia
amongst older inpatients in general hospitals was 31 per cent; the prevalence of depression was 29 per cent, and 20 per cent also suffered from
delirium. These conditions were independent predictors of adverse
outcomes, including loss of function, institutionalization and higher
readmission rates. One third of stroke survivors develop vascular
dementia. Late referral to old-age psychiatry also means that opportunities may be lost to prevent deterioration, or to intervene while people
still have the cognitive capacity to make decisions, including the ability to return home with support. Older people with dementia are also
less likely to have intermediate care services available to them, or to be
referred for palliative care. Recognizing the interaction between physical and mental health problems requires both holistic assessment and
facilitated access to appropriate supplementary resources.

Quality standards

Quality for older people in residential care is again a combination
of process and final outcomes. Regulation seeks to ensure that staff-
ing levels, care routines and residents' experience are monitored

against accepted standards. Contracts with care home residents are also subject to guidance from the Office of Fair Trading (2003) stressing the legal nature of the relationship. Before private care providers of residents placed by the local authority were made subject to the Human Rights Act 1998 (from December 2008), a requirement to observe human rights principles of due process, respect for privacy and humane treatment would commonly be contained in contracts with the local authority for the residents for whom they commission care. The vulnerability of private residents, however, remains. There is also no statutory guidance on how care home closures are managed (Williams and Netten, 2005). Residents are licensees who can be asked to leave after a period of notice, and not tenants protected by a statutory process. Legal protection for older people in residential care is therefore limited, and social workers operate with a system which contains ambiguities about the status and rights of older people, and the responsibility of agencies for their well-being. Residential care thus acts as a microcosm of more general concerns about the status and protection of older people.

The status of carers

The system of community care was predicated upon the willingness and capacity of informal carers to support growing numbers of older people. Approximately 70 per cent of carers provide support for older people (Audit Commission, 2004a), covering a variety of relationships from being a spouse, a family member, a neighbour or a friend. The term 'carer' is a contested one, but has become increasingly formalized in policy and legislation. The term 'family carer' has also been accepted into general usage, in preference to that of 'informal' carer. In developing a typology of carers, Twigg and Atkin (1994) see carers as a resource, as co-workers or as co-clients; in addition, carers can be 'superseded' as the person for whom they care moves into a different care setting or dies. Applying this typology, Manthorpe and Iliffe (2005) found that social workers predominantly view carers as a resource to draw upon within the care planning process. Carers therefore are in considerable jeopardy in the care planning situation. The first principle must be that they are free to withdraw from this role, or to limit their input. Yet caring is rarely a matter of negotiation, and more often a culmination of an emotional or family commitment. Assessment of carers has its legal basis in the Carers (Recognition and Services) Act 1995, the Carers and Disabled Children Act 2000 and the Carers (Equal Opportunities) Act 2004. Carers have a right to an assessment of their ability to care and to continue to provide care independently of the person whom they support; local authorities may also provide services for carers, or direct payments in lieu of these, and caring for adults now attracts protection in employment situations (McDonald and Taylor, 2006).

Guidance from SCIE (2007) emphasizes that strategic planning for carers is the responsibility of all agencies, not just health and social care. Caring for others is a significant issue for older people. Young et al. (2006) examined changes in the characteristics of carers based on data from the 2001 census. The peak age for care-giving was 50–59, but 5 per cent of those aged 75 or over are themselves carers. Carers are therefore predominantly 'older people' themselves. There are proportionately more carers in economically disadvantaged groups, and in more deprived areas. People from Bangladesh and Pakistani ethnic groups were more likely to be carers than those from other ethnic groups. Women were more likely than men to combine care-giving and paid work, especially those working in the public sector. Another potential source of care is adult children living in the same household. However, only about one-fifth of co-resident children were providing 20 or more hours per week of care; in about 5 per cent of these intergenerational households, it was likely that the older parent was providing care for the adult child.

Care planning for carers

Reciprocity in care-giving is a theme within the literature. Arksey and Glendinning (2007) make the case for a more comprehensive approach to policy for carers, whereby the interests of both carers and those receiving care are considered together: choice for carers is essentially limited by the constraints of their care-giving role. On the same theme, Seddon et al. (2006) present the need for practitioners to engage with carers as partners in the care planning process. Key issues to be resolved are confidentiality (Rapaport et al., 2006), balancing costs with rewards (Quereshi et al., 1983), and the need for information (Arksey et al., 2000). O'Connor et al. (1988) ask us to reconsider the taken-for-granted assumption that a wife will undertake care tasks and the risk of undermining her sense of competence by raising expectations that she could do more than is feasible. They therefore advocate the reframing of situations as 'extraordinary' rather than as unattainable demands for assistance which are within the usual assumptions of family relationships. Being supported in such situations is thus a matter of entitlement, though support will only be acceptable if achieved in partnership, rather than imposed on a deficit model. The UK government's *Carers Strategy* (DH, 2008a) identifies support for carers as a continuing priority, calls for recognition that carers have their own work and leisure interests to balance with caring, and pledges support for them to have necessary breaks from caring and also proper financial rewards.

Focusing specifically on carers of older people, Philp (2001) has identified the following types of support from formal services as particularly valuable:

1 Emotional support: listening; showing concern; providing a trusting, reassuring and professionally intimate relationship; giving the feeling that one is cared about.

2 Informational support: enhancing preparedness for taking on the caring role; supporting the development of new coping resources and responses.
3 Appraisal support: giving feedback that affirms self-worth, leading to the achievement of autonomy; dealing with feelings of guilt and inadequacy.
4 Instrumental support: providing direct aid and services to meet practical needs.

For support to be appropriately pitched, it is essential that carers' opinions and expertise are incorporated into the assessment process (ibid.). Carers' own coping strategies may range from the problem-focused to the emotion-focused (Lazarus and Folkman, 1984) thereby requiring different types of intervention. Recognizing the limits of their own resources is, however, a necessary first step in the care-giver's acceptance of external help (Philp, 2001). For some people, accepting external help may be difficult; in the earlier part of their relationship, a partner may have exerted power over the decisions that were made. O'Connor et al. (1988) therefore argue that issues of power must be explicitly addressed; this may involve presenting services as non-threatening and something that the husband reciprocally can do to support his wife, rather than placing the wife in a position where she has directly to take responsibility for challenging assumptions upon which their prior relationship was based.

User-directed care planning

Despite the traditional focus on services rather than cash for care, a number of options have developed to enable individuals to plan their own care, and recent policy developments have promoted such arrangements as the bedrock of the personalization of care agenda. Direct payments, as an alternative to services provided either directly or through contracts by the statutory sector, have been available to older people since 2001, though the original legislation, the Community Care Direct Payments Act 1996, applied only to adults under the age of 65. Direct payments arose out of the consumerist philosophy of extending market choice in care, and the interests of the disability movement in promoting independent living. Direct payments are also available for carers' services, where such services are available. Legally, a power to provide direct payments in lieu of services has, as a result of regulations, been turned into a duty (McDonald and Taylor, 2006). Despite the rhetoric of personal budgets, the only legal means directly of transferring funding from local authorities to individuals is through a direct payment to cover either the whole of or part of a package of care (Law Commission, 2008), with all the eligibility criteria for managing public funding that this entails.

In their study of the take-up of direct payments by older people,

Leece and Bornat (2006) argue that one of the outcomes of a shift to a market economy is that social care provision is treated progressively as a commodity to be bought and sold. Other European countries have also instituted 'cash-for-care' programmes for older people, and Timonen et al. (2006) have evaluated schemes in Ireland, Finland and the Netherlands, as well as in the UK (England). They found that such schemes have not radically transformed care provision except in Ireland, where the restricted availability of alternative forms of service provision means that the extension of cash-for-care might shift care provision significantly towards private provision and financing. In England, Clark et al. (2004) have described the benefits of direct payments for older people in emancipatory terms, but concluded that older people could probably derive more benefit from direct payments if it were not assumed that they also prioritized personal care and that they led a restrictive lifestyle. Older people themselves experienced age discrimination when crossing administrative boundaries between 'adult' and 'older persons' services. Although care managers were key to giving older people access to direct payments, these were not yet part of the culture of care management. Direct payment users, however, experienced a positive impact on their social, emotional and physical health; they felt that they, rather than the service providers, were now in control. So, proactively, older people might make use of direct payments to restart their social life, or to provide respite for carers through a trusted friend or supporter in whom they have confidence, and who would be able to provide continuity and flexibility in the use of time and tasks. Such an approach is therefore much less socially disruptive than the provision of direct agency care, and also much more flexible and personalized.

There are wide variations nationally in the amount of money allocated to direct payments. Research by Fernandez et al. (2007) showed that only 0.8 per cent of social care budgets for older people were spent on direct payments, though 15 per cent of the budget for physical disability teams was thus spent. However, the average weekly rates paid to employ live-in carers for older people was higher than the cost of residential care. There did not appear to be any relationship between devolving budgets to care managers and the take-up of direct payments. Particularly in relation to older people, the research showed that there were low expectations of autonomy, and a medical model of vulnerability and dependency prevailed. Class and ethnicity were overriding factors for indicating the ability to manage a direct payment, or to meet needs that could not be accommodated within mainstream services.

Factors hindering take-up have remained constant over the history of direct payments. They include concern about managing payments, staff resistance and problems with the supply of personal assistants. The provision of direct payments is thus not simply a complex logistical exercise; it is key to social workers' commitment to user control and the theoretical constructs according to which those deserving of state-funded support are distinguished from those less deserving who will receive only a residual service. Ellis (2007) further explains barriers to the development of direct payments in terms of 'street level bureaucracy' (Lipsky, 1980), which rests on the discretion that welfare professionals have in the interpretation of guidance. Specifically in relation to direct payments, there is potential conflict between the ethical obligation to value self-determination and the legal obligation to monitor resources and provide a safe system of care.

The fragmented nature of funding for care was a difficulty noted in the White Paper (DH, 2006c) which proposed the piloting of individual budgets, drawing together different streams of funding, including council-provided social care services, housing support from the Supporting People programme, and disabled facilities grants. The individual older person would then be able to spend their allocation of funding according to their own rather than agency priorities. The commitment to individual budgets was also made in *Opportunity Age* (DH, 2005b) as a person-centred planning approach capable of delivering improved outcomes for individuals for the same, or fewer, resources. Unlike direct payments, individual budgets give a joined-up package of support; and the allocation need not be in cash: it can be in services. At a community level, it is important that there is enough demand to support service innovation, but there are important political as well as personal gains in encouraging participation and innovation rather than isolation and dependency.

Building on direct payments, pilots of individual budgets (IBs) bringing together diverse funding streams have been evaluated by Glendinning et al. (2008). Initial consumer response has been that IBs are easier to manage than direct payments, though there was a need for brokerage or advocacy to get the most out of systems and to manage the support. How to facilitate choice and longer-term monitoring of services for people who do not have family or other informal support appears to be a major challenge for personalized payment schemes. The social work role will also change: from an emphasis on entrepreneurial skills within care planning, to a brokerage role assisting individuals to make their own choices and to act as navigators through the process. More fundamentally, the individualized budgets signify a shift in power, making people more aware of their own needs in a transformational process, within which providers of service have to adjust to user demands in a way in which the 'contracting out' of services has failed to do. As time devoted to 'care management' is freed up, social workers will be able to explore with individuals what matters in their life, rather than what they are eligible for, and to engage directly with service users in managing the risks associated with their care (Demos, 2007). There is continuing concern that not all older people may benefit from such targeted support. Paradoxically, those most likely to be disenfranchised are the better off.

One of the risks that wealthier older people face is exclusion from formal support either because their needs are deemed not to meet eligibility criteria, or because they are self-funders (Henwood and Hudson, 2007). Screening systems post-assessment often deflect self-funders towards private provision for care planning. Within Henwood and Hudson's research, those 'signposted' elsewhere without a care plan were observed to be inadequately followed up, and in many cases had to rely on word of mouth or 'feel' in choosing services, or assessing their quality. The conclusion is that the private individuals who contribute to 50 per cent of the cost of social care nationally are not well served by current arrangements which focus services on reaching eligibility criteria. Personalized budgets, by contrast, ask people what matters in their life, and use the answer to that question to support individuals in designing services. For people who do not want directly commissioned services, the social work role would then shift from gate-keeping and care management to brokerage, sourcing available services, advocacy and advising; the challenge is to ensure that such support is available to all those who are interested in receiving it. The social worker's continuing role in monitoring change, responding to risk and safeguarding older people while maintaining choice and control is considered further in the next chapter.

Conclusion

The mixed economy of care has meant that services increasingly are not directly provided by the statutory sector, but are commissioned from the voluntary, private and independent sectors. This has changed the role of social workers into care managers. Though greatest emphasis has been placed on securing services, monitoring quality is equally important, as is ensuring appropriate outcomes for service users. More recently, schemes have been developed to enable service users to commission their own care through direct payments and individual budgets. This in turn may see the atrophy of traditional forms of service provision, as individuals prioritize social and leisure activities over the personal care tasks that are currently emphasized within packages of care. Social workers will develop new, more creative, roles to support older people in making these choices.

Chapter summary

1 Care planning is a process which identifies the most appropriate ways of achieving the objectives identified by the assessment of need. It includes the identification of service providers and the commissioning of resources.

2 Outcomes may be categorized as change outcomes, maintenance or prevention outcomes, and service outcomes. However, providers may face difficulties in developing an outcomes-focused approach

if services are allocated according to a task-based or time-limited model.

3 Older people are likely to reject service outcomes which are incompatible with their concept of independence or self-image.

4 In the commissioning of services, three main types of contract are employed: block contracts, cost and volume contracts, and individual or spot contracts. Care managers create a package of care by contracting for services for a particular individual. Direct payments and individualized budgets devolve control and choice to the level of the individual service user.

5 Conventional services such as domiciliary care, day services and housing or residential care are becoming more flexible in their provision in order to meet a range of needs, Nevertheless, most support is provided by family, neighbours and friends, who have the right to an independent assessment of their ability to provide or to continue to provide care, and who may be entitled to services in their own right.

Key lessons

1 The personalization of care provision is a major challenge to the social work task of matching services to needs.

2 Dignity in care provision includes respect, privacy, autonomy and self-worth. How care is experienced and the outcomes that can be achieved for individuals, families and groups should direct the social worker in planning services.

3 There is a need to involve older people in the planning as well as the receipt of services.

4 Care managers mediate older people's choices through the decisions that they make as purchasers of care; independence for older people may be achieved through self-directed care, and this will involve a change of role towards brokerage and navigation of care.

5 Working with carers takes place within a framework that sees carers variously as a resource, as partners or as clients. Support may continue when the caring role formally comes to an end.

Activity

Research the availability of domiciliary care in your own area

1 What is the balance of provision between the statutory, voluntary and private sector?
2 How is quality assessed within the sector?
3 What charges are made for the service?
4 How adaptable is the service to different needs?
5 Can service users themselves alter the timing of calls, or the tasks that care workers perform?

Further reading

H. Clark, H. Gough and A. Macfarlane, *Making Direct Payments Work for Older People*. York: Joseph Rowntree Foundation, 2004.
An early analysis of how older people use direct payments, the importance of support services and the perspectives of care managers.

K. Stalker, *Reconceptualising Work with 'Carers'* (Research Highlights in Social Work 43). London: Jessica Kingsley, 2004.
This looks at how the term 'carer' has been socially constructed, and examines different types of relationships which may be contained within the description of 'caring'.

6 Monitoring and Review

Issues considered in this chapter:

- monitoring and review as opportunities to assess the outcomes of social work intervention and as important, though often neglected, stages in the process of care management;
- barriers to the empowerment of older people and opportunities for older people to be proactive;
- risk and risk management;
- safeguarding and protection.

Managing change, monitoring the impact of intervention and reviewing the provision of services are essential to an outcomes-focused approach. Monitoring and review have in general received less attention than assessment and care planning, and monitoring has been made more difficult by the separation between purchasers and providers of services and by the adoption commonly of short-term models of intervention. Review as a formal process may be allocated to workers who are separate organizationally from assessors, raising questions about continuity of approach. For older people, for whom initial intervention may take place in a crisis, and whose health and supports may be fragile, effective monitoring is essential. Monitoring, however, needs to be focused and purposive. As Goldberg and Warburton (1979) found in their study of local authority social workers, anxious visiting by social workers was ineffective in situations that were inherently unpredictable; more useful as a means of monitoring was building a circle of support around the individual which could report changes as they happened.

Key concepts in dealing with change and challenges to the integrity of older people's lives are empowerment, risk and protection. This chapter will examine these concepts for their relevance to social work practice. Cross-cutting issues include the impact of change on family relationships and attitudes which reflect cultural differences between older people. Monitoring and review, which may be presented as 'good practice' opportunities to assess the outcomes of interventions in social work and social care, are not necessarily experienced positively by people whose circumstances are thereby reconstructed according to agency preferences or public concerns. The two case studies presented here are used to illustrate how transitions which are the outcomes of monitoring and review may raise issues about the autonomy of older people.

Case profile

Shaun Taylor is a 75-year-old man with angina and chronic obstructive pulmonary disease. He has lived alone since his wife died 12 months ago. Shaun's only daughter is suggesting that he moves into sheltered accommodation where there is a resident warden. Shaun lives in a semi-detached house with a garden. His nextdoor neighbour pops in most days to see how he is, and he employs a cleaner, as well as receiving meals on wheels. Shaun is finding it difficult to climb stairs, and is no longer able to walk to the local shops. Sometimes he forgets to take his medication, and he has had three hospital admissions in the past year.

Case profile

Olive Preston is 63 years of age and lives with her partner Paula, who has recently retired from employment. Olive has had multiple sclerosis for 15 years and is currently supported by a social worker from a physical disability team. Olive was one of the first people in her area to receive a direct payment with which she employs a team of personal assistants, effectively to provide 24-hour care in her own home. In addition, she is able to visit friends in another part of the country twice a year, accompanied by a personal assistant, and to attend the theatre and ballet whenever possible. Olive has been informed that at the age of 65 she will be transferred to an 'older person's team', and that she will then be reassessed, and her needs reviewed.

Organizational arrangements may incorporate ageist assumptions into their structures; in Olive Preston's case it is her age alone which has prompted a formal change in her status as a user of services. Critically important for Olive will be whether 'older people' in the locality receive the same level of service provision on the same terms as younger people. Olive's identity as a disabled person is overlaid with the identity of 'older person'. The transition provides an opportunity for her need (as defined by the agency) to be reviewed. Olive's accumulated experience in using direct payments to direct her own case is not given priority over organizational opportunities to reallocate and to ration. Shaun Taylor is at risk of being uprooted from familiar surroundings at a critical time after the anniversary of the loss of his wife and of this emotional risk being outbalanced on review by a more overt physical risk.

Empowerment

The meaning of empowerment has a particular resonance for older people and those who work with them. So Thompson and Thompson

(2001) argue that the empowerment of older people involves working beyond 'the care model' whereby older people are passive recipients of services, and focusing instead on involving them in service planning and delivery. Access to and engagement in social networks may also be facilitated by timely and sensitive social work intervention; for example, following hospital discharge (McLeod et al., 2008). The importance of tangible outcomes and real choices is reflected in a report from CSCI, *Real Voices, Real Choices: The Qualities People Expect from Care Services* (2006a): people who use social care services say that they don't just want to be asked for their views about the services they use – they want to see their lives changing for the better as a result.

Yet real barriers exist at the personal, cultural and structural levels for older people seeking empowerment (Thompson, 1997). At a structural level, patterns of inequality assign older people like Olive Preston to a particular social position with significant implications for the differential allocation of life choices, status, credibility, power and social resources (Thompson and Thompson, 2001). At a cultural level, the empowerment of older people requires a challenge to powerful discourses which create stereotypes of older people as weak and dependent (Thompson, 1997). At an individual level, personal empowerment is dependent upon the individual (or group's) ability to recognise and develop aspects of their lives over which they have direct control (ibid.)

Fundamentally, 'deep rooted cultural attitudes to ageing' in local public services have been acknowledged to restrict improvements in health, social care and other public services for older people (CSCI, 2006a). When planning and commissioning public services such as healthcare and transport, a lack of priority is given to the particular needs of older people: the CSCI report showed that 95 per cent of older people had not been asked their views on NHS or council services in the previous year, and 80 per cent did not think that they influenced the planning of services (ibid.). In some instances, there may be a lack of congruence between access to services and community needs, particularly in the case of people with low income, dementia, or those from minority ethnic groups where available services are not accessible (McLeod et al., 2008). Older people themselves may internalize discrimination as low self-esteem and not feel 'entitled' to ask for more and better services. Conversely, factors that appear necessary to sustain a sense of well-being in old age are linked to overcoming cultural and social isolation, and having the capacity and opportunity to be involved in different types of social and leisure activities that connect with people with whom there are shared interests and experiences (Godfrey at al., 2004). It is important that services are proactive, that change is managed sensitively and that appropriate resources are made available to deal with complex needs at times of transition.

Proactive services

It is timely to be reminded that the National Service Framework (NSF) for Older People (DH, 2001) emphasized:

- person-centred care;
- joined-up services;
- a timely response to needs; and
- promotion of health and active life.

Choice, control and responsibility are key phases (ibid.: 2), and transition points for older people, such as healthcare crises, provide opportunities to reinforce the value of focused and timely interventions. The CSCI report on hospital discharge (2005) found that services designed to rehabilitate and improve mobility can make a real difference to people's lives, that anticipating and planning for crises can help prevent hospital admissions, but that loneliness, chronic ill-health, depression, poverty and feeling unsafe in one's neighbourhood are major risk factors that contribute to the deterioration of health and quality of life in old age. Though all of these factors may be present in Shaun Taylor's case, it is important that strengths as well as deficits are acknowledged. Here, there is good support from neighbours, and Shaun's physical problems with mobility could potentially be overcome with the use of assistive technology. There are also dangers in moving from a familiar environment so recently after a bereavement. Shaun's attachment to his house and garden as 'home' needs to be explored; also, his willingness to move to what will be smaller accommodation where there is an element of communal living. The forgetfulness with medication and history of hospital admissions would indicate a need for better healthcare monitoring, alongside social solutions.

Community health services are also critical in monitoring need and in responding to changes in functioning. *The NSF for Long-Term Conditions* (DH, 2005a) targets those like Shaun who are identified as high users of secondary services for intensive case management. Community matrons lead on this part of a strategy to support self-care and link health and social care. There has also been a rapid expansion of intermediate care services, designed both as a step-down from acute hospital care and as an alternative to acute admission, though there are concerns that some services have simply been relabelled, and that GP engagement is weak (Young and Stevenson, 2006). Although some intermediate care services may be too small, inadequately targeted or insufficiently integrated to achieve a whole system change to services for older people, the underlying principle of intermediate care in the sense of multi-agency working, comprehensive shared assessments and a rehabilitation approach are principles that could be translated more generally into care in the community (ibid.). Such an approach might benefit Shaun, whose health needs are complex, but capable of responding to targeted intervention.

Managing change

Changes in the needs of older people have an impact upon the individual's sense of self, confidence and plans for the future. They also have an impact on family carers and formal services. Gooberman-Hill and Ebrahim (2006) have looked at informal care at times of change in health and mobility. They describe the adaptations within relationships which are required in response particularly to the onset or escalation of immobility. Three main ways in which participants dealt with recent changes in health and mobility in the context of relationships were:

- working together to enable recovery;
- working together to maintain independence; and
- working together to face the difficulties experienced in coping.

Those who experienced a sudden decline in health found it easier than those with gradually deteriorating conditions to work on recovery. Adaptation to change took place in the context of pre-existing relationships, and prognosis and expectations of improvement were crucial to emotional coping. So Shaun's daughter's adaptability to her father's changing needs is critical to his maintenance in the community, and future intervention might more appropriately be focused on her anxieties than on harm.

Parker (1993) has also considered the impact of acquired impairment on the marital relationship. Help from family and neighbours tends to be marginal, physical care is carried out by the spouse, but the transition from intimate partner to provider of physical care involves a reassessment of role. Paula's position is in some jeopardy now that she has given up work; though not having formally adopted the role of carer for Olive, she may find herself cast in that role as Olive's identity as a disabled person is subsumed under that of 'older person'. As well as these psychosocial adjustments, same-sex partners face particular issues in relation to being providers of care. Formal services may be reluctant to involve them in decision-making; if they do not have the status of 'next-of-kin', medical decision-making in particular may exclude them and care planning processes may leave them marginalized (Price, 2008).

Facing death and bereavement

The loss of a partner will profoundly alter the social situation of older people. Holloway (2007) comments on the absence of an explicit 'older person's' agenda in the theorizing of death and dying, especially given the prevalence of chronic illness in this age group. For older people, especially for the very old, there has been a cultural shift away from home to 'institution' as the site of death and, partly as a result of this, the experience of a period of instability, movement and change in the weeks leading up to death. Yet even within the away-from-home experience, there are age differentials, with younger people more likely than older people with the same diagnosis to be cared for in a hospice setting. There is no evidence, however, that the fear of death is abated in old age; it remains consistent over the lifecourse, although for older people this focuses more precisely upon the fear of the circumstances of death, and the desire not to be 'a burden' (Holloway, 2007). For staff in care home settings, dying is a process that has to be managed alongside care of the living.

Secularization has removed (ibid.), or at least muted, the moral, philosophical and social underpinnings of death, The shift is particularly significant for older people who may retain beliefs and expectations that are not congruent with the current practice of medicalizing and institutionalizing death and dying. Holloway challenges expectations that bereavement is necessarily a process that ends with 'reinvestment' of energy elsewhere than on the deceased; in older age, reinvestment in new relationships and occupations may be neither desired nor practical (ibid.). Preserving memories and continuing bonds with a departed spouse or child, through preserving rituals and visiting of the grave, may be an appropriate 'end' stage of bereavement for people who have lost significant relationships (Kellaher et al., 2007). Bereavement for an older person may mean loss of social contact, financial support and sexual expression, which is irreplaceable. Particularly problematic is 'untimely dying', when the 'wrong one' in the relationship dies first. Thus the sudden death of a wife who for years has cared for a husband will be an emotional as well as a practical crisis for her widower. Suddenly faced with a reassessment of roles, the older man is less likely than a younger person to be able to manage on his own, or to find adequate substitute domiciliary support. The death or serious illness of a caring spouse is thus a common precipitating feature for entry into residential care. Assessment of the bereaved partner is made more difficult by the experience of confusion, forgetfulness, fatigue and neglect of self-care that commonly follows on from bereavement (Holloway, 2007). Thus the common advice not to make major lifestyle changes immediately upon bereavement has a sound psychosocial foundation; however, pressing care needs may make such changes unavoidable. Shaun Taylor, in our example, finds himself pressed to make decisions about his own care when bereft of a significant relationship.

Changes in relationships

A survey by the Relatives and Residents Association (Clarke and Bright, 2006) looked at the experience of people who had a partner who had moved into a care home. The main concern was funding and paying for suitable care, ensuring the receipt of good-quality care and dealing with the negative experiences and emotions associated with such a move. Between 7 and 10 per cent of residents in care homes for older people are estimated to be the long-term partner of someone living in the community. Numbers of men and women with a partner in long-term care are likely to be approximately equal (Hancock and Wright, 1999). Couples were likely to have been receiving very little help up to the point that the decision was taken for one of them to move into a care home; few people made their decision without intervention from other family members, or from health or social services professionals. The most common and persistent emotion was guilt, often connected with a perception of the quality of life of the home's residents. Against this, Clarke and Bright consider the 'unavoidable hierarchy' that 'the first focus must be the needs of the prospective resident and helping him or her to make the right decision about his or her own care' (2006: 12). Much good practice on planned admissions is redundant if hurried decisions are forced upon people; full pre-admission assessment should focus on support through transition as well as acquiring knowledge of previous relationships. Communities or families may put pressure on a spouse to continue to care, and children from previous relationships may question the entitlement of a second spouse to make decisions. The social status of the remaining spouse is also unclear; to some extent they are 'widows' or 'widowers' even though they are still living their partner's life (ibid.: 13), meaning that the change in the relationship is more profound than for children whose parents move into a care home. Couples tried to maintain a normal relationship, often with daily visiting, though many were excluded from care plans: privacy and dignity in visits was also found to be an issue (ibid.). Such partial change, where community presence overlaps with residential care, is particularly challenging to manage both practically and emotionally.

Risk assessment and risk management

Monitoring of change from a baseline measure is often used for the re-evaluation of risk. 'Risk' is a contested concept, but one which is increasingly pervasive in modern life (Beck, 1992). The state's responsibility for risk management through resource allocation and monitoring is central to the delivery of health and social care services. Governments display their risk choices in the framing of social policy. The distribution of risks has arguably become more emphasized than the distribution of wealth, and the avoidance of harm is a greater concern than the pursuit of the collective good (Kemshall, 2001). This may affect older people particularly if services are targeted on those who are most frail, and if 'keeping safe' is given a higher priority than developmental choices. Economic well-being in older age through pensions policies is increasingly seen as an issue of personal responsibility; the same is true of personal responsibility for maintaining a healthy lifestyle. Yet, case-finding approaches to professional intervention are based on the idea of systematic pre-detection of individuals who are likely to find self-help more difficult. Monitoring the impact of interventions on well-being must be alert to stigmatizing older people and providing surveillance of their ability to maintain what are seen by others as acceptable lifestyles. Comparing, for example, the lifestyles of Olive Preston and Shaun Taylor, Olive is positive and assertive in maintaining her independence, while Shaun is struggling to maintain his independence and is therefore more vulnerable to assertive interventions from others, based, most likely, upon assessment of risk.

There are number of ways of understanding 'risk' which may be relevant to the particular position of older people:

1   *Legal notions of risk* are based on the idea of foreseeability. They are based on the likelihood of an event occurring, and on the existence of a duty of care owed to those who are sufficiently proximate to be affected by the reasonably foreseeable consequences of another's actions. The law of negligence determines culpability within a forensic process which seeks to attribute blame. So the older person who is a resident in a care home is owed a duty of care by the owners of the home to provide a safe environment. A breach of that duty of care will lead to liability for reasonably foreseeable consequences – for example, a broken leg as a result of a fall in circumstances when staff assistance with walking is required, but is not available. A key issue is causation: did the lack of assistance make the fall more likely, or the consequences more severe? But determining liability continues to be a balancing act. Is the 'cost' of taking precautions so high that it would be unreasonable to expect that the hazard of walking unaccompanied should be covered in all circumstances? Relevant considerations here would not only be the cost of staff time in ensuring that all residents are always accompanied, but the restriction of individual freedom involved in such close monitoring. Again, the cost has to be balanced against both the likelihood of harm occurring as the result of a fall, for example, and the severity of its consequences. So it may be necessary always to provide staff support to residents previously assessed as having a propensity to fall (and negligent not to do such an assessment), and to provide support to the very frail for whom a broken leg and subsequent immobility may be a disastrous consequence. Risks may extend beyond the individual to the environment: the risk to residents leaving the building without the knowledge of staff would require greater precautions if the building were located on a busy road, or if the residents were known to wander.

2   *Actuarial notions of risk*, used in the calculation of insurance premiums, see risk in terms of the probability of events occurring based on statistical analyses of whole populations, or subgroups. Although this may be useful in identifying, for example, older widowers with poor health as statistically more likely to experience depression, it is only the starting point for looking at the issues relevant to the particular individual, their strengths and their networks of support.

Predictive criteria do not determine events, nor do they necessarily uncover solutions (Steele, 2004); the notion of risk as predictability, inherent within this approach, has therefore tended to be replaced with that of risk as uncertainty, with a focus on risk management which is more solution-focused (Kemshall, 2001).

3 *Risk as a scientific reality*: this view of risk as normative and amenable to measurement is located within positivism and is concerned with the correction of poor 'risk choice'. For example, government guidelines may set out a recommended level of alcohol consumption for the general population based on research into the effects of alcohol on health and social functioning. In some instances, for example drink-driving, recommended levels of consumption may be reinforced by criminal sanctions for their breach. Conformity with such guidance depends upon individuals being capable of making rational choices, based upon evidence presented to them.

4 *Social constructivism*: the role of the social in the construction of risk meanings and their legitimacy is seen as critical here. As it has become increasingly socially unacceptable to drink and drive, for example, so the 'risks' of drink-driving have been incorporated into cultural norms. For older people generally, social constructivism may limit the tolerance of risk-taking behaviours in a way in which younger people would not be so limited. Older people at risk of falling may be constrained in a way which would not be considered appropriate for young people who might injure themselves through taking part in sporting activities. Whole new areas of concern for older people, around abuse by family members, have also been 'constructed' in response to greater awareness of the incidence of physical and emotional assaults.

5 *Subjective perceptions of risk* are influenced by individuals' life history and belief. Older people may have been lifelong heavy drinkers, or believe that alcohol does them no harm. Subjective views explain why people fail to act on 'expert' advice, which is not congruent with the way in which they see themselves. Olive, in our example, has 15 years of expert experience of monitoring and accommodating her condition and associated risks.

6 *Postmodern views of risk*: postmodern challenges to rationality, progress and cohesion emphasize uncertainty and fragmentation. The loss of faith in reason militates against the idea of objective truth; risk is an illustration of the weakness of human decision-making in the face of hazards and the unknown. Postmodern views of ageing therefore emphasize diversity and the specificity of individual experience. So the physical risks to Shaun Taylor resulting from his immobility, the nature of his physical condition and his relative isolation are apparent; yet, balanced against these must be the risk of upheaval by a move, the risk of undermining his self-esteem by seeking to control his decision-making and the unknown risks of the new environment.

Kemshall (2001) sees risk as having replaced need as the key criterion for welfare intervention. Risk assessments are increasingly conflated with assessments of the need for community care services and of eligibility for service receipt. In addition, the social worker may feel personally at risk through anxiety about making mistakes in decision-making, and the organization itself may be at risk of adverse consequences. The focus on 'risk' may be a threat to self-determination or to freedom of action. It may also be a threat to the rights of individuals not to be deprived of their liberty except by legal mandate. The focus of risk also individualizes work and pathologizes people whose circumstances are interpreted to fit narrow service definitions; this detracts from the wider view of 'who/what' could help in this situation (Smale et al., 2000). Risk management in the sense of putting together a package of support to sustain a tenuous situation takes this broader view – for example, setting up a network of family and friends to assist the older person who wishes to remain at home, or to identify contingency plans if that network should break down. 'Protection plans' for the safeguarding of vulnerable individuals are inherently a device for managing risk and allocating responsibility for assessing volatile situations.

Professional risks

Professionals may be at risk within their organization for the quality of their decision-making. Also professionals themselves may exacerbate the risk in situations requiring careful judgement, by operating alone and unsupported, acting without a theoretical base, avoiding recognition of and dealing with their own personal feelings and values, and operating within undefined boundaries, roles and responsibilities. Also, professionals will be acting unsafely if they work without clear procedures to guide intervention, good supervision to provide a challenge over the management of cases, and a safe, containing environment (Thompson, 2005).

It is the interaction between the individual and the environment which is the most powerful factor, if the defences of denial, projection and displacement are understood not only in an individual context, but in the relationship between the worker's anxiety and the unsupportive organization. This idea of organizational strain is further discussed in chapter 8, but its existence means not only that changes in an individual's circumstances must be monitored, but so too must the quality of the service that is being delivered, including the social worker's own ability to perceive and respond to change.

Independence, choice and risk

The Department of Health's guide, *Independence, Choice and Risk: A Guide to Best Practice in Supported Decision-Making* (DH, 2007a) seeks to develop a common set of principles for organizations to use as the basis for supporting people in making decisions about their own lives and managing any risk in relation to those choices. The recommendations are for a personalized approach to risk, collective discussion of risk management strategies and clarification of rights and responsibilities, incorporating individual, collective and legal approaches to risk. Generally, the approach taken is a legal/organizational one: 'Ultimately, the local authority has a statutory duty of care and a responsibility not to agree to support a care plan if there are serious concerns that it will not meet an individual's needs or if it places an individual in a dangerous situation' (ibid.: 7).

Nevertheless, the governing principle behind positive approaches to choice and risk is seen to be that people have the right to live their lives to the full as long as that doesn't stop others from doing the same. To put this principle into practice, people supporting users of services have to (ibid.: 9):

- help people to have choice and control over their lives;
- recognize that making a choice can sometimes involve an element of risk;
- help people understand their responsibilities and the implications of their choices, including any risks;
- acknowledge that there will often be some risk, and that trying to remove it altogether can outweigh the quality of life benefits for the person;
- continue existing arrangements for safeguarding people.

Examples given include enabling a 97-year-old lady in a care home to continue to make tea for herself in the morning, as she had done at home. She herself accepted shared responsibility for any risks of scalding or falling, and the home arranged for tea-making provisions to be left out in the dining-room for her. In another example, a woman in her 50s with Huntington's disease and motor neurone disease, supported at home by a package of health and social care, refused the offer of a stomach tube to increase her nutritional intake. Although her family and doctor were concerned about her choice, they respected her wishes based on her mental capacity to make decisions, but agreed to revisit the question on a regular basis. There are always parameters within which risk assessments take place that cannot be ignored, though they may need to be challenged. These include culturally informed values and norms, agency expectations and the amount of information and time available. Also required is an individual, team and agency strategy to manage caseloads to ensure that cases are allocated at the most appropriate level of expertise and with sufficient time for reflection.

Protection and safeguarding

The developing awareness that older people, like other vulnerable adults and children, might be subject to abuse in the domestic setting and when they are in receipt of care has led to changes in policy, legislation, research and practice. Definition, though vital, has proved contentious; once an issue has been defined in a specific way, methods of investigation and the possible solutions are encrypted within the original definition (Dobash and Dobash, 1992). So the formulation has variously been abuse (Eastman, 1984), a violation of trust (Action on Elder Abuse: www.elderabuse.org.uk) or the violation of human and civil rights (DH and Home Office, 2000). Emphasis may be on the intention or otherwise of the perpetrator, or on outcomes, regardless of motive. The focus may be on parallels with domestic violence (Mullender, 1996) or child abuse (Stevenson, 1996), or upon the abusive power of the state (Biggs, 2004) or criminality. The charity Action on Elder Abuse creates a focus for older people to take compensatory action for previous neglect of their needs as a group.

No Secrets (DH, 2000) provides an institutional response to the abuse of vulnerable adults by the setting up of inter-agency procedures, including strategy meetings and case conferences on a child protection model. The prevalence of abuse of older people has been assessed in research by O'Keeffe et al. (2007) as involving 4 per cent of the UK population; abuse is attributed to family, close friends, care workers, neighbours and acquaintances. 'Mistreatment' is broken down into neglect (1.1 per cent), financial abuse (0.7 per cent), psychological and physical abuse (both 0.4 per cent) and sexual abuse (0.2 per cent). The majority of incidents involved a partner or other family members, followed by a voluntary or paid care worker (13 per cent). The extent of the responsibility owed by family members to older people is less clear than parental responsibility towards children, which makes issues of attribution more complex. The research did not cover abuse in care homes, or in respect of people with dementia. From O'Keeffe et al.'s research, there appeared to be no correlation between the strain of caring and the likelihood of abuse. Other factors included the quality of relationship, the gender of the victim and the type of abuse. Eastman and Harris (2004) call for a citizenship approach to abuse, emphasizing prevention and protection. The emphasis would thus shift from a medico-legal approach to that of 'safeguarding' through community involvement and recognition.

Understanding why abuse occurs enables appropriate interventions to be pursued (McCreadie, 1995). Explanations may variously lie in a process associated with a change in role, from cared for to carer; in behaviourist explanations of the perpetuation of family violence; and in the psychopathology of the abuser. Interventions, whether through use of the criminal law, the provision of community care services or the use of domestic violence legislation, need to be matched to theories of why abuse occurs. Though most victims of neglect are female, men are vulnerable to financial exploitation (O'Keeffe et al., 2007). Research by Pritchard (2002) directly involving male victims of abuse found strong evidence of past vulnerabilities, and a desire for long-term support beyond the crisis stage. What older people did not want was crisis-driven intervention, which then left them without support in the longer term. Mechanisms within *No Secrets* for the holding of strategy meetings and case conferences and the writing of protection plans are designed to allocate responsibility within a multidisciplinary environment, but the lack of duty on any professional to report on those whom they suspect of abuse, and the absence of a legal duty to investigate, to secure entry to domestic premises or temporarily to remove the older person to a place of safety means that the protection of vulnerable adults is less robust than that of children, and professionals are less well supported in their decision-making (McDonald and Taylor, 2006).

Evidence gained from the range of CSCI's regulatory and inspection functions across councils, care homes, homecare agencies and other social care agencies (see CSCI, 2008c) showed that current arrangements for safeguarding adults are applied inconsistently. There is a correlation between good performance on safeguarding and general quality performance indicators. Different practices in defining abuse and instigating procedures meant that the previous year's increase in referrals across services ranged from 10 to 150 per cent. To date, no council has a system for safeguarding people who direct their own support. There were particular shortfalls in the provision of effective information for service users who might have concerns about abuse, shortfalls in advocacy services and unacceptable failures in auditing casework recording and monitoring outcomes for individuals. Definitions remain in need of clarification; in particular, there should be:

- a theoretical shift to the recognition of human rights and citizenship;
- greater emphasis on prevention;
- clarification of terminology;
- a clearer boundary between what is considered to be and what actually is poor practice; and
- consideration to be given to additional legislative powers and duties.

In addition to policy change, changes in practice are seen to be necessary. Older people, once in the system, may lose control over events, and there is variability in the quality of support provided for those who have experienced abuse. With respect to residential services, support is needed at an individual level; it is not simply at the organizational level that work should be provided to drive up overall standards. There is a correlation between staff training and service quality. Worryingly, in only 61 per cent of cases did service users feel confident that concerns would be acted upon; service users' confidence in formal systems of monitoring are therefore not high.

Evidence from the CSCI study (ibid.) also showed that legal remedies in cases of suspected abuse were not widely understood by frontline staff and the use of legal powers was very patchy. There was also variability in standards of practice relating to case management. Essential components of good practice were seen as: a clear chronology of events, a risk assessment, clear case recording and a protection plan. Proper use of the Mental Capacity Act 2005 should facilitate an assessment of capacity which should be recorded to show the ways in which wishes and feelings are taken into account, together with the views of family members and friends. In cases where there are potential conflicts of interest, an Independent Mental Capacity Advocate may be appointed to inform decision-making. Such an approach is protective of the older person's autonomy, but also of their right to be presented with alternative ways of managing family and financial relationships.

Case profile

Phyllis and Ernest Jones are both 75 years of age and have been married for 50 years. They have no close relatives apart from Phyllis's niece, Sandra, who visits them on average once a month. Phyllis and Ernest have always had a turbulent relationship and there have been many arguments over the years about Ernest's drinking and accusations from Phyllis that he has hit her when drunk. Sandra has become increasingly concerned about Phyllis, whose physical health seems to have deteriorated; she has lost a lot of weight and seems tired all the time. Ernest shouts at her to get moving, but she does not seem able to respond. When Sandra last visited, there was very little food in the house, but a large number of whisky bottles were in the dustbin. Phyllis had a black eye and told Sandra that Ernest had hit her when she refused to give him more money for drink. When Sandra challenged Ernest about this, he told her to leave the house and not to come back. Sandra is concerned at leaving her aunt on her own with Ernest and seeks advice.

Issues to consider:

- the support available to Phyllis and Ernest through an assessment for community care services or onward referral for further assessment;
- the prognosis for change in behaviour or in the content of the relationship;
- the legal position.

Locating Phyllis and Ernest's situation within the ordinary process of assessment, care planning, monitoring and review assumes that continuing strengths in their 50-year relationship can be supported through external intervention. The process of safeguarding involves the creation of a care plan with outcomes of keeping Phyllis safe, improving her well-being and enabling Ernest to acknowledge the impact of his drinking on their ability to function together as a couple.

Phyllis's increasing frailty means that the ways in which they have previously constructed their relationship and the roles that they have assumed within it are no longer viable; Phyllis is unable to be coerced into action, nor can she retaliate as she used to. It may be that further medical investigation of the causes of Phyllis's weight loss is needed. There may be an organic cause for this, or it may be due to a remediable lack of nutrition. Specific legal interventions may reflect the criminality of Ernest's behaviour or indicate the use of domestic violence remedies if there is a need to protect Phyllis to enable her to remain at home. Matrimonial remedies are significant for older people; having a property which she can adapt or later sell gives her a wider range of options when planning her future care.

Conclusion

The empowerment of older people depends upon a negotiated stance being taken on issues of risk, choice and protection. Risk is a contested concept, and older people's perceptions of 'the risk that is worth taking' may differ from those of professionals. Where individuals are unable to express a preference or are being unduly influenced by others, protection systems have evolved to safeguard those who are vulnerable. Processes here are at early stage of development, and the legal framework for safeguarding older people is at points unclear. Careful recording of decision-making is required, and effective and challenging supervision of complex cases.

Chapter summary

1 Monitoring and review functions of care management have generally received less attention than assessment and care planning.
2 Change and loss have an impact both upon the sense of self and on relationships; the needs of partners and families must also be considered.
3 Choice, control and responsibility are key factors in the promotion of health and well-being for older people.
4 Services designed to rehabilitate people following a crisis, intermediate care services as a step-down from acute hospital care and planned admissions to residential care all require careful monitoring by professionals in order to allow for time for recovery and for informed choice.
5 Empowerment, risk and protection are key concepts in analysing the decision-making context of work with older people.

Key lessons

1 Social workers need skills in supporting carers when their relationship with the older person must adapt to changes in health and

mobility; this may involve a change in role which is unanticipated and stressful.

2   Decisions to enter long-term care are affected by a range of personal factors, but also by pressures on other services, and the availability of places. Social workers need to acknowledge the influence of these factors on their decision-making.

3   Family carers should be included (where they wish) in care plans in residential care; spouses remaining at home may need particular support in revising their relationships.

4   Feeling unsafe, physically, mentally and financially, is a major factor in the deterioration of quality of life in old age; social work intervention in such circumstances needs to be multidimensional and preventative.

5   Social workers need to be aware of professional risks when dealing with complex cases, including the protection of older people. Clarity of role, support and supervision are essential for safe practice.

Further reading

Action on Elder Abuse, *Hidden Voices: Older People's Experience of Abuse*. London, Help the Aged, 2008.
This is essential reading for anyone involved in the care and support of older people's human rights. It is based on analyses of more than 10,000 calls to the Elder Abuse Response helpline over six and a half years.

D. Carson and A. Bain, *Professional Risk and working with people: Decision-Making in Health, Social Care and Criminal Justice*. London: Jessica Kingsley, 2008.
This presents a positive view of risk assessment and risk management, informed by analysis of the vocabulary of risk for communication, across professional groups.

PART III

SOCIAL WORK METHODS AND INTERVENTIONS

7 Working with Individuals

Issues considered in this chapter:

- a rights-based framework for working with older people, and the application of the Mental Capacity Act 2005;
- the agendas of older people and responsive social work practice;
- working in partnership with older people;
- understanding behaviour and therapeutic interventions, with particular reference to mental disorder in older age.

Working with individuals requires an examination of different theories and methods of social work intervention, chosen for their relevance to older people. This in turn requires a reconsideration of different ways of conceptualizing ageing. The application in practice of social work values is key in balancing rights and risk, enablement and protection. For the practitioner, there are dilemmas both in decision-making and in challenging barriers posed by structural issues and by the working environment. Particular issues arise when working with people whose capacity to make decisions is in doubt. This chapter will explore different approaches to working with older people as individuals in a social context either to understand their situation, to support decision-making or to effect change.

Reference was made in chapter 3 to Howe's (1987) taxonomy of social work theories which explain the core assumptions that underpin social work practice. So social workers may be functionalists (or fixers), interpretivists (seekers after meaning), radical humanists (raisers of consciousness) or radical structuralists (committed to revolutionary change). Social workers may work with and within systems, easing communication and understanding, but also seeing systems as the target for change. Alternatively, the focus of the intervention can be the individual and their treatment, support and maintenance. Such interventions may be psychoanalytic, seeking to understand the individual and their world, or behaviourist, seeking to intervene to change problem behaviours. But for each of these approaches the aim of the fixers is to recover the individual or the social system to proper healthy and harmonious functioning (Howe 1987: 57). Interpretivists accept that social reality is constructed from shared meanings, and practice within this paradigm is avowedly client-centred, helping individuals to recognize and value their own experience. The social worker is not the expert fixer, but the facilitator. External forces may, however, negatively label older people or place burdensome expectations upon them. Enabling people to recognize the inequalities in their situation which are socially created places the locus of change away from the individual and onto the organizations of society. Radical action then tackles the political causes of personal problems.

So older people who may not have a need for services to support daily living may nevertheless benefit from psychosocial interventions to address psychological and emotional needs and barriers, as in the case profile given here.

Case profile

Arthur Bertram served as a soldier in the Second World War. A number of his friends were killed during the war, and Arthur was badly wounded. He has never really spoken about his experiences during that time, except to say that he would never want to set foot in a hospital again. Recently, Arthur has been unwell, and his GP suspects lung cancer. Arthur refuses an appointment to attend his local hospital for tests, and is becoming increasingly anxious and distressed.

Arthur not only faces a difficult diagnosis, he also has to face past losses. Though his distress may indicate a psychosocial intervention, there are also issues of rights to consider in the rejection of medical treatment. The context in which the social worker has to operate is a multidisciplinary one, and the referral from the GP is directed towards maintaining the integrity of the medical system of diagnosis and intervention as much as exploring Arthur's interpretation of his situation.

Arthur is facing a crisis generated by his transition into the role of patient. Previous coping mechanisms which have enabled him to suppress past memories are being challenged. A situation which would be challenging for a younger person is occurring for Arthur at a stage in life at which Erikson (1980) identifies the chief psychosocial conflict as ego integrity versus despair. So Arthur will need to review his identity as a survivor of past trauma, placing it in the context of a life well lived. Harsh impatience with his unwillingness to pursue what might appear to others to be the sensible solution of accepting the proffered hospital appointment may reinforce feelings of worthlessness and of being undeserving of life – major risk factors for depression in older age.

The social worker working with Arthur will need an understanding of crisis theory (Rapoport, 1962) and its associated feeling of being out of control, accompanied by a loss of usual skills in maintaining a steady state of being. An understanding of responses to loss, actual or anticipated (Worden, 2008), will enable the social worker both to interpret Arthur's responses and to seek to move him from a stage of denial or rejection to one of acceptance. Particular methods of intervention may include cognitive behavioural approaches (Roth and Fonagy, 2005), counselling (Scrutton, 1999) and task-centred approaches (Reid and Shyne, 1969), which enable the task of being able to accept medical assistance to be broken down into small measurable steps agreed with Arthur. Networks may be used to reframe an individual issue as a collective experience, for example by putting Arthur in touch with veterans' groups or fellow patients. The radical social worker would seek to understand Arthur's situation in terms of systemic neglect throughout the lifecourse of soldiers once asked to fight for their country and later rejected as a burden on health and social care systems.

Rights-based approaches

Rights-based approaches emphasize the social contract between individuals and the state in terms of reciprocity of obligations. There is a recent but growing interest in the rights of older people, often from the basis of their accumulated investment in civil society through their labour and past financial contributions. Discussion of individual rights may arise from a philosophical, political or legal analysis. Rights may be seen as an essential attribute of being a person, when the discussion may range from basic human rights of sustenance to more sophisticated rights to be supported economically, socially and developmentally in order to make maximum use of the opportunities that are available, albeit located within a particular historical period or culture. Political rights embrace citizenship and an entitlement to contribute to decision-making and reciprocally to receive support and protection from the state in exchange for service and adherence to societal expectations. Legal rights may variously be considered as having their basis in natural law in the sense of being inalienable by legislative means, or may be presented from a positivist standpoint as the creation of national law or international conventions (McDonald, 2007).

Rights, decision-making and therapeutic intervention with individuals are the themes of this chapter: how individuals become aware of the decisions that they have to make and how they respond to those opportunities are not fixed in time, but may be subject to change within the context of a professional relationship. This means that the application of rights involves a dynamic process within which individuals may make new and differently informed challenges to conventional ways of describing the status of older people.

Being a bearer of rights in the abstract does not, however, guarantee that those rights will be effectively supported and enforced. As a corollary of having a right, some other person or organization must be under a duty to respect or give effect to that right. There may also be administrative discretion in the interpretation and enforcement of rights, leading to variable experiences depending upon who the decision-maker is. Finally, rights are ineffective without remedies for their breach, and mechanisms by which decision-makers and the state itself can be called to account for inadequacies in the support that individuals, or groups of individuals, receive. Conversely, interference with rights to autonomy on 'welfare' grounds is specifically constrained; in the UK, deprivation of liberty must be in accordance with the Mental Health Acts, or for those who are incapacitated, in accordance with due process and best interests decision-making under the Mental Capacity Act 2005. Since neither of these appears to apply to Arthur, his present refusal to accept referral for hospital treatment must, within a discourse of rights, be respected.

Contemporaneous with the modernizing agenda of health and social care has been the development of a human rights discourse constructed around the implementation of the Human Rights Act 1998 in the UK and the effective incorporation of the rights guaranteed by the European Convention on Human Rights (McDonald, 2007). Yet the two may be incompatible: if rights depend upon the existence of a correlative duty to respond to claims for services, then the development of eligibility criteria and rationing of services has intensified the experience of receiving social care as being in receipt of a 'privilege' or a 'concession', rather than an entitlement. The discretion of decision-makers in the provision of health and social care services also means that the content of such rights as 'the right to life' (Art. 2 of the European Convention) and the right to respect for privacy and family life (Art. 8) may be differentially interpreted according to geographical location, personal status and, arguably, age. This is so even though Art. 14 prohibits discrimination in the enjoyment of rights on a number of bases, including age as well as gender and race. The majority of rights are in fact not absolute but qualified, being subject to a proportionate interference by the state within a democratic process. Furthermore, the individualist focus on civil and political rights within the Convention has no relevance to equal economic and social enjoyment of natural resources or community-generated goods (Ife, 2001). The rights which are guaranteed are those that the state has chosen to allocate according to its own formulation of priorities beyond the basic level. In the UK currently, discrimination against people on the basis of age is outlawed only in relation to employment and training and not in respect of the provision of goods and services, as is the case with disability, race or gender discrimination. The rights of older people therefore receive limited protection from the law – a situation which may be attributed to their lesser social and political status.

To what extent then do older people currently have 'rights' in the UK, and what are the relevant areas for development? In their 2002 policy position paper on the Human Rights Act, Age Concern saw that one of the most important aspects of the implementation of the Act was the extent to which it was interpreted as placing obligations on the state positively to support older people and to raise their social position. Such an interpretation also needs to be reflected in agency practice and in the decision-making of individual practitioners.

Key areas in which discussion about the engagement of rights is particularly relevant for older people are (Age Concern, 2002):

- access to life saving treatment, and general standards in health and social care;
- protection from abuse and neglect;
- detention without consent;
- care home closures;
- the rationing of services necessary to enable people to remain in their own home or to maintain social and family relationships;
- policies that preclude older people from parenthood;
- protection from age discrimination; and
- procedural rights in giving older people a greater say in the decision-making processes that affect them.

Evidence from the Audit Commission (2003) showed that few public bodies had made general information on the Human Rights Act available to the public, and that this was attributable to a fear of litigation and a reluctance to rework policies to fit a rights agenda. Ellis (2004) found that at an operational level, talk of rights was subsumed within a more conservative assumption that those who were able to had to create their own welfare; frontline social care staff viewed social rights as largely conditional upon meeting obligations, rather than as absolute attributes of citizenship. So the dominant discourse concerned self-help, contributing to the economy and avoidance of dependency. The British Institute of Human Rights has produced guidance (BIHR, 2004) on ways in which older people may benefit from a human rights agenda, including dignity in the provision of care services and the state's obligation to provide protection. Formal guidance on the interpretation of the Human Rights Act is based on the premise that its principles will be readily absorbed into decision-making. However, pressure on resources, a managerialist context for decision-making rather than a professional approach to exercising discretion, and limited acceptance of the legitimacy of challenging traditional ways of working mean that guidance alone will not be sufficient to effect change (McDonald, 2007).

There are opportunities to bring human rights principles to bear in situations commonly affecting older people if there is sufficient knowledge of the law and a facility in using rights-based arguments. For example, the decision to discharge a patient directly from hospital to residential care against the wishes of their family may engage the right to respect for family life. Regimes in residential care which amount to degrading treatment or unwarranted invasion of privacy may also be challengeable on human rights principles. Failure to protect people who experience domestic violence through adequate housing or support services may also threaten the right to life. The interplay between the legal protection of human rights, even in the current stage of development, and social work values of respect for persons and empowerment mean that there is a positive dynamic at work to support individual work with older people. The importance of human rights principles to the legal structure within which social workers with older people operate means that claims to ethical and legally correct practice have to be validated to the maximum extent possible in accordance with principles of non-discrimination in the general enjoyment of Convention rights. This means that social workers cannot ignore the imperative to support the claims of older people as part of their legal professional brief.

The agendas of old age and their relationship to changing social work practice

Individual work with older people should begin with an awareness of issues common to older people in a developmental, social and political sense and the experience and interpretation of these issues by individuals in the context of their life experience so far and personal aspirations for the future. The traditional way of providing services to older people as a group, which was the hallmark of the welfare state, focused on needs based on deficiencies in economic and social well-being. The delivery of services within formal bureaucratic structures created an identity for social workers as bureau professionals. This model remained largely intact through the development of care management in the 1990s as a method of targeting services at those most at risk of developing higher dependency needs. Although the provision of services was shared between statutory, voluntary and private agencies, individuals had little opportunity to influence commissioning decisions or to make lifestyle choices which went beyond the remit of 'services for older people'. The focus of care management on task-centred work with measurable outcomes meant that either the counselling role was lost to social work and privatized elsewhere, or else the need for emotional and social development in older age was ignored altogether. Modernizing services for older people has therefore meant devising new ways of delivering support which focus on the individual and acknowledge the importance of a largely preventative agenda in maintaining or retrieving well-being in older age. In consequence, for Arthur Bertram, a psychosocial intervention addressing present dilemmas in the context of the losses experienced at an earlier stage in his lifecourse is a 'service' which social work can provide at this point to enable him, if he wishes, to take advantage of the healthcare interventions which are open to him.

Thus the personalization of care, first of all through the development of direct payments, then through the creation of individual budgets, has moved the balance of power away from professionals towards older people by making funding directly amenable to their own choices and preferences, albeit within an assessment framework which is professionally led. Not only has personalization of care been a radical challenge to traditional agency-based ways of working, it has also been an expression of a change in the value base of service provision which has great potential for widening the traditional agendas of social work with older people. Trusting individuals to set their own priorities has been a significant aspect of the individualizing process of care planning for older people, focusing on the diversity of interests and needs of older people, their ability to make choices and the respect that is due to individual lifestyle preferences. Personalization is therefore an expression of a humanist value base, and a practical response to the marginalizing of individuality. Issues over which personalization is important are gender, sexuality, ethnicity and the particular needs of people with dementia. Providing user-centred care has become a mantra for good practice, but unless these human rights dimensions are addressed, opportunities for designing and matching services incontrovertibly to need are lost.

Translating the personalizing agenda to meeting the emotional needs of older people creates an opportunity for social workers legitimately to be involved in therapeutic work with them alongside or as an alternative to providing practical support. Clearly, identifying agendas for older people should not fall into the trap of stereotyping older people and their needs. Yet there are a number of issues and transitions which commonly call for resolution and which may be encountered in the relevant counselling agendas (Scrutton, 1999). The setting of agendas for older age links to themes of ageing which may variously emphasize loss (of occupation, of health, of relationships), or transitions (to retirement, to grandparenthood, to living alone), or activity (leisure opportunities, greater community involvement or learning of new skills). A diversity of experiences is possible which may in turn be influenced by structural factors and previous life chances. Old age may offer the opportunity for diversification: from Jung's point of view (2009) that the second half of life enables previously suppressed identities to be explored to Tornstam's view (1996) of 'gerotranscendence' – a shift from the material and rational to the spiritual and meditative. Throughout, it is important to bear in mind that the experiences and views of older people themselves should not be marginalized in the development of professional and academic practice, and that the experiences of older people offers a different, but valuable form of knowledge. Levy (2003) makes us aware of the impact of stereotypes on older peoples' self-esteem, and the importance therefore of a focus on strengths rather than deficits or professional anxieties.

Acknowledging the rights of older people to be heard, to be helped or to refuse interventions means that there is no mandate for social workers to intervene unless the role is either statutory (in narrowly defined circumstances requiring protection) or explicitly negotiated with the older person. So, in our case profile, Arthur Bertram must be willing to accept a referral to engage in an examination of the past experiences which are acting as a barrier to receiving the medical care that he has been assessed as needing. The physical crisis that he faces may attenuate fears for his mortality, 'guilt' at surviving when his comrades did not, and a breaking down of the barriers that have protected him previously from being overwhelmed by those anxieties. Although addressing these issues may be framed in terms of a series of tasks to be worked on with Arthur, precipitated by the current crisis, the legitimacy of social work intervention in such a case raises ethical issues about privacy, trustworthiness of professionals, skills in developing relationships and the availability of longer-term support which are difficult to accommodate within a functional model of care management.

Rights, empowerment and choice

It may be useful when discussing issues of rights to return once more to consider the context within which rights-based practice is located. Responding to older people as citizens means not only asking for their views on services, but also acting on what they say (CSCI, 2006a). Thompson and Thompson (2001) challenge practitioners to look beyond the 'care model' – the paternalistic and medicalized approach to social work with older people, which has tended to dominate service provision in the past – to a model of empowerment which replicates that of the disability movement and of people who use mental health services. The social work role in an empowerment model is that of facilitator and enabler, rather than that of 'expert'. Self-awareness by social workers of the role that is being undertaken is critical because, as Dalrymple and Burke (2006) describe, the legal framework within which services are provided following a professional assessment of need prioritizes 'welfare' over self-determination. It is important, therefore, that principles of human rights and user self-determination are at the forefront of professional awareness when embarking upon work with older people. The impact of ageism at an institutional and personal level must also be brought into consciousness and considered. Obstacles to older people being in a position to voice their needs are identified by Thompson and Thompson (2001: 65) as:

- structural oppression, and ageist assumptions about 'not wanting to be a nuisance' that have been internalized;
- lack of information, exacerbated by emotional factors such as grief reactions leading to feelings of hopelessness and defeatism; and
- the very complexity of the circumstances in which older people find themselves.

These three factors make the task of empowering social work with older people more complex. A superficial response to the refusal of services or the rejection of support by withdrawing from the situation may fail to engage with the felt needs of older people that they are unable for the time being sufficiently to express. Looking at the provision of services, it is clear that, first of all, core knowledge, personal confidence and a degree of stamina are needed to spot opportunities, to take advantage of them and to follow them through. This is particularly so if systems over-emphasize consumerism and self-sufficiency. Faced with these barriers, an appeal to 'choice' is ineffective, particularly so when faced with a confusing marketplace of services.

If individuals are left unsupported in establishing and making choices, because of an adherence to liberal values which unrealistically ignore the complexities of financial markets and quality control, the danger is that 'the language of choice can act as a screen and effectively hide conditions of social neglect and isolation' (Neysmith, 1999: 11). For older people, making effective choices may thus require a partnership with professionals, rather than an abandonment to market forces, as well as the provision of advocacy and therapeutic tools to support decision-making. Effective social work with older people will most likely therefore require a combination of entrepreneurial skills and interpersonal approaches which enable older people to be supported in order to achieve a position within which they can genuinely exercise self-determination.

Working in partnership

The social worker's contribution to partnership with older people, Thompson and Thompson assert (2001: 66), should be:

- a set of interpersonal and problem-solving skills geared towards helping older people go beyond internalized oppression to raise confidence and self-esteem;
- an understanding of the services, resources and other problem-solving opportunities likely to be available; and
- the ability to analyse complex social and personal circumstances and identify a number of constructive ways forward.

To this might be added:

- an awareness of the psychosocial aspects of ageing which explain or predict behaviour and complexities in relationships;
- skills in negotiating with gate-keepers and resource holders; and
- an ability to anticipate and plan for changes in needs.

These skills map onto a range of social work methods which enables older people effectively to understand and express their wishes and to bring about solutions to problems. So, the use of task-centred methods not only enable specific issues to be identified and worked upon, they also enhance general problem-solving skills for the future (thus raising confidence and self-esteem). Care management processes also harness the expertise of the professional 'helper' to broker for services and to enable such services to be monitored and reviewed. Solution-focused approaches will always be helpful as long as they do not deny the reality of physical restrictions or relationship breakdowns. The focus is looking to break free from past obstacles, identifying old age as a continuing developmental stage. Thus the social worker in a technical sense has a range of methods of intervention, which singly or in combination can be used to support older people. Working in partnership, however, requires social workers to be explicit both about possible tensions within their role as gatekeepers of agency resources alongside that of advocate for the older person, and also about any powers of compulsory intervention that they may or may not have.

Mental capacity

Arthur Bertram is rejecting a referral for tests that his GP is assuming will be in his best interests. The position of older people whose capacity to make decisions is in doubt poses particular challenges for professionals. The mandate to intervene requires careful analysis and an awareness of rights, values and decision-making processes.

Decisions that older people have to make may be complex and life-changing, such as refusing medical treatment, or deciding whether to move in with relatives or to enter residential care. They may also be routine, such as what to have to eat, how to spend their money, or whether to take medication. The ability to make such decisions is defined by the legal notion of capacity, previously a matter of common law but now governed by the Mental Capacity Act 2005. This legislation defines what capacity is, how it is to be expressed and how substitute decisions are to be made in accordance with 'best interest' principles. It will be a vital piece of legislation for family carers as well as professional workers; the Act protects them from liability for the consequences of their decisions if the terms of the Act are followed. This makes it important for decisions to be explained and to be justifiable. Because such decision-making now takes place within a statutory framework, social workers need to be aware of the ultimate role of a redesignated Court of Protection in challenging their decisions for nonconformity with the Act and its principles. The Act also requires a considered and informed approach to assessment which recognizes individuals' hesitancy and uncertainty about making decisions.

The Mental Capacity Act will be particularly relevant for people with dementia or other medical conditions which lead to 'an impairment of, or a disturbance in the functioning of, the mind or brain' (s.2(1)). This includes people with learning difficulties, those who remain affected by a stroke and those incapacitated by drugs or alcohol misuse. Such lack of capacity may be permanent or temporary, but it is decision-specific – that is, a person may be able to decide what medication to take, but not how to invest their money. Those who have capacity may delegate in advance the power to make 'welfare' decisions, as well as the power to make financial decisions, to another person through the making of a Lasting Power of Attorney. The Act also enables advance decisions to refuse treatment to be made, which are binding on medical professionals. Amendments to the Mental Capacity Act 2005 introduced by the Mental Health Act 2007 authorize 'deprivation of liberty' subject to certain safeguards, for people resident in care homes, as well as those admitted to hospital. This may include preventing people from leaving the premises or having contact with visitors. Independent Mental Capacity Advocates (ICMAs) are also to be appointed when the provision of serious medical treatment by an NHS body is under consideration or when the provision of long-term accommodation is proposed; the duty arises when there is no one – for example, family or friends – that it would be appropriate for the professionals to consult when making such decisions. IMCAs may also be appointed when care is reviewed, or adult protection procedures are engaged. There is a lengthy code of practice on the application of the Act to which decision-makers are to 'have regard'.

The Mental Capacity Act 2005 has had a long genesis, but is welcome protection for vulnerable adults from arbitrary decision-making. It incorporates respect for the autonomy of the individual, insofar as it requires appropriate efforts to be made to communicate information before a decision of incapacity is made, and requires participation of that person as far as it is practicable in any 'best interests' decision-making. The Court of Protection is given the power to decide disputes concerning capacity, and also has the power, similar to powers of the courts under the Children Act 1989, to decide questions of residence, contact and other specific issues relating to people lacking capacity or their property. The court can also appoint 'deputies' to make such decisions. The Mental Capacity Act 2005 is underpinned by a number of principles and values, shown in the box on p. 122, and has considerable potential to steer practice towards a more conscious application of rights-based arguments (for further details, see Dawson, 2007).

So, in Arthur's case, the presumption is that he has capacity. Practicable steps to enable him to make a decision would involve making available information about the benefits and risks of the hospital tests that are proposed, involving a third party such as a relative in explaining the consequences of refusing or delaying a referral, or postponing a decision until Arthur is less anxious about his situation. However, he is not to be treated as unable to make a decision merely because he makes an unwise decision. It is only if he is unable to make this decision for himself that substitute decision-makers can act in his best interests; even then, he should be involved in the decision that is made, and if there is a choice of intervention, the course of action that is less restrictive, though still in his best interests, should be chosen. The Mental Capacity Act thus challenges professionals properly to explain their reasons for the recommendations that they make to older people, to include them in a staged process of decision-making and to consult with significant others.

Mental Capacity Act 2005 (s.1)

The following principles apply for the purposes of this Act:

1 A person must be assumed to have capacity unless it is established that he lacks capacity.
2 A person is not to be treated as unable to make a decision unless all practicable steps to help him to do so have been taken without success.
3 A person is not to be treated as unable to make a decision merely because he makes an unwise decision.
4 An act done, or a decision made, under this Act for or on behalf of a person who lacks capacity must be done, or made, in his best interests.
5 Before the act is done, or the decision is made, regard must be had to whether the purpose for which it is needed can be as effectively achieved in a way that is less restrictive of the person's rights and freedom of action.

Questions

1 How would you apply the principles of the Act to particular cases?
2 Are these principles helpful in practice?

Advocacy

People who have the capacity legally to make decisions for themselves may nevertheless benefit from the services of an advocate to represent their interests. Older people may need different forms of advocacy at different times, or indeed at the same time in different situations, but the connecting thread in advocacy is about 'stating a case, influencing decisions, ending assumptions, getting better services, being treated equally, being included, protecting from abuse, redressing the balance of power, becoming more aware of and exercising rights' (Dunning, 1995: 11). Dunning distinguishes, in relation to older people, between different types of advocacy (ibid.: 20):

Citizen advocacy	an ongoing partnership with a trained volunteer
Crisis advocacy	a 'one off' involvement focused on a particular task or specific situation
Peer advocacy	support for another who has experienced or is experiencing similar difficulties or discrimination
Complaints advocacy	narrowly focused to pursue complaints about or within particular services
Public advocacy	the activities of organizations that campaign on behalf of or alongside particular groups of people

Professional advocacy	includes those who are paid to carry out a particular advocacy service, or for whom advocacy is part of their role. Dunning includes social workers in this
Self-advocacy	the experience of a person expressing their own needs and representing their own interests
Group advocacy	Self-advocacy groups or organizations which offer mutual support, skills development and a common call for change

The provision of advocacy services may be coupled with the giving of information or advice relevant to decision-making. Research by Quinn et al. (2003) found that older people generally did not distinguish clearly between information, advice and advocacy. However, there were observed to be barriers at different stages in becoming aware that there was help available (of whatever nature) to assist older people in their situation, gaining access to it and receiving practical assistance. Older people were found to value information that was topic-based, rather than the more usually available agency-based information. Continuity of contact was also liked in order to avoid having to retell one's story to different people. A follow-up service to ensure that a solution was achieved, rather than referral on, was also preferred. Focusing on the problem and finding a solution, rather than adhering to differentiations between agencies and giving consistent support through the journey, thus appears to be what older people say they want – a useful message also for social work involvement.

Advocacy comes into its own when professional views are divided; it is an evidence-based way of informing decisions and particularly valuable when no obvious solution presents itself – hence its use within the Mental Capacity Act. When the older person is unable to give instructions to the advocate, the term 'non-instructed advocacy' is used. Even within this term there are different approaches (Henderson, 2007). Rights-based advocates take a watchdog-negotiator stance, ensuring that the person for whom they are an advocate gets their full share of resources. This sort of approach will emphasize vigilance, for example in the application of the Human Rights Act to decisions concerning older people. In rights-based advocacy, there is not necessarily a relationship between advocates and the person they represent, as there is when the alternative model is chosen and the advocate acts as an 'articulate friend'. Henderson (2007) considers that this issue of judgement is a key factor in defining non-instructed advocacy – that is, judgement in relation to the nature of the individual's concerns, the best methods of seeking redress and the criteria for a successful outcome. Such an approach in turn demands greater accountability for the process and outcomes of decision-making, and so advocacy, by its very nature, may act to improve the quality of bureaucratic decisions, not only by emphasizing legality but also by exploring the meaning of rights for particular individuals.

Understanding behaviour

Practical interventions with older people must necessarily be based on an understanding of developmental issues within particular social and personal contexts. Within this, particular attention must be paid to those who experience mental distress in old age, not only because of the impact of this on their own functioning and understanding, but also to understand – and in some cases challenge – the response of others. 'Earlier experiences, attachment experiences and events in a person's life history help to determine the way in which they will deal with old age, and the problems in it' (Miesen, 1992: 112).

Understanding behaviour leads in turn to the opportunity for therapeutic interventions. Despite the complexity of accumulated issues in older age, there has historically been a lack of interest in therapeutic interventions with older people. Scrutton (1999: 3) queries whether there is an assumption that older people do not require theoretical constructs such as counselling, and that their needs can be accurately assessed and readily satisfied by an emphasis on the practical, rather than the emotional. On the contrary, the complexity of accumulated needs in older age may point to a need for reparative intervention, which goes beyond a superficial service-based response.

Attachment theory provides a relationship-based approach to social work with older people that the introduction of proceduralized care management models has tended to submerge (Phillips and Waterson, 2002). Shemmings (2005) notes how the nexus around which decisions are made concerning, for example, an older person's entry to residential care is more likely to be competence, consent or cash than relational dynamics. Yet a breakdown in caring relationships is the most important precipitating factor for entering permanent care (Levin et al., 1989). Shemmings (2005) accordingly explores the value of adult attachment theory in helping social workers to understand how people feel and act within close relationships, particularly in stressful situations.

Attachment relationships in adulthood are different from attachment relationships in childhood because they are bi-directional, in the sense that either party will give and receive support (ibid.). But a basic understanding of attachment theory explains strengths and risks in these relationship patterns. Adult attachment theory, developed from the work of Sperling and Berman (1994), raises questions about the extent to which attachment styles remain relatively constant across the lifespan, whether uniqueness and irreplaceability are distinctive features of attachment relationships that distinguish them from, for example, friendships, and whether close relationships in adulthood offer both parties an opportunity to re-evaluate, or re-experience relationships. Bretherton and Mulholland's 'intergenerational transmission hypothesis' (1999) raises the question of whether our own experience of being parented affects the way in which we parent a future generation. In this way, attachment styles in childhood create internal working models the potency of which can endure throughout the lifecourse.

Attachment styles developed in infancy are seen by Bartholomew and Horowitz (1991) to map in adulthood onto a secure mode (the balanced style) and three insecure modes (the preoccupied, dismissing and fearful styles). Balanced individuals are the most able to respond with resilience to stress, and to nurture others. Preoccupied individuals, as a result of their attempts to maintain contact with inconsistent caregivers, hypersensitively monitor negative emotions, worry about being rejected and enter into dependent relationships that fail to reduce that anxiety. The dismissing style combines a positive view of self with a negative view of others, while the fearful style combines negative views of both self and others. Shemmings (2005) considers how individuals with these different internal working models experience and express emotions (affect regulation), and deal with conflict and tensions in relationships. While securely attached individuals are able to acknowledge distress and to turn to others for comfort and support, dismissing/ fearful individuals may reject support and not acknowledge distress. While differently styled 'pairings' may complement each other, opposite pairings can lead to aggression between close partners when there are stresses such as ill-health or financial worries or loss. Professionals themselves also respond differently to stresses in their relationships according to their attachment style. 'Not only do social workers need to consider how their attachment organisation affects conflictual relationships with family members and service users, they may also choose to reflect upon what happens when they experience tensions and disagreement with other professionals' (Shemmings, 2005: 26).

So, at a time of stress, such as that which Arthur Bertram is currently experiencing when faced with the prospect of admission to hospital for investigative tests, old conflicts will revive. Family and friends may be experienced as a source of support, or they may be rejected or anxiously monitored for their loyalty and availability. Such friends may also be in conflict with each other, or, alternatively, seek to avoid an uncomfortable outcome by terminating their involvement. Differences in attachment styles may thus explain why some carers cope well when faced with changes in the person with whom they were previously in a different type of relationship, while others faced with similar stressors become unable to provide consistent or adequate care.

Mental health in older age

Mental health in older age is not just the absence of mental disorder (though this is the most likely means by which professional involvement is triggered); it is also a sense of well-being and satisfaction which enables stresses that occur as a result of ageing to be dealt with. Scrutton (1999) identifies key therapeutic agendas for older people as coping with loss, the legacy of life history (as above) and dissonance between the 'ideal' self and the actual self. Yet there are also obstacles within the helping process itself which reflect ageist assumptions about older people (by the counsellor, as well as by the person being counselled); most importantly, an assumption that growth and change is either not possible, or that nonconformity to an image of old age as a time of 'peace, tranquillity and serenity' (ibid.: 6) is a sign of weakness. At the same time, it is important to be aware of structural situational constraints on freedom of expression: older people may have been subject to a greater number of what Scrutton calls 'moral imperatives' in their lives than younger people, as society's attitude to sexuality, for example, has changed. Also, some older people who become dependent on care provided by others may curtail an honest and healthy expression of how they feel (ibid.: 38). All these factors may impact on therapeutic work with older people. Further complexity is introduced by the onset of mental disorder in older age. Individual, professional and societal reactions to mental health and well-being in old age thus need to be explored.

Understanding depression

Depression is the most common form of mental disorder in older age. Estimates of its prevalence vary at between 10 and 20 per cent of older people in the community, and up to 40 per cent of care home residents (SCIE, 2006b). The most common symptoms of depression (in people of all ages) are:

- a prevailing feeling of sadness;
- a loss of interest in life and inability to take pleasure in things;
- tiredness and sleep problems;
- loss of appetite;
- poor concentration and memory;
- anxiety and agitation;
- hopelessness;
- feelings of guilt and worthlessness;
- thoughts of suicide.

Older people tend not to complain of being depressed, and are more likely to refer to physical symptoms; conversely, some symptoms of physical illness are similar to those of depression (ibid.). Clearly, careful differential assessment is needed, and in Arthur Bertram's case this will be one of the diagnostic issues of which to be aware. But risk factors in depression are social as well as biomedical, and reflect the diversity of older people (Moriarty and Butt, 2004); only social interventions may target such factors. Social isolation, bereavement and multiple adverse events or changes in circumstances may all trigger or exacerbate depression. Community involvement, conversely, can reduce social isolation, provide support and increase the sense of self-worth (SCIE, 2006b).

Social and economic factors are also linked to depression, particularly a lack of close confiding relationships and an absence of occupation (Murphy, 1982). Not surprisingly, therefore, suicide is a significant risk for older people who are depressed. Bereavement, poor physical health, alcohol abuse and access to the means to commit suicide are the key risk factors, As with depression, older people may not speak openly about suicidal intent, but social workers and others need to be aware of actuarial figures which say that older people, and particularly men, are more likely than younger people determinedly to pursue suicidal intent (SCIE, 2006b). Older men aged 75 and over, and especially those who are living alone, pose a significant risk of successful suicide and self-harm and any referral should be approached with this knowledge in mind.

Self-harm in older people should always be taken seriously. An analysis of 76 older people who presented to a specialist self-harm team (Dennis et al., 2007) found that the majority had high suicide intent and 69 per cent were depressed, the two being correlated. The study highlighted the need for adequate recognition and management of depression in older people in primary care, and of risk factors located in living alone with an isolated lifestyle and poor physical health. Such people are already known to services: 59 per cent of older people in the sample had seen their GP in the previous month, 29 per cent had reported a previous episode of self-harm and 21 per cent were in contact with psychiatric services. A key finding is the importance of assessing the whole range of factors – depression, physical problems (and to a lesser extent relationship difficulties) and social isolation – as part of a comprehensive assessment of social as well as healthcare needs, and recognizing the particular vulnerability of older men.

Understanding dementia

The idea that a diagnosis of dementia defines the individual negatively as a sufferer from a predominantly organic and deteriorating illness has been challenged by Kitwood's (1997) seminal exposition of the 'personhood' of people with dementia. Critical of the 'standard paradigm' of the medical model, Kitwood focused on the social construction of dementia through personal relationships. His approach, based on the strengths that the individual person with a diagnosis of dementia retains, depends significantly on the context of recognition and approbation from others. The task of those working with people with dementia is thus to reinforce 'personhood' (ibid.: 8) as a 'standing or status that is bestowed upon one human being, by others, in the context of the relationship and social being. It implies recognition, respect and trust'. He defined the basic needs of people with dementia as

comfort in the face of loss, responsiveness to attachment needs, inclusion, occupation and identity, in the sense of a 'narrative' to present to
others. Yet, as Kitwood observed, a 'malignant social psychology' may
exist in dementia services as part of a cultural or organizational process which separates or 'others' people with dementia in ways which
undermine personhood. Kitwood's exposition of the ways in which
'malignant social psychology' manifests itself have become a classic
definition of unacceptable practice in dementia care . The elements of
malignant social psychology are (ibid.):

1 Treachery, deception or manipulation – for example, taking advantage of an individual's disorientation in place and time covertly
   to secure their attendance at a day service or their admission to
   residential care.
2 Disempowerment – excluding people from involvement in decision-making or choice.
3 Infantilization – automatically addressing older people by their
   first names, or using nicknames.
4 Intimidation – for example, threats that if cooperation does not
   improve, services will be withdrawn.
5 Labelling – giving older people a reputation as a troublemaker or
   source of difficulty for others.
6 Stigmatization – attributing negative social status to older people
   or excluding them from services because of their complex needs.
7 Outpacing – failing to adapt speed of speech or movement to the
   capacity of the older person.
8 Invalidation – refuting or ridiculing feelings of anxiety or loss.
9 Banishment – placing people with behavioural difficulty in isolation or excluding people from social interaction.
10 Objectification – treating people as objects of concern or bundles
   of medical symptoms rather than as individuals.
11 Ignoring – not responding to requests for attention or assistance.
12 Imposition – not asking the permission of the older person to carry
   out routines of care or programmes of activity.
13 Withholding – using the withdrawal of attention or concern as a
   punishment, or not meeting basic physical or emotional needs.
14 Accusation – blaming people for things which are unintentional,
   such as incontinence or shouting.
15 Disruption – interfering without permission in others' routines, such
   as imposing set bedtimes or the abrupt ending of visiting times.
16 Mockery – holding individuals up to ridicule because of their
   appearance, views or behaviour.
17 Disparagement – discounting the opinions of the person with
   dementia as invalid.

So, social workers who cajole an older person into accepting services
that he or she does not want by using the authority of their position
are guilty of treachery as well as disempowerment. By denying the

older person's adult status as a citizen, they are guilty of intimidation. By labelling the person as incompetent to express an opinion, they stigmatize and invalidate the older person's contribution on the basis of a diagnosis of dementia. The cleverness of the social worker, speaking quickly and arranging hastily, outpaces the older person, who may have information about choice or legal rights that are being withheld. Any protests that the older person may make are ignored or disparaged. Even well-meant protective measures may be malignant if imposed on the individual, through an objectification of their individuality as an 'object of concern'.

Conversely, the person with dementia may need positive input in order to preserve their personhood. Miesen (1992: 116) discusses how diminishing defensive reactions mean that it is likely that old pain can no longer be suppressed and therefore resurfaces in older age; for example, war trauma, unfinished grieving and past disappointments. Focused intervention to address past trauma may thus be indicated when cognitive abilities which had functioned previously to protect the individual are diminished. In addition, the onset of dementia may present a further crisis which is experienced differently by different individuals depending on their previous cognitive strengths and social supports. The idea of personhood in dementia makes it inappropriate to talk about the disorder as if it had taken away the individual that existed before; rather, the onset of dementia operates to remove a veil which had previously disguised past, unresolved conflicts.

Aminzadeh et al. (2007) have examined the emotional impact of a diagnosis of dementia on patients and carers. Their empirical research found three broad categories of response:

- lack of insight and/or active denial of the diagnosis;
- grief reactions/emotional crises related to actual or anticipated losses associated with dementia; and
- positive coping responses to maximize outcomes.

Dealing with disclosure has been cited as one of the most difficult aspects of dementia care by both professionals and family carers (Arksey et al., 2004; SCIE, 2006b). The dilemma for people with dementia themselves is balancing the desire to maintain a prior sense of self against the need to reappraise and reconstruct an identity.

Focus group interviews with carers in Aminzadeh et al.'s research (2007) showed how the emotional response to the diagnosis of dementia could be delayed, indicating a need for continuing involvement. A minority of patients in the same study expressed a sense of relief and validation in having a reason to explain changes that they had noticed. There is therefore a range of possible responses to the diagnosis. Not surprisingly, questions about the accuracy of the diagnosis, and conflicting messages from people in the social network, made decision-making and future planning more complex. For some patients there was an increase in attachment behaviours. Diagnosis is thus not just a medical process, but a social act which removes a person to a new social group that is highly stigmatized, and in addition may impact on the development of the condition through the threat to and destruction of self (Cheston and Bender, 1999).

Psychological therapies with older people

Psychological therapies with older people have been limited by negative stereotypes about the treatability of older people, and by limitations in theoretical models and expertise (Hepple, 2004). The dominant model has been the biological model of illness and pharmacology, Murphy (2000, cited in Hepple, 2004) conducted a survey of mental health and social care professionals and found that 87 per cent felt that their services failed to deliver a good enough therapeutic service to older people. Referral rates for patients over 75 comprised only 1 per cent of all referrals, even though this group accounted for 9 per cent of the population. Nevertheless, there are a number of approaches advocated as positive for older people (Hepple, 2004), as well as a range of interventions developed specifically in response to their needs. Some of these are considered below, not necessarily as an alternative to pharmacological intervention (because this may be a prerequisite to enabling individuals to focus on therapy), but as a positive intervention for consideration in appropriate cases. Proactive intervention to improve access to psychological therapies for older people has recently been announced (DH, 2009b); a flexible and accessible approach is advocated, and social workers are seen as a potential source of referrals to challenge the perceived discrimination against older people within mental health services, and the reluctance of older people themselves to seek out appropriate interventions.

Cognitive behavioural therapy (CBT)

Cognitive behavioural therapy has been shown to be an effective intervention in depression for general populations and for older people (Roth and Fonagy, 2005). Intervention is based on Beck's (1992) cognitive theory of depression – that it is the way in which individuals view and interpret the world that are key vulnerability factors for the onset and maintenance of depression. The theory helps to explain why some people become depressed in adverse circumstances and others do not. Solomon and Haaga (2003) explain the aetiology of depression as comprising:

- rigidly negativistic beliefs regarding personal inadequacy or loss (e.g. 'I am all alone in the world'), in combination with the overvaluation of certain outcomes ('Life is not worth living as I am all alone') – taken together, such beliefs create vulnerability to the onset and maintenance of depression;

- core dysfunctional beliefs, learned primarily through childhood experiences, such as helplessness in the face of external changes, or unlovability – such core beliefs are reactivated (and/or reinforced) by negative experiences;
- the appraisal of day-to-day experiences, systematically distorted to conform to the core negative belief, through the use of overgeneralizations, dichotomous thinking, magnification or personalization – such 'cognitive distortions' act as a negative filter for events and ideas; for example, a failure by acquaintances to acknowledge the depressed person would, through a negative filter, be seen as rejection rather than oversight;
- 'automatic thoughts' are conclusions drawn from negative distortions – such thoughts are intrusive, repetitive and seemingly involuntary;
- other aspects of depression, such as lethargy, lack of concentration and interpersonal conflict, are aggravated by and in turn strengthen such negative beliefs; there may also be a belief that such symptoms must be attributable to a physical cause such as cancer or disease, and somatic symptoms may result.

Therapeutic intervention using CBT is a collaboration with the patient, teaching them skills for questioning and re-evaluating negative automatic thoughts. Behavioural methods are used to challenge negative thoughts through the provision of compensatory positive experiences. Core beliefs are then challenged in the light of these new ways of thinking about and experiencing the world. The focus is on the 'here and now' and future behavioural change rather than a direct interrogation of difficulties in the past. Hepple (2004: 236) considers that cognitive behavioural therapy should be the first-line approach for pronounced anxiety symptoms and panic with avoidant behaviour, and is particularly valuable in 'complicated' depressive illness, for example after bereavement.

Cognitive analytic therapy (CAT)

Cognitive analytic therapy takes a cathartic and reparative view of past trauma, using the therapeutic relationship to create new meaning and understanding. Ryle (2000) emphasizes the sustaining of personality in conversations that we have with ourselves and with others, a conversation with roots in the past and learning points for the future. Hepple (2004) sees CAT as helpful for individuals who have a history of traumatic experiences in childhood, the impact of which may re-emerge in later life. He provides a case vignette of Mrs Y, aged 67, a patient on an adult psychiatric ward with a diagnosis of depression who has regressed into a childlike state of withdrawal and frozen watchfulness (ibid.: 374). Therapeutic intervention gave Mrs Y the opportunity to communicate the pain of sexual abuse in adolescence to a trusted other. CAT may also be appropriate where somatic symptoms (distress without a physical cause) can be linked to past trauma.

Case profile

An application of CBT in practice might be illustrated by the case of Mrs Kay, who had always been quite socially isolated, and never (in her words) 'a good mixer'. Following the death of her husband 12 months ago, Mrs Kay had become increasingly anxious about being alone, fearing that her house was being targeted by local youths; she was constantly telephoning her daughter for reassurance. Mrs Kay's daughter was now starting to talk about residential care for her mother. Following a referral, the social worker identified Mrs Kay's negative beliefs: 'I cannot rely on anyone but my family for support'; 'If they do not protect me, dangerous people will prey on me.' Mrs Kay's late husband, a retired policeman, had been her 'defender'; now that he had gone, children playing in the street were seen by Mrs Kay as a threat to her and her property. The social worker arranged for a crime prevention officer to visit Mrs Kay to advise her on installing a burglar alarm, and she was also subscribed to a community warden service. The social worker also arranged for Mrs Kay to attend a luncheon club at a local community centre. Despite initial reluctance and fears that no one would speak to her, Mrs Kay recognized some familiar faces there from her younger days. Staff responded to her fears that they would ignore her by facilitating conversations between Mrs Kay and former neighbours. Mrs Kay found that the grandchildren of some of these renewed acquaintances were the same children who were playing in her street. Generally, her dependence on her daughter diminished, and she became more confident of her place in the community. She no longer wished to consider residential care. So, although the social worker may not have practised 'therapy' with Mrs Kay, a cognitive behavioural approach enabled identification of negative beliefs, cognitive distortion and repetitive, but unproductive thoughts. The death of her husband acted to make Mrs Kay vulnerable to being overwhelmed by such thoughts, which were instrumental in pursuing her towards a negative outcome.

What other approaches might you use with Mrs Kay, or (when you have read chapter 8), with her family and with her community?

Life review and reminiscence

Understanding current needs in the context of past experience provides principles and an approach, rather than a 'tool' for therapeutic intervention; as such, it need not be at odds with operational imperatives of being problem-focused if it is an integrated part of a care management process. What is forgotten, as well as what is remembered, may become the focus of therapeutic work. Seeking coherence over the lifecourse, including recognition of limitations and failings, fits with Erikson's (1980) sense of the psychosocial task of old age as achieving ego integrity. Integrating new service needs into the narrative also allows present circumstances to be adjusted to 'fit the story', rather than be experienced as 'worthless appendages' (Coleman, 1994: 9). So the unplanned-for 'new' event of physical impairment, bereavement or relocation in older age becomes another chapter in the story. Coleman (1997) sees two separate challenges here: one, 'self preservation', focuses on the maintenance of worth and value in circumstances of life which changed dramatically and may be accessed through reminiscence; the other, 'life review', focuses on the formation of an acceptable identity with which to face death. Different responses are required to each. Reminiscence valuing life experience for the preservation of the self is something to be shared with others and may be carried out in group settings; life review is a personal activity to be undertaken systematically over a period of time.

Coleman (1994) adds a further category of 'storytelling' to show how reminiscence could fulfil a social as well as a psychological function, as an outcome of the social need to teach and inform from one's own life experience. Enabling older people to share their knowledge of the past with younger people is a source of both consolation and cultural enrichment. This 'public' aspect of reminiscence is seen by Coleman (ibid.) as important to prevent reminiscence by older people from being merely a 'sentimental journey' or a flight from the present. Gibson (2004) goes on to describe the use of reminiscence and oral history within community development. Its value lies not only in bringing together different generations, but in its potential for challenging conventional accounts of history by a wider range of participants than those who usually have access to the construction of formal records. A radical, political aspect of reminiscence can thus sit alongside a personal therapeutic role for older people.

Reminiscence has thus been defined as 'the vocal or silent recall of events in a person's life, either alone or with another person or groups of people' (Woods et al., 1992). Four processes are often mentioned to explain the contribution of reminiscence to successful ageing: identity-forming and self-continuity; enhancing meaning in life and coherence; preserving a sense of mastery; and promoting acceptance and reconciliation (Bohlmeijer et al., 2007). Reminiscence may, however, reinforce negative behaviour as well as positive. Wong and Watt (1991) defined types of reminiscence as integrative, instrumental, narrative, escapist and obsessive, of which only integrative and instrumental reminiscence were found to correlate to successful ageing as ways of identity synthesis or therapeutic problem-solving. Individuals may reminisce with different functions in mind, and Webster (1993) has developed the Reminiscence Function Scale to measure eight functions: boredom reduction, death preparation, identity-forming, conversation, intimacy maintenance, bitterness revival, teaching/informing and problem-solving. High levels of bitterness revival have been found to correlate with both higher levels of anxiety and depression. Caution therefore needs to be taken in undertaking reminiscence work without such analysis of its impact on particular individuals.

Carers may also benefit from the learning contained in reminiscence. Gibson (2004) describes positively the benefits of small group work in care settings with people with dementia in rediscovering the rules of conversation and enhancing communication with carers. Memory boxes, containing memorabilia on themes like cooking and holidays, and themed spaces that recall previous ways of living can provide opportunities for conversation which can counteract the isolation caused by memory loss and associated language difficulties. Reminiscence work undertaken with carers can also enhance their sensitivity towards the past strengths of the person for whom they are caring, enabling them to see that person's life more coherently. So Arthur Bertram, no longer only 'the patient', is also the 'former soldier' and survivor of past trauma.

Life review is consonant with a view of ageing as a continuous process of adaptation to life events and challenges (Baltes, 1987). In terms of his final psychosocial task of ego integrity versus despair, Erikson (1980) opened up opportunities for the process of life review to be used in a therapeutic way with older people. In a meta-analysis of reported studies, Bohlmeijer et al. (2007) found that life review had a significant effect on psychological well-being in older age. Life review as an intervention is structured, systematically addresses the whole lifespan, focuses on both positive and negative events and is evaluative. After reviewing the different life events separately, the focus is on synthesizing the positive and negative experiences with themes. Life review may be combined with other approaches, such as cognitive therapy or narrative therapy, in a counselling context. It provides the opportunity to revisit past events in order to provide a coherent view of the life that has been lived. For people like Arthur Bertram who have faced traumatic events at earlier life stages, life review seeks to make sense of those experiences in the context of a 'life well lived' and understood as a coherent whole.

Therapeutic interventions with people with dementia

Allen (2001) has explored ways of communicating with people with dementia using observation and rapport to seek to understand their preferences and needs. Gibson (2004) uses the analogy of a game of tennis to describe communication with people with dementia where the worker must serve to begin a conversation; what is batted back and forth is a message, often about underlying emotions and a sharing of pleasure. Killick (1994) uses poetry to capture the symbolism and metaphor of the words used by the person with dementia. Communicators need to be aware of power imbalances, taking care not to ask leading questions and outpacing older people (Phillips et al., 2006).

Communication tools may be of assistance in facilitating the involvement of older people in decision-making. Talking Mats (www. talkingmats.com) offers a low-tech communication framework to help people with dementia to communicate. Topic cards which can be placed on a mat in front of the individual can be moved around 'options' on which a visual scale expresses 'happy', 'unhappy' or 'not sure'. Talking mats enable people to think about services on offer, explain what they would like to do on a day-to-day basis, and say where they would like to see improvements made. Photographs of the completed mats can provide a permanent record of the views of a person with dementia. An evaluation of the effectiveness of talking mats carried out by Murphy (2004) found that it was a system that was accessible to most people at any stage of dementia and, importantly, it enhanced the reliability of information provided through a more focused concentration on the here-and-now.

Working with people with dementia therapeutically in groups may also be effective in developing social interaction and acceptance. Group counselling for older people generally may offer both a secure environment in which to explore personal issues and an opportunity for the testing out of social skills. Group psychotherapy for people with memory problems may help to overcome feelings of shame and fear by the sharing of narratives (Miesen and Jones, 2004). Dementia care mapping, which explores the quality of group care interactions, may also serve to model good practice for staff (Chenoweth and Jeon, 2007).

For people with dementia and for their partners, the concept of the Alzheimer's Café, a meeting place for people with dementia and their carers, combines formal meetings with entertainment and refreshments and the opportunity to talk informally. These are real meeting places and have been introduced internationally from their original location in the Netherlands – they are informal spaces where people can sit and converse. For those who find counselling too challenging because they are struggling with denial and avoidance, the Alzheimer's Café provides greater anonymity and an educative and supportive function. Miesen and Jones (2004) have three objectives for the Alzheimer's Café:

- to provide information about the medical and psychosocial aspects of dementia;
- to emphasize the importance of speaking openly about emotional problems in an atmosphere that promotes recognition and social acceptance; and
- to prevent the social isolation of persons with dementia and their families.

The idea of mutual support using everyday opportunities for meeting has also been developed by individuals with dementia. People with dementia who have taken a proactive approach to supporting each other have formed an internet group DASN International (www.dasn-international.org) As experts on dementia, they 'see the world from the inside out' and offer mutual support and advice.

Principles, beliefs and values of DASN International

- we are autonomous and competent people diagnosed with dementia, and our loyal allies;
- we believe that shared knowledge is empowerment;
- we believe our strengths provide a supportive network;
- we are a voice and a helping hand;
- our purpose is to promote respect and dignity for persons with dementia, provide a forum for the exchange of information, encourage support mechanisms such as local groups, counselling, and internet linkages, and to advocate service.

Reality orientation

Reality orientation (Taulbee and Folsom, 1966) developed as a method of enabling people with memory difficulties to remain in touch with the present. The emphasis in reality orientation is on the here and now, and in organizational settings provides cues within a total care environment. So '24-hour reality orientation' includes notice boards and calendars stating the date, time, weather and current activities, and the use of colour coding and labelling of doors to designate, for example, bathrooms and sleeping areas. Gibson (2004) is critical of reality orientation as focusing on lost rather than retained abilities and, disregarding the different time orientation of people with dementia, imposing the values and priorities of staff in ways which could be confrontational. The legacy of reality orientation is, however, apparent in building design for people with dementia, with bright colours giving clear messages about the use of space. Gibson describes the way in which reality orientation has been succeeded by cognitive rehabilitation as a collaborative strategy for coping with memory difficulties. Such strategies include diaries and reminder notes, some of which may be supported by assistive technology.

Validation therapy

Therapeutic approaches which depend upon psychological insight, and are focused on personal development, may not, it is argued, be appropriate for some individuals with dementia who have progressed beyond the stage where they are able to respond to opportunities to recognize and deal with unresolved life tasks before reaching very old age. Validation therapy (Feil, 1992) addresses itself to those who are disorientated, time confused, or retreating to earlier developmental stages. People who are unable to find new ways of coping in old age, with no residual capacity to reflect, need empathy for negative emotions and validation of their feelings. In working with such people, carers need to set aside their own feelings, and enable themselves to be used in the present time as a sounding board for emotions not expressed in the past. Relatives similarly may need to accept change, disappointment, fear and guilt so that they can enter the emotional world of people with dementia. Common reactions from people who are disorientated are to blame others as a way of covering up their own grief and fear. So carers may be accused of stealing money that has been mislaid, or of moving precious objects that have already been sold. People who are time confused may keep track of memories, not time, so they may prepare meals for a long-dead husband, or children expected home from school. Validating the need to care for others or pride in past homemaking skills is seen as a more empathetic response than reality orientation which would remind the older person of their loss. In the final stage of dementia, there may be a retreat to pre-linguistic movements and sounds, with searching behaviour seeking reassurance or crying seeking comfort. Validation is thus not concerned with objective 'truth', but with coming alongside people and supporting them in expressing emotion and meaning at the end of life.

Conclusion

Working with individuals requires both a commitment to rights-based approaches and an understanding of the psychosocial needs of older people. Particular skill is needed where capacity is in doubt, or where the personhood of people with dementia is threatened. A number of techniques are available to engage with older people; the major challenge is to recognize the appropriateness of doing so.

Chapter summary

1 Working with individuals requires an examination of generic social work theories and methods, and of those which are specific to older people. Such theories reflect different ways of conceptualizing ageing.

2 Risk interacts with independence, choice, protection and rights in direct work with older people. The legal framework for intervention requires consideration of the capacity of older people to make (supported) decisions, and of the nature of the mandate for substitute decision-makers to act in the best interests only of service users.

3 The Human Rights Act sets out clear principles for interventions which must respect the rights of older people against unwarranted interference, but which also imposes obligations positively to promote their welfare.

4 Confident practice in direct work with older people remains in need of development, informed by the voices of older people themselves.

5 There is, nevertheless, a range of direct interventions with older people, some of which are particularly appropriate for those with cognitive impairment.

Key lessons

1 Structural, organizational and individual factors affect decision-making by social workers, and can create professional dilemmas when rights, risks and resources are in conflict.
2 Social workers as well as service users are affected by interpretations of 'risk' which inform their professional judgement, and which hold them accountable for the outcomes of their actions. 'Safe' practice for organizations and for individual professionals requires consideration of support, boundaries, a secure base and containment.
3 Assessments of mental capacity are part of the social work task; social workers cannot deny their responsibility to make such judgements and to act as substitute decision-makers even when the liberty of the individual is at stake. Structured decision-making leads to justifiable decisions.
4 Working with advocates for older people is becoming a significant part of the social work role.
5 Therapeutic interventions, including counselling and life review and the development of theories of personhood specifically in working with people with dementia, require a range of knowledge and skills on the part of practitioners which transcend the care management role.

Further reading

M. Baltes, *The Many Faces of Dependency in Old Age*. Cambridge: Cambridge University Press, 1996.
    A landmark book which considers resourceful adaptation to loss. Observation as a research methodology is also used to describe and understand older people's response to decreasing independence.
R. Cheston and M. Bender, *Understanding Dementia: The Man with the Worried Eyes*. London: Jessica Kingsley, 2000.
    This constructs a psychological model of dementia, and challenges the limitations of the organic model, taking a person-centred approach.

8 Working with Families and Groups

Issues considered in this chapter:

- family relationships in older age, and effective interventions;
- promoting equality and recognizing diversity;
- developing support networks;
- living in groups and understanding the residential environment.

Working with families and groups involves an understanding of the relationships between individuals, of the patterns for living together which older people experience and of the culture within which these develop. This chapter will look at social work with older people and their families and will also look at other group experiences of older people such as day services and living in collective housing or in residential care. The provision of care at the end of life is also dealt with in this chapter. For many people there will be a progression from receiving family support, to having that support enhanced by respite services, to experiencing shared care with others and to facing the end stage of life, possibly in a different location. Structural factors, including the availability of resources, will determine the experiences of older people; however, the quality of interpersonal relationships remains important in defining the quality of those experiences and the extent to which older age is supported as a developmental process.

The autonomy of older people may be either enhanced or curtailed by those within their environment. Family carers have their own needs, as well as rights which are acknowledged by legislation. There is great diversity in family 'types' and expectations, which needs to be acknowledged; re-partnering in older age and the impact of changing family structures on older people's experiences illustrate the extent to which old age is a developmental stage in itself, not simply the culmination of previous experiences. Everyday life in group settings, in day services or in residential care is affected by the meaning that participants bring to the situation and by the dynamics of the relationships within it. Younger people, and other family members, may have assumptions about how older people should behave in relationships as is illustrated by the case profile presented here.

In this case, previous patterns of behaviour within the relationship between Laura and David are having an impact in the present. The balance of power, however, has changed, as Laura has gained financial and

> ## Case profile
>
> Laura and David Cohen are a retired couple who have been married for 40 years. David has been diagnosed with Alzheimer's disease. The couple has always had a turbulent relationship, with frequent arguments which in the past centred around David's long working hours, and his accusations that Laura frittered away their money. David now accuses Laura of hoarding money so that she can leave him. Laura says that all the money goes on household expenses, but that she is tired of living with David and would welcome a chance to 'escape'. Janet, their only daughter, is shocked that her mother is talking in this way, and says that if her mother should leave, Janet and the grandchildren will have nothing more to do with her.

decision-making control. Symbolic interactionism (Mead, 1934) shows how social roles are developed in the interactions between individuals. David's role within the family has been a traditional one of breadwinner and head of the family. He has now been forced to step down from this role and is finding it a threat to his identity. Laura has been positioned in the socially constructed role of carer, a role for which she has had little preparation. Money has always been a potent source of bargaining power between Laura and David, so it is not surprising that this remains as a significant issue in defining conflicts within their relationship. The onset of dementia will heighten past sources of anxiety for David as he struggles to deal with challenges to his sense of himself as an individual whose status was strongly linked to his earning power and control over money. Janet, as the child, is unwilling to acknowledge the necessity of changing her perception of how both her parents should live in older age. She may also be contemplating her role in middle age as a potential carer for her parents. She is having to reassess her father's role in the family and also expectations culturally of how women should respond to changes in family cohesion. Feminist social theory would enable us to analyse how Laura's economic dependence on David has defined their relationship, and that of others in similar situations. Janet will also have observed in her own upbringing the relative financial dependence of women and the expectation that marriage comprises duty and commitment which for women is exchanged for financial support. The wishes of the grandchildren are not explored. We need to know how old the children are and whether they are able to articulate their wishes in this situation. What those wishes are may depend upon the previous relationship they had with each of their grandparents and their ability to understand that David's behaviour will now be different because of his dementia.

Promoting equality and respecting diversity

Relationships within families and between generations are not confined to the private sphere. The personal status of older people is defined by their social, economic and legal status. The onset of illness, reductions in financial status and changes in role which are common in older age are experienced as personal challenges, but are socially constructed according to the status which older people and their concerns have within society.

The social situation of older people creates inequalities which impact on personal experience. In this way, private rights – such as rights to a reasonable income in retirement, adequate support through illness and support for families – are to a large extent dependent on the creation of public law rights. Though there may be public law duties of non-discrimination under the Equality Act 2006, and rights to equal treatment of older people under Art. 14 of the European Convention on Human Rights, such rights will not reflect the lived experience of older people unless there are proactive means of promoting them. So, the ability of families like the Cohens to preserve their equilibrium is dependent upon society's investment in services for, for example, the timely diagnosis and treatment of dementia, the provision of adequate financial support and a sufficient investment in social care services to give them a real choice about whether and how they will continue to support each other. Finally, if such services as the state makes available are not delivered, then there must be proper forms of redress.

Such a functionalist view of society, which is predicated upon social cohesion and maintenance of existing institutions and relationships may be challenged. Thompson (1997: 24) describes how existing power relations are maintained and reinforced by ideas which operate at the ideological level, such as disablism and ageism. For Laura, in our example above, gendered expectations of duty and submissiveness are also potent reinforcers of status within relationships. Such power may be manifested in formal decision-making about the allocation of resources, or in professional discourse, but it will also exist within personal relationships. Biggs (2004) makes us aware of 'age imperialism' and the danger that official recognition of ways of ageing is confined to those who are seen as successful or productive – an attempt to regulate identity in later life to fit the agendas of other age groups. So, the consequence of David's apparent 'failure' to remain economically successful and productive in older age will have to be absorbed personally by him and his family. The emphasis on sameness belies diversity and assumes a baseline that is not drawn from later life itself (ibid.: 104). Biggs acknowledges that older people will age differently according to past life experiences, so David and Laura Cohen's present experience of older age is uniquely based on their past social and personal histories.

Gender significantly influences the experience of ageing and the distribution of resources in old age (Arber et al., 2003). Law and social policy have traditionally been focused on the nuclear family and have thus shaped the experiences of older women (Estes, 2001). The devaluation of caring work is also seen as an outcome of the low status of older, working-class women who are the chief recipients (and sometimes providers) of care (Cancian and Oliker, 2000). The failure of the state to adopt a universal policy of free long-term care means that women are obliged to accept responsibilities for care work which is unrecognized and unpaid (Estes, 2001). A lifecourse perspective draws attention to interlocking oppressions throughout life (Dressel et al., 1997), which operate at individual and family as well as cultural levels. Walsh et al.'s research in Canada (2007) also explored the extent to which cultural factors, ageism and gender characterized elder abuse, and found that those with less community support, those from minority ethnic groups and gay/lesbian older people were particularly vulnerable to prolonged abuse. Deference to authority and the emotional hegemony of the care-giver magnified an acknowledged reluctance to disclose mistreatment within the family.

In our case study, Laura is rejecting the role of carer, and is also responding to an awareness of how her position is being socially defined. The social worker presented with a referral for the Cohens must not only acknowledge Laura's legal right as a carer to a separate assessment of her needs, but should also understand the ways in which the definition of her role has been both socially constructed and personally experienced through her experiences as a wife, mother and grandmother.

Changing families

As family life has changed in response to greater geographical and social mobility and greater variety in possible relationships, previous expectations of continuity and support have modified the experience and expectations of older people. Ogg (2003) sees the growth of intimacy as an important quality of contemporary relationships, alongside normative family roles such as parent and grandparent. The growth of intimate relationships outside traditional family ties enables people to seek and receive support from friends and partners with whom they have no legal relationship. Although Phillipson et al. (1998) show that living apart may not have weakened essential family ties, new patterns are emerging: there is a growth of 'intimacy at a distance' (Rosenmayr and Köckeis, 1963), with people living separately, but engaged in close relationships, and an important role for friends as providers of direct support and as mediators (Ogg, 2003; Jerrome and Wenger, 1999). Relationships with children may not involve an expectation of support in old age, and there is a commensurate fear amongst many older people of 'being a burden' to their families (Godfrey et al., 2004). Research by Gierveld and Peeters (2003) found that people over the age of 50 (in Holland) were more likely to choose cohabitation or 'living apart together' than remarriage. However, within these two groups of cohabitees and non-resident partners, bonds with children became weaker. Children then, even in adulthood, have expectations of parental exclusivity that are threatened by re-partnering in older age. This may manifest itself in legal disputes with the surviving partner following the death of a parent.

However, as well as receiving assistance from families, older people also contribute emotionally, practically and sometimes financially to the welfare of their own children. Grandparents may provide substitute care for working families or take on responsibilities for children who would otherwise enter the public care system. Key policy debates about work/life balance, and inheritance, centre around older people and their place in the workforce, their ability to provide unpaid care for the children of working parents, and the availability of accumulated capital to provide access to the housing market for younger people. The emotional, social and economic needs of older and younger generations within families therefore remain enmeshed.

Age, gender and life after work are being redefined in changing social contexts, though traditional roles are likely to endure in intimate relationships. Women in older age take primary responsibility for maintaining social networks (Arber et al., 2003); men living alone are therefore more likely to be socially isolated. Men who take on caring roles in respect of a disabled partner retain power in that relationship by adherence to structure and routines (Davidson et al., 2003). Previous social roles and skills therefore persist into older age; what is unknown is the extent to which the increased longevity of older men, and the decrease in marriage coupled with the increase in divorce, will enable 'new' identities to emerge as living alone becomes more a positive choice than a situation created through loss.

The gendered construction of old age impacts also on the experiences of gay, lesbian, bisexual and transgender older people. Age Concern's 'Opening Doors' policy (Turnbull, 2002) has focused on the needs of older lesbians and gay men in terms of both planning for old age and securing services which are not discriminatory. Turnbull's literature review revealed a paucity of research, but found positives in terms of role flexibility, strong friendship networks and supportive sub-cultures. CSCI (2008b) examined the extent to which appropriate services were available and the particular needs of lesbian, gay, bisexual and transgender people were considered at assessment and review. Of the respondents to the CSCI survey, 45 per cent said that they had faced discrimination in using services either directly or indirectly, in the sense of being put at a disadvantage by the way in which needs were met in terms of supporting identity and community. Only 9 per cent of service providers said that they had carried out any specific work to promote equality. CSCI thus sees the responsibility as sitting with the service provider rather than the user to improve services.

Family interventions

Changing family structures have had an impact on methods of intervention by social workers and others. Curtis and Dixon (2005) describe how family therapy and systemic practice with older people has developed in response to the erosion of traditional roles, routines and institutions. While the changing cultural context potentially provides an opportunity for the deconstruction of negative stereotypes, it can also generate feelings of confusion and anxiety. Family therapy may enable people to negotiate new ways of sharing tasks after retirement which are different from traditional gender expectations. Other transitions, such as illness and bereavement, will provide psychosocial challenges to families, sometimes with the opportunity to address longstanding interpersonal tensions. So, Curtis and Dixon (2005: 51) employ Hargrave and Anderson's (1992) concept of 'relational ethics' to explore issues of reciprocity within families. Relational ethics is 'the balance of fairness between entitlements and obligations built up over a lifetime of a relationship; and in parent–child relationships begins with the care given to a baby by its mother and father' (Curtis and Dixon, 2005: 31). This understanding may be used to explore conflicts based on different recollections of care, or abuse, in childhood, and it also serves to explain tensions in reconstructed families in which there is little 'credit' upon which to draw.

In formulating effective interventions, Curtis and Dixon identify systemic practice as being relevant for much day-to-day work within services for older people, exploring the relationships that maintain and support older people within families and communities. Working in a systemic way requires confidence in managing situations in which conflicting views are expressed, but also it means that solutions must incorporate concurrent demands on carers from their own families, work and communities, and that they cannot focus on only one of these issues. Levine and Murray (2004) draw attention to the lack of congruence between carers and professionals when looking at what support can feasibly be provided for an older relative. While carers may need to prioritize their own work/life balance, the social worker (and indeed the older person) may see their potential contribution as a resource to be built into a care plan. So Janet, the daughter of Laura and David Cohen, will have responsibilities to help her children to balance obligations that she may have towards her parents against those she has towards her children. Entitlement and obligation will be coloured by past experiences of parental care and support. Recognizing and needing to respond to the frailty of parents is a challenge to even the adult child's sense of security and independence, particularly if the parent behaves in unexpected ways.

Cultural expectations of receiving and providing care must be set alongside individual biography. Guberman and Maheu (1999) have looked at ageing and caregiving in ethnocultural families in the United States where the process of assisting with activities of daily living confronted families with questions of values, meanings, norms and attitudes concerning such themes as sickness, dependency, care, family dynamics and gender relations (Guberman and Maheu, 1999: 127).

Their findings were that family availability was limited, despite a continuing adherence to family solidarity, but also that care-giving was unequally divided between men and women. Structural socioeconomic changes, such as women's participation in the workforce, small housing units, geographical distance and increased life expectancy of people with chronic health conditions, had impacted on personal relationships. The actual tasks of care-giving did not vary significantly between different ethnic groups and involved specialized hands-on care, mobilization and coordination of services and resources, and negotiation with other demands on the carer's time. Lack of services and their inadequacy affected the amount of outside assistance that was sought. For some groups, going outside the family was seen as a transgression of traditional values, older people were seen in terms of being dependent and requiring solicitous surveillance, and there was a suspicion of external authorities. Negotiations with families (from whatever background) will therefore be needed to explore what is culturally and structurally, as well as personally, acceptable when offering services or support.

General social work theory can also be helpful here as a tool for problem-solving. Crisis theory (Rapoport, 1962) is a useful framework for understanding the 'plea for removal' that relatives of older people may make if their equilibrium is threatened by an unexpected external event or disruption to routine. In crisis theory, the intervention is short term and seeks to support existing strengths to restore equilibrium, perhaps by providing a period of respite. Alternatively, such intervention seeks to reinterpret the situation as a natural progression from a state of being that cannot remain stable. So, the onset of ill-health, or the need for care which is a threat to established roles or power relationships between couples, will precipitate a crisis, within which the professional may be called upon to act as interpreter or arbitrator.

Support networks

Pierson (2008) draws a distinction between support networks and care networks. The size and strength of support networks able to provide emotional and practical support involving visits, errands and phone calls depend not only on continuity of personal ties, but also on the ideas and views that these networks have about how much support should be offered and how much accepted. Support networks themselves diminish with older age, with the loss of same-generation relatives and friends and the tendency to put energy into only the closest of relationships (Keating et al., 2003, cited in Pierson, 2008). Care networks tend to be smaller and based on notions of reciprocity within close relationships. Such networks might provide help with domestic tasks, personal care and paying household bills. 'Mixed' networks of family and friends provide the most efficient systems for the sharing of tasks, and relieve tensions in the carer/cared-for dyad in cases where a primary carer is identified,

Reed et al. (2004) suggest that as opportunities beyond the family open up as a result of socializing or hobbies, older people are more likely to form connections that range from close emotional connection, to friendship or companionship. These activities may involve reciprocity and intimacy, but need not do so. Referring to a study by Cheang (2002) of older people meeting in a fast-food restaurant, Reed et al. conclude that older people enjoy 'casual' relationships and 'fun' in the same way that younger people do. As a result, older people may not describe themselves as 'lonely' even though they may have lifestyles and interaction patterns which could suggest otherwise (ibid.: 121). Older people will not rely exclusively on picking up friendships from earlier life stages, where the focus is on continuity in activities, relationships and lifestyles; they will also continue to make new friends, as relationship patterns and priorities change (ibid.; Jerrome and Wenger, 1999).

The function of day services

Many of these opportunities for socializing will, however, depend upon reasonable health, sufficient income and transport networks. The development of community support for older people is discussed in chapter 9. For older people who are housebound, or otherwise isolated, the traditional service model has been that of day care, in a formal setting. Clark (2001) has observed the trend to deconstruct day care, into 'day services', not necessarily located in a particular venue, but often still bringing people together in groups to socialize, to have access to information and advice, and to provide personal services such as food and bathing. A corollary, or a trigger for, day-service provision is the desire to provide respite for carers. Research by Moriarty and Webb (2000) among people with dementia and their carers found not only that was day care highly regarded as a break from routine, but also that it was an effective resource in delaying admission to permanent care. However, to balance this view of the benefits of day care for people with dementia, we must also consider Innes and Sherlock's (2004) research exploring the views of people with dementia in rural communities on the experience of the day care that they received. Although all service users praised the services particularly for the companionship provided there were also negative aspects. Some service users found frequent staff turnover led to poor relationships, while others found the experience tiring or disorientating. Careful assessment and matching is thus needed between potential service users and services. What is not known is the extent to which the introduction of individualized budgets will narrow opportunities for day-service provision, based on communal funding. The obvious conclusion is that day-service providers should anticipate this threat, and work with service users to incorporate their views of what a good-quality service should look like.

For some service users, day care is a service which leads on to residential care. Many care homes have day-care units, or take day visitors. Achieving a balance between respecting the privacy of the home for permanent residents and enabling respite for day-care users needs careful management. Not only do practical arrangements have to be considered, but staff need to be aware of the psychological implications for day-care users of the transition from autonomy at home to contemplating a situation where they have to acknowledge that their situation at home is not sustainable.

Living in group care

Older people's well-being in residential group care settings requires a sensitivity to relational issues and a set of skills which is beyond the 'everyday' experience of most older people. For social workers, the opposite is true; they have a familiarity with group living environments which may lead them not to appreciate the strangeness of this situation for most older people. There is a range of group living situations for older people, ranging from warden-supported sheltered accommodation through extra care housing, often with 24-hour assistance available, to care home provision. Though the majority of older people live in ordinary housing, those who are struggling to manage in such accommodation will feature heavily on social workers' caseloads. For most people, the move to supported housing or residential care is a first experience of group living, and the decision to make this transition is often unwelcome and precipitated by circumstances such as bereavement or illness. The dominant model for residential living is 'care', though Bland (1999) shows that a 'hotel' approach may offer a more acceptable model for older people's retention of autonomy.

Oldman (2000) found that housing schemes received an informal subsidy from care by relatives which residents of care homes on the whole did not receive. As such, moving to a housing scheme can be a way of enabling family intimacy to be retained albeit at a distance, whereas the full responsibility for formal care that care homes provide excludes relatives on the whole from continuing to provide physical or intimate care. Though extra care housing is difficult to define, the emphasis has shifted away from bricks and mortar provision to the 'home for life' concept and easy access to round-the-clock care services, often including the provision of meals. A lack of consensus on what extra care housing should provide may create a source of difficulty for the social worker if not all needs can be met, or if an individual's condition deteriorates. What is regarded as eccentric behaviour by others may be more difficult to tolerate in communal settings. Acknowledging the risks involved in embarking upon communal living is therefore important preparation for making this choice.

Living in a group setting such as a residential home involves living a private life in a public place (Willcocks et al., 1987). External roles are left behind, and the 'patient' or 'resident' takes on a new social role; staff acquire authority to scrutinize everyday activities, and may take on the 'parental' role which infantilizes older people (Hockey and James, 1993). As institutional practice recreates social identities, sustaining a sense of self in the homogeneity of residential care is a challenge. Though it may be achieved positively by taking on familiar roles (as 'greeter' of new residents, or by becoming a 'carer' of those who are more frail), individuality may also be expressed as deficiencies, by aggression or by deliberate incontinence. Group norms may be enforced, such as the segregation of men and women, by the fear of gossip, or by the avoidance of difficult emotions. So Frogatt (2007) describes how even death and dying in care homes is regulated and inspected, with 'minimum standards' for inspectors to report upon – a regime that is instituted from good motives, but which has the effect of denying the diverse needs of older people.

Numbers of older people in residential care have declined by 90,000 since 1992, despite the growth in numbers of older people (CSCI, 2008d). Currently, 420,000 people live in care homes for older people or for those with physical disabilities; this is about 5 per cent of the older population. The number of people supported by the local authority has declined by 12 per cent since 2003, and 28 per cent of the total are entirely self-funding. This means that the proactive involvement of social workers in placing and reviewing older people in care homes has been diminished. Increasing numbers of older people are in receipt of top-up payments by relatives to enable them to remain in the care home of their choice. Under the Health and Social Care Act 2008, responsibility for the inspection of all health and adult social care services will reside with the Care Quality Commission from April 2009. The system of national standards to measure compliance is to be replaced by themed inspections that focus on human rights and well-being. There have therefore been significant changes to the role of the state in assuring quality of care for older people, with a greater emphasis on neo-liberal values of personal autonomy and responsibility.

Residential environments

As Clough (2000) describes, residential work is about the interplay of people and systems; the combination of tasks and personal relationships. Clough purposively uses the words 'residential work' rather than 'residential care': the notion of 'being looked after' symbolizes loss of independence, whereas the idea of care work is more positive, symbolizing a relationship of assistance. Much of the perception of self is founded on daily living activities: in getting up, eating, washing, choosing one's clothes, keeping house, talking directly or on the phone, doing things on one's own or with others (ibid.: 14). It is important therefore that residents have a choice of routines and that regimes are sufficiently flexible to allow this. Willcocks et al. (1987) thus see staff as 'creators' of the experience of residents Traditionally, roles were dominated by physical care tasks and routine, with cleanliness and good order dominating – an important function for the 'legitimacy' of formal care for those who have struggled at home with domestic tasks. Inherently, there is a conflict between the personal needs of individual older people for flexibility, continuity and friendship, and staff employment needs for a safe environment and structuring of their day. In their classic analysis of residential care for physically disabled people, Miller and Gwynne (1972) commented on three different models: the warehousing model, wherein residents were 'housed' and processed; the 'horticultural' model, with an emphasis on developmental potential; and the 'organizational' model, enabling residents differentially to choose dependence, independence or support. Crucially, the environment within the home has to meet a wide range of needs, such as:

- security and control;
- a reflection of personality and values;
- permanence and continuity;
- a place for relationships with family and friends;
- a centre of activities;
- a refuge from the outside world;
- an indicator of personal status.

Individual residents may seek different combinations of these 'meanings' of home at different times. The challenge for the institution is both to recognize and to respond to such needs.

Residential care has been analysed in psychodynamic terms both in terms of organizational function and as a site of group work (Ward, 2007). Though the organization may provide a secure base for those within it, organizational anxieties, provoked by working in difficult emotional circumstances, may lead to avoidance or projection. So care of residents may be routinized, or scapegoating of difficult groups of residents may occur, when staff perceive the management of the organization as unsupportive or negative. Conversely, the environment, or 'milieu', may provide a therapeutic community environment within which divisions between staff and residents are minimized, and the power of the group in affirming and developing individual strengths is used as a therapeutic tool. Formal group work with older people in residential settings thus may be pragmatic (Brown, 1992), in terms of an economical use of staff times, it may be focused on particular issues (for example, reminiscence), or it may be remedial, in helping individuals to change behaviour.

The meaning of residential care

Hospital discharge, the views of GPs and of families and responses to sudden changes such as bereavement are potent factors in the admission to residential care, and will colour individuals' and families' understanding of the meaning of residential care. Opportunities for families to contribute to caring when a relative enters a care home, or for the resident to maintain friendships and routines in the community, will increase the permeability of the boundaries of residential care (Jack, 1998). O'Connor and Vallerand (1994) suggest that long-term adjustment to residential care is better served by an environment that gives opportunities for autonomy that are always slightly greater than one's initial level of self-determined motivation. Lieberman and Tobin (1983) found that people who were more assertive and with a stronger sense of self were the most resilient, and best able to resist institutionalization. The 'difficult' resident, whose individuality is retained, may therefore function more appropriately than the resident who is passive and amenable to staff demands.

Ever since Goffman (1961) described the various ways in which institutions exercised power over individuals by subjecting them to routines which stripped them of their previous identity and status, commentators have analysed residential care in terms of power relationships. The very design of buildings around a 'panopticon', which enables staff to observe residents' every movement, is a means of exercising control and promoting conformity (Foucault, 1991). The welfare tradition, dating back to the poor law, may itself be seen as a tradition of control, whereby impoverished institutional inmates pay the price for their dependence by relinquishing property, social rights and ultimately the self (Willcocks et al., 1987). From a critical perspective, Neysmith (1999: 10) observes how routine care procedures are powerful sites for reproducing gender, race and class devaluations among older women and those attending to them. From a social policy perspective, Drakeford (2006) examines the growth of private care provision, and concludes that regulation has failed to deliver the improvements in service delivery and quality which were hoped for it. CSCI (2008d) found that in 2006–7, care homes achieved only 79 per cent compliance with national minimum standards; this reduced to 56 per cent for compliance with care planning requirements. Decisions of the courts that private care homes are not public authorities and are thus not subject to the Human Rights Act 1998 (McDonald, 2007) further marginalized the citizenship of care home residents. This position was only rectified in December 2008 when the coming into force of s.145 of the Health and Social Care Act 2008 meant that private care homes were acknowledged in law as well as in fact as performing functions of a public nature, though even this was limited to residents placed by a local authority.

Research in the UK was collated by Towers (2006), who found that staff too are affected by this institutional environment and by low expectations, though training can ameliorate this. Poor wages and poor career structure lead to high staff turnover, which will, in turn, have an effect on residents' ability to develop supportive relationships. Better outcomes for care home residents are linked to a number of factors: continuing family involvement, feelings of control and focused planning to enhance staff involvement with residents. Family involvement both enhances the quality of personal care given and also functions as a monitor for nursing home policies and quality of care. Feeling in control was, according to Towers, found to be important in 'making a place feel like home', and was a strong predictor of well-being. Key features of control were:

- being in control when friends or relatives visit;
- being able to live in the home for as long as was wanted;
- having control over how you spend your time;
- being able to come and go as you please;
- being able to arrange your room to suit your own tastes; and
- being allowed time alone when wanted.

Staff interactions

Staff interaction with residents is a particularly potent therapeutic tool, especially when older people are experiencing mental disorder. Ward (2007) refers to opportunity-led work which can happen in the course of carrying out day-to-day activities, and which enhances a sense of belonging. Training for staff to enable them to understand the meaning of behaviour, rather than simply to observe its negative effects, enhances the total quality of life of the care environment between residents and staff. Lyne et al. (2006: 402) found that training for care assistants in alleviating depression amongst residents not only produced an improvement in the quality of care, it also increased morale and confidence among staff. Positive outcomes were attributed to the development by care staff of a greater appreciation of the resident as a person with a history, and, particularly, with a history of difficulty in making transitions which needed to be understood in a personally meaningful way. Staff training programmes for behavioural problems among older people with dementia were also seen to lead to a positive change in the interpretation that nurses placed on behaviour; job satisfaction and retention rates among staff also improved.

Systemic family therapy approaches have also been applied to care homes, focusing on the system rather than individual residents, through an emphasis on relationships (Curtis and Dixon, 2005). An organizational commitment to supporting and valuing staff and providing a holding environment for their anxieties is seen as essential to changing cultures where traditional emphases on 'looking after' older people are replaced by a focus on supporting older people to become empowered to meet the life challenges they face in adjusting to a new environment (Thompson and Thompson, 2001).

Social exclusion in care homes

Bruce (2004) identifies issues of social exclusion for residents of care homes as being similar to issues of dependency and control in the community. These are particularly heightened for people with dementia through the operation of an 'inverse care law' within which, as the dementia becomes more severe, the likelihood of appropriate care for emotional, physical, occupational, spiritual and social needs decreases (ibid.). This is attributed to a lack of skills amongst staff, a pessimistic orientation, and a lack of positive feedback. The urgent need for better staff training and the paucity of time available to interact individually with residents is key. However, the consequences for residents of staff seeking specialist advice can be either removal to an EMI unit or hospital admission (ibid.).

Similarly, Savishinsky (1991) describes the contradictory nature of the 'nursing home'; that it is not a 'home', and that there is no 'cure'. Bruce (2004) also explores the difficulties inherent in living in a closed system where opinion leaders amongst staff tend to set up a dominant view of the person and their needs in which every action was capable of being interpreted (negatively) to support their dominant view. Thus, the organization becomes a 'total' institution within which all aspects of life are observed and controlled (Goffman, 1961). As the body regresses to a weaker state, old conflicts between disorder and cleanliness can resurface. So staff will anxiously observe bodily functions, particularly for the onset of incontinence, seen as not acceptable in an adult body. Patients, in turn, may 'return the shame' (Sevenhuijsen, 2004) by deliberate fouling, as a reconstitution of power over the staff. The body, as a site for interventions which emphasize a lack of control and intrude on privacy and gendered identities, is particularly vulnerable in old age. Understanding the often hidden emotional meaning behind actions and language may assist in resolving conflicts prompted by change; group work, presenting a 'community of voices' to express the lived experience, is particularly helpful for people with dementia to help them assimilate and 'normalize' the changes that are happening to them.

Interpreting behaviour in terms of past identities and current conflicts is key to understanding the experience of residents and their relationship with staff. Bornat (2001) focuses on the power of narrative, telling one's story, as a way of connecting with the past and reconstructing the self in a novel environment. So, residential workers need to listen to accounts of past strengths and interests and to provide occupational activities for continuation of previous skills and choices, whether these involve intellectual, social or emotional strengths. Residents may also adopt roles that facilitate their inclusion in the group, such as 'top dog', 'staff pet', 'brave forbearance', being a character', making people laugh, or becoming an honorary member of the staff group (Bruce, 2004) Thus, not all roles in the group are necessarily positive. Coleman (1997) considers it necessary for staff to intervene to emphasize group norms of respect for others and the commonality of residents' interests if some members of the group seek to perpetuate social hierarchies based on earlier life chances within the group of residents. When attempts to assert the self become narcissistic or bullying – for example 'I used to be a teacher so I am most important' – staff need to strike a balance between acknowledging identity and protecting others. Discussing the need to acknowledge the sexuality of older people in residential care and to make opportunities for the continuation and development of relationships, Archibald (2004) describes the ways in which sexual expression can be reformulated as 'challenging behaviour', thus infantilizing older people. Nevertheless, there is a duty on managers to protect staff from the 'halo' effect caused by this diminishing of the adult status of residents, acknowledging ambiguities within the residential setting which are not protective of workers: 'In residential care there is an ideology of home and the family that places a heavy burden on care workers to tolerate and, arguably, not to name this behaviour as sexual harassment' (ibid.: 106).

Acknowledging diversity

CSCI (2008b) surveyed the provision of appropriate services for people from black and minority ethnic groups in group care and have proposed measures of quality. In residential settings, equality and diversity require that service users should be asked for preferences not only concerning food and the decoration of their own rooms and communal areas, but also in the ways in which personal care – for example, skin and hair – is carried out. Religious practices must be respected and multi-faith calendars provided, giving the message that significant events for different cultural groups will be celebrated. Specific support needs should be written into care plans and explored through the use of open questions. The use of staff as cultural experts is, however, questioned, both because it may leave institutional racism unchallenged and because it may limit career progression on the part of workers. Protection from discriminatory abuse must also extend to the actions of other service users. Staff attitudes and continuity of care are seen as important in recognizing and responding consistently to cultural needs.

Knocker (2006) has produced a resource pack for those working in care homes and extra care housing to enable them to meet the needs of older lesbians and gay men. There are a number of challenges identified by CSCI (2008b) to providing appropriate services. The use of person-centred planning to promote equality and diversity and the use of open-questions at assessment to enable individuals to identify and define their own needs are seen as critical. In care homes, retaining links with the wider community is vital to identity; support from staff is important and choice of personal assistance may be critical in the performance of personal care if the body does not match the gender identity. On entry to residential care, it is essential that positive introductory information is available, and that there is clarity about confidentiality. CSCI found however that only 7 per cent of care homes for older people had carried out any specific work on promoting gender equality. When Hubbard and Rossington (1995) carried out a study of the housing and support needs of older lesbians and gay men on behalf of Polari Housing Association, they found that 91 per cent of women and 75 per cent of men would have welcomed separate accommodation. Their survey of wardens of sheltered accommodation and care home managers found many examples of open antagonism. In 2008, CSCI found that 45 per cent of service users had faced discrimination in using services and only 24 per cent felt that their needs were adequately considered. Freedom from discrimination and support for the lifestyle of the person in care therefore appear to be continuing challenges for care services.

End-of-life care in residential settings

Holloway (2007) has commented on the absence of an 'older person's' agenda which is explicit in the theorizing of death and dying. Especially for the very old, there has been a cultural shift away from home to 'institution' as the site of death and, partly as a result of this, older people may experience periods of instability, movement and change in the weeks leading up to death, as they are moved from one care setting to another. Increasingly, admission to residential care signifies the end stage of life: residents, families and staff will be aware that for most people there will be no 'going home'. For older people and their families as well as for care staff, the taboo of death needs to be removed, and care-givers need to know where they stand on important issues such as resuscitation, medication and the disclosure that no more can be done. As well as actual grief, there will be anticipatory grief, and the definitive failure of dreams, wishes and expectations. For staff in care home settings, dying is a process that has to be managed alongside care of the living. There is no evidence, however, that old age abates the fear of death, which remains consistent over the lifecourse, though for older people this fear focuses more precisely upon the fear of the circumstances of death, and the desire not to be 'a burden' (Holloway, 2007).

The Department of Health's *End of Life Care Strategy* (2008c) seeks to promote high-quality care for all adults at the end of life. Older people are less likely than younger people to receive specialized end-of-life care. They are also more likely to have co-morbidity of symptoms, making single pathways for care, such as those in existence for cancer services, less appropriate. Most deaths of people aged over 75 follow a period of chronic illness. Ensuring good-quality care is seen as both a measure of society's compassion and a litmus test for health and social care services (ibid.). A good death is seen to depend upon the following factors:

- being treated as an individual with dignity and respect;
- being without pain and other symptoms;

- being in familiar surroundings;
- being in the company of close family and/or friends.

Care plans should therefore contain an agreed set of actions reflecting the needs, wishes and preferences of older people. In the community, 24-hour services can avoid unnecessary emergency admissions and enable more people to live and die in their chosen place.

Social care staff will have a range of experience in dealing with end-of-life issues. They may come into contact with death only infrequently, they may encounter dying patients frequently in the course of their work or they may be employed in settings such as palliative care where dealing with death is a major part of their role. There thus exists a range of knowledge and support in dealing with death and dying. Currently, the focus of palliative care is biased towards cancer patients. There is the potential for adopting a palliative care approach to other life-threatening conditions such as chronic heart failure, which is common amongst older people; these are people with unacknowledged palliative care needs, including symptom management, but without a terminal prognosis.

There are no existing tools which are adequate to help decision-making about referral for palliative care, and the perspectives of older people on community palliative care for chronic illness are missing from the debate (ibid.). In order to raise awareness of the particular needs of older people from black and minority ethnic groups for a culturally appropriate provision of end-of-life care, the Policy Research Institute on Ageing and Ethnicity has developed the Palliative Care, Older People and Ethnicity Project (PALCOPE) (www.priae.org). The purpose of the project is to develop materials and resources for service users and for workers which can overcome the social exclusion of older people from minority ethnic groups. The experience of illness and of dying is seen as increasing the salience of identity as people become more sensitive to the impact of ethnicity, gender and faith.

Understandings from palliative care are particularly significant in dementia, which Van den Berg sees as a continuous loss of 'a person's entire conscious and subconscious interpretation and perceptions of life' (2006: 394) for an understanding of the progression made from 'the threatened self', 'the submerged self' and 'the withdrawn self'. Validation therapy as developed by Feil (1992) recognizes that, in the later stages of dementia, what is needed is empathy, not confrontation: 'There are too many physical and social losses and the person retreats' (Scrutton, 1999). It is precisely in this situation that palliative care may be helpful in supporting the individual in their loss. Similarly, spiritual concerns, which are increasingly recognized as a dimension of personhood (Gilbert, 2003) will need nurturing in a palliative care environment. Helping residents to have 'a good death' requires sensitivity to their personal wishes and fears. Yet, as death takes place in a communal setting, other residents need to be prepared and, if willing, to be involved in paying respect to and commemorating the deceased.

Quality assessment tools in residential care

Impersonal assistance and a task-oriented approach undermine dignity and can lead to passivity and withdrawal. Seeking to understand the experience of living in a care home from the perspective of people with dementia has produced new approaches to assessing quality. CSCI (2008a), in conjunction with the University of Bradford, has developed an assessment tool known as SOFI: Short Observational Framework for Inspection. SOFI is a brief version of Dementia Care Mapping, which details the quality of the care provided for up to five individuals over a period of two hours in communal areas of the care home. By looking in detail at how staff relate to residents and at the activities with which they are engaged during an ordinary day, inspectors can look beyond the surface of care routines and assess in detail the emotional well-being of residents. There are three core questions: (i) Are my wishes respected and my views taken into account? (ii) How am I treated and how do staff communicate with me? (iii) Do I have opportunities to relate to people who are important to me?

CSCI's findings against these measures were derived from 100 such thematic inspections. Better performance against these standards was related to smaller size of unit, active management and staff training. However, the built-in environment had no impact on the quality of interactions and having a dedicated EMI unit did not necessarily mean a more appropriate response from staff. The survey showed that communication between residents was limited; 42 per cent of those surveyed did not interact at all with other residents, and a core of 22 per cent withdrew from activities with which others were engaged. A significant finding was that 'neutral' communication from staff – for example, when residents were being fed but not spoken to – led to low well-being. Only positive engagement from staff, sitting down with residents and welcoming visitors, resulted in positive engagement with people who had moderate to advanced dementia. Also, in one-third of homes, care plans did not meet statutory requirements and in some homes staff were not involved in the care planning process. Active engagement of staff therefore appears to be necessary to prevent residents with dementia being passive and silent recipients of care.

The account (see case profile) of Alfred Blake's situation takes no account of his culture, race, religion or sexual orientation. He is defined by his age and by his gender, which does not acknowledge the interlocking nature of his experiences and possible sources of discrimination (Dominelli, 1998). Given the circumstances of his admission to Castle Dell, he is probably feeling isolated, 'dumped' and discounted. Previous experiences of being 'cared for', which could be explored with Alfred, will colour his perception of his present situation. Being the only

Case profile

Alfred Blake is 85 years of age and has been a resident of Castle Dell care home for six weeks. There are 16 residents and Alfred is the only man. The manager of Castle Dell is Edith Francis, and the staff are all female. Edith describes Alfred as 'a sad man, tired and neglected'. She is receiving complaints from staff that Alfred is not cooperative when they are washing him and are helping him to dress. On occasions he has kicked out at some of the younger staff, who say they are frightened of him. At other times, Alfred sits quietly in the lounge with the residents watching TV. He has been invited to join a music and movement group and a craft group, but he has declined. Alfred has had no visitors during his time at Castle Dell. He was an 'emergency placement' at the request of his GP following a fall. It seems unlikely that his physical condition will improve.

Alfred's terraced property is privately rented and in a poor state of repair. A review of his placement is imminent.

Questions

1 What is the 'meaning' of residential care for Alfred?
2 How can the dynamic between Alfred, the care staff and the home manager be understood?
3 When developing a care plan for Alfred, what factors should be taken into account, and what outcomes should be considered?

man in the home emphasizes gender issues and Alfred may need further explanation of why it is necessary for young, female staff to assist with private functions; he may be genuinely confused by their role if it has not been explained to him. The staff also have little information about Alfred to inform their responses to him: we do not know, for example, whether his behaviour or mood has changed in any significant way since his admission to Castle Dell. In the absence of any more positive information about Alfred, his actions are viewed negatively and somewhat patronizingly. The possibility of recovery is discounted.

Cut off from his former environment, Alfred is defined in terms of Castle Dell's expectations of residents and their conception of residential care. He may be worrying about the state of his property and his landlord's view of the situation; the social worker here is a vital link between the residential world and the community. There may also be friends and family who can be sought out to support Alfred or to give insights into his preferences and needs. Any assumption that his physical condition will not improve might be challenged by the involvement in the care plan of specialist healthcare professionals focusing on his well-being, not on his age. Assessment of his mental as well as physical health is also timely. Most important is Alfred's own view of his situation and his capacity positively to contribute to decision-making to ensure that continuation of the placement does not happen by default and continues to be reviewed. The principles of the Mental Capacity Act 2005 support good practice in such cases by assuming that all available means will be used to involve individuals concerned in decision-making processes, or that sufficient will be known about their previously expressed wishes and feelings to enable an informed 'best interests' decision to be made. Importantly for Alfred, the renewal of links with the community need to be explored, and a decision taken of the most appropriate place for him to receive care. Links between older people and their communities are addressed in the next chapter.

Conclusion

A knowledge of working with families requires adaptation to new family forms and relationships. Such skills may also be transferred to work in group settings where social exclusion is a risk and staff dynamics affect the service users' experience. Particular attention needs to be paid to the psychosocial needs of older people at the end of life.

Chapter summary

1 Understanding culture and tradition respects the diverse experiences of older people within families and groups.
2 Care-giving takes many forms, and is understood in different ways. Despite social changes and geographical separation, most older people have significant links with their families, though friendship networks are increasingly also recognized as important reciprocal arrangements.
3 Understanding family dynamics facilitates working with new challenges in key transitions such as physical and mental changes, reconstitution of family relationships and entry to residential care.
4 Group settings, providing day services, housing support or residential care, have a functional role to play, and have their own organizational dynamics.
5 Good practice in group settings requires acceptance of old age as a developmental stage with an emphasis on outcomes as well as processes within a regulatory framework which ensures minimum standards and respects rights.

Key lessons

1 In order to work effectively with older people in groups and within families, social workers need knowledge of different cultural forms, skills in identifying and working with group dynamics and values in promoting the claims of older people.
2 Social workers view carers differentially as colleagues or as service users in their own right. Carers who provide a substantial amount of

care on a regular basis are entitled to a separate assessment of their needs, and may be given services in their own right.

3 The range of skills that may be employed include work with couples, family therapy approaches and group-work facilitation.

4 Traditional service provision for day care and residential care has moved towards a resource model, which facilitates the personalization of care. The social worker may act as a broker in arranging such care, but has a continuing role in monitoring the responsiveness of the care-giving environment to individual needs.

5 Group settings for older people enable 'opportunity-led' and relationship-based work to take place, but staff need to be aware of the social and personal meaning for older people of becoming a care home resident.

6 Palliative care is a concept which can be expanded to enable a wider range of older people with chronic life-threatening disorders to have choices in end-of-life care.

Further reading

J. Bayley, *Elegy for Iris*. London: Picador, 1999.
John Bayley, the literary critic, writes of his life with Iris Murdoch, writer and philosopher, and his wife of 42 years, who died with Alzheimer's disease in 1999.

P. Beresford, L. Adshead and S. Croft, *Service Users' Views of Specialist Palliative Care Social Work*. York: Joseph Rowntree Foundation, 2006.
Publication of a participatory project undertaken with people living with life-limiting illnesses and those facing bereavement. Personal and relationship strengths and working in partnership were particularly valued.

9 Working with Communities

Issues considered in this chapter:

- the meaning of community and different models of focusing on communities;
- developing community well-being;
- measures of community involvement;
- proactive and virtual communities.

Location in time and place has a specific meaning for older people, who are vulnerable to changes in local as well as national policy. Having considered direct work with older people as individuals and in groups in previous chapters, this chapter looks at the social situation of older people within communities, and at opportunities for strategic interventions. Paradoxically, the personalization agenda will necessitate a review of the needs and understandings of the whole population for health and social care services. Strategic decisions will have to be made about the amount of funding that needs to be freed up to support personal budgets for the few, alongside a broad range of accessible services for the majority of the older population. This is an opportunity to engage with communities to identify resources that will support well-being and choice.

Johnson (2002) considers the situation of older people in terms of social justice, carrying an entitlement to care in terms of their significant contribution to and heavy investment in the welfare state. Key aspects of social work and care management impact disproportionately on older people; these include developments in residential and nursing care, charging for care and the shifting boundary between health and social care. The citizenship of older people is jeopardized by the processes involved in identifying those at future high risk, as services to those with low-level needs are cut back (Tanner, 2003). Against this background of political and social isolation, Postle and Beresford (2007) see a possible solution in terms of an alliance between social workers and older people Such an alliance would be developed through self-help and campaigning, and through capacity-building in user-controlled organizations. Formal modes of political participation which seek to preserve and maintain rather than challenge existing institutions are seen as ineffective to achieve change. This is because communities may be sites of surveillance and control as well as mutuality, and power may operate through traditional associations to regulate social identities and practices (Chambers, 2006). Far greater potential is seen in what may be called critical democracy (Blaug, 2002): a grass-roots movement which is resistant to elite governance. While user-led groups may have the freedom to initiate action where professionals do not, professionals may inform the issues to be considered, and may provide relevant organizational skills and contacts.

Proactive involvement within and by communities is part of the social inclusion of older people, and is a key indicator of citizenship. Involving older people in the development of policy and practice gives them a voice in constructing services and in neighbourhood revival. Communities may be differentially defined either as communities of place, based on geographical location, or as communities of interest, where older people with common concerns or with a shared culture work together to provide support and regeneration. Working beyond the individual model enables social workers to tap into these strengths, and to direct change at structures and organizations. There is a strong preventative core in work with communities focusing on quality of life, which contrasts with the trend of statutory services to identify and target high-risk individuals. Some models have been taken from children's services, for example the Sure Start initiative, for application to older people. There are also particular issues relating to rural communities which are presented in terms of accessibility, distributive justice in the location of services, isolation and stigma (Pugh, 2000). The social work skills required for effective work in communities require consideration in terms of work with key individuals and with groups. Skills in planning, negotiation and challenging exclusion are necessary attributes of the community social worker.

Case profile

Washbrook is a former mining village in the East Midlands. The pit closed in 1988, and, since then, unemployment amongst men has been high. Few local businesses have survived. There is a high incidence of drug misuse amongst younger people, and older residents complain about intimidation from gangs of youths, and of vandalism. Those in employment travel to the nearest town, which is 10 miles away, mostly by car, as the bus service is infrequent. The local post office is threatened with closure.

Older residents of Washbrook (see the case profile) will have experienced fundamental shifts in their expectations of continuity of life for themselves and security for a younger generation. Such changes are attributable to economic and political decisions at a structural level. Community cohesion is threatened and isolation is a significant risk. What then is an appropriate social work role for the older inhabitants of Washbrook?

Looking at community

Putnam (2000) has developed the idea of social capital as a measure of social ties which describe the extent to which the individual is productively linked to the community. There is a particular resonance with liberal ideas of communitarianism, in the sense of social responsibility (Gilchrist, 2004). Such liberal notions have, however, been challenged by Bourdieu (1986), who saw that wealthier and better-connected individuals and groups could perpetuate inequalities through the dominance of their networks. This then raises the issue of how we describe community and how we measure the value of involvement therein.

Hawtin and Percy-Smith (2007) distinguish different models of focusing on communities, through community assessment, community consultation, social audit or community profiling. Which approach is chosen depends largely upon the purpose of the exercise, who is initiating it, the extent to which people within the community are directly involved, the scope of the exercise and who has determined this. Modes of involving older people are fundamentally different within each model as described below (ibid.:3):

1 *Needs assessment.* Carried out chiefly by statutory agencies, needs assessments look at demographic characteristics in order to plan future services. There will not necessarily be any opportunity for direct community involvement. Practitioners 'mapping' communities to understand the positive and the challenging aspects of life in particular communities may also carry out small-scale needs assessments of the areas within which they work, often networking with other agencies.
2 *Community consultation* looks for responses to local problems or proposed initiatives. Community consultation seeks a response from the community itself through, for example, focus groups or citizens' panels. Critical here is the question of who sets the agenda for the consultation, whether that is formal organizations or the community itself.
3 *Social audit* looks at the social and ethical impact upon the community of the organization which is being audited. The focus is on identifying inequalities both anticipated and unanticipated, for future action. As the example of Washbrook shows, older people will have an interest in the outcomes of services such as those designed for younger people, in which they do not directly participate.
4 *Community profiling* may be carried out by any organization; it challenges departmentalization by looking across agency boundaries to identify needs and resources. It is carried out with the active involvement of the community (however defined), usually with a view to developing an action plan to change the overall quality of life of the community and to enhance well-being.

What is community well-being?

Hird (2003) has examined the idea of 'community well being', and sees it covering social, economic and environmental issues each of which is present in the case profile of Washbrook (see p. 161). One theme that is very poorly measured (if it is measured at all) as an aspect of community well-being is 'community involvement' or 'community empowerment'. Yet having robust indicators can help to show what interventions help communities to regenerate and why some interventions are effective where others fail. Showing a breadth of support for community initiatives can help to support a community's application for funding, or help policy-makers to differentiate between different options (ibid.).

Chanan (2004) sees community development in terms of reciprocity – a sense that everyone's fulfilment (individual or organizational) adds something to the quality of everyone else's life as well as their own. Mapping the environment of Washbrook produces a profile of the community that illustrates the extent to which older people are involved with, and are able to be supported by, their community. Community approaches to well-being counteract statutory agencies' focus on rationing services on the basis of individual need. 'All Our Tomorrows: Inverting the triangle of care' ADSS/LGA, 2003) seeks to turn the emphasis from the provision of targeted services for a few older people towards a strategy of community engagement, within which a range of agencies work in partnership. Pierson (2008) accordingly sees well-being as requiring more than attention to personal comfort, cleanliness and good accommodation, and observes how fear of crime, poor transport and inaccessible buildings can all undermine choice (ibid.: 137). Equally, risks are not only physical, but include risk of exclusion, of diminished status in society and of disjointed networks. Conversely, older people may be drawn into active roles in communities through paid and unpaid work, and social activities.

Measures of community involvement

Community involvement may be measured across a number of factors which can be used to illustrate the extent to which individuals, groups and formal organizations are active in a community and differentially contribute to community development. Measures of community involvement (Chanan, 2004) may be individual, horizontal, vertical or cross-cutting. The focus may be on service provision and economic development, or on the provision of support and empowerment of community and voluntary sector infrastructures. Individual involvement may be measured by the level of volunteering or involvement in community activities; more fundamentally, it may be evidenced by the resourcefulness or resilience of individuals in the face of personal difficulties. Horizontal community involvement measures the number, range and connectedness of community and voluntary organizations active in the area. Vertical community involvement measures opportunities to influence policy at a higher political level. Cross-cutting measures of involvement look at the extent to which specific neighbourhoods or sections of the population, by age, gender, income, ethnicity or disability, can affirm their identity and share in the level of inclusion achieved by others. Economic development measures the extent and range of public services and social enterprises. The empowerment of communities may depend upon support from public services and inter-agency partnerships, and upon the community infrastructure which is able to develop.

A high congruence between these different measures when observing the interactions between the individual and the community lends support to Pierson's (2008) argument that the division between individual experience and the social structure is obsolete. Location plays a major role in the development and sustenance of the sense of self, and shapes expectations and experience of quality of life. Involved individuals, conversely, play a role in shaping the environment which defines them.

Pierson thus sees social work intervention as being possible at two levels: community-level intervention (capacity building) and community-based intervention (focused on individual experience) Community-level intervention addresses structural issues affecting the availability and distribution of resources for community activities, such as luncheon clubs and leisure opportunities, while community-based interventions deal with the impact of social change on individuals' and families' well-being. Social workers' understanding of the lifecourse within a social and interactive framework places them in a particularly strong position professionally to bring together community-level and community-based interventions in a transformative way. The value-base of social work will drive the imperative of working to challenge social exclusion and discrimination against individuals or groups within communities. For example, the social worker in Washbrook, having identified depression in older men as redundant miners as a particular problem, may thus work to create social opportunities for bringing old workmates together to recreate a sense of solidarity and mutual support.

Building a good life for older people in local communities

In partnership with older people's groups, Godfrey et al. (2004) have looked at factors that make for a 'good life' for older people in local communities. They found that central to a 'good life' is the value attached to interdependence, with an emphasis on mutual help and reciprocal relationships. As people become less mobile, their lives are increasingly affected by and bounded within their immediate physical and social environments. The conclusion is that locality-based service models offer the potential to connect the values and preferences of older people with statutory services.

Significantly, relationships based on social exchange models (Van Sonderen et al., 1990), friendships and social networks are experienced positively by older people, as a counter to the isolation of living alone (Ogg, 2003). Ogg observes a continuing movement towards independence, but not necessarily towards individualism, with different strategies being used by older people to elicit social support, whether from neighbours or from other community groups. He also produces evidence that women are better at forming and maintaining social networks than men. Psychologically, individuals' assessments of well-being are related to their attachment to particular communities; Godfrey et al. (2004) found that shared memories of places, people and experiences during different stages over the lifecourse provided a sense of continuity with the present and the basis for refashioning friendships in old age.

Structural, social and psychological factors therefore point to the importance of community life for older people, but also a need to facilitate the development and maintenance of supportive ties. Such facilitation is an appropriate role for social workers in building, or seeking to rebuild, in the case of communities like Washbrook, an integrated network of support for older people.

Inclusive communities

The experience of social exclusion is identified as particularly acute in later life for three reasons (ODPM, 2006):

- difficulties that people who are excluded in mid-life have in breaking this cycle;
- the impact of key life events such as bereavement;
- the impact of age discrimination.

The Sure Start approach is seen as bringing together the full range of services – health and social care, housing, transport, finance and social activities – into local centres located in communities. There are three drivers for this: the development of progressive, personalized services to meet need; a commitment to social justice; and a commitment to economically efficient services through better prevention and joined-up working (ibid.: 9).The recognition that difficulties in mid-life persist into older age is consistent with a lifecourse approach to ageing, recognizing the impact of earlier inequalities on life chances. Tackling discrimination against older people is necessary to counteract the cumulative effect of ageism upon other sources of discrimination in communities such as race and disability. Social work in communities thus necessitates an exploration of individual experience as well as an awareness of structural sources of exclusion. Working with older and young people to support access to employment, social activities and community regeneration enables older residents to create new alliances, and younger people to contribute to a sense of continuity and pride in local achievement.

Proactive older people

Chambers (2006: 94) describes how 'participatory capital' can lead to joint accomplishments. Such capital may be created by the exercise of rational choice in creating new alliances as well as natural association, but trust is key, as connections amongst individuals are based on norms of reciprocity and connectivity (Putnam, 2000). Involving older people in their communities requires a range of skills together with an awareness of the particular susceptibilities of older people to marginalization by others with traditionally stronger voices. A study of Chinese older people engaged in policy and practice (Chau, 2007) found that experiences of involvement, both in their own community and the wider society, were diverse. Participants gained a sense of achievement when change happened, and an increase in friendship and respect; however, involvement of time and energy could also bring stress and anxiety. Caution was expressed about the use of link workers whose role, as 'staff member' or 'leader', was unclear. Isolation by language was an important barrier to involvement, and English-speaking communities were observed to be insensitive to the disabling effects resulting from a lack of language support. Care therefore needs to be taken when supporting older people's involvement in community issues, so as not to overwhelm individuals with a model of consultation based on consumerist notions of service provision, but instead to follow the pace of older people themselves, according to their agendas. Support to enable people to express their ideas directly, rather than in a 'representative' way, also needs to be in place.

For some older people, particularly those living in rural communities, a lack of transport, distant services and, particularly, not having a car all impact on quality of life. Davey (2007) found that, while 'serious' transport requirements may be catered for by alternative means, the 'discretionary' trips that contribute significantly to quality of life may be lost when private transport is not available. Davey sees lack of transport not just as a single issue, but as a metaphor for the experiences of social exclusion amongst older people. Formal services in rural communities may adapt to problems of distance in innovatory ways (for example, by developing peripatetic services), but the fragmentation of traditional communities that follows as a result of new inhabitants commuting to nearby cities to work may lead to social isolation and to an absence of a community leadership that is able to express the voices of those with the strongest ties to the neighbourhood.

Shucksmith (2000) found that locality based interventions in rural areas were often insufficient to address diverse needs, and older people in particular needed services to be targeted directly at them. It should not be assumed, therefore, that generally available services will be taken up by older people in ways which address their particular experiences of isolation. Patch working, whereby social workers build up knowledge of the range of statutory, voluntary and private sector resources within a particular community, and work with other professionals and services such as churches and special interest groups, can be an effective way of generating broader community involvement (McDonald, 2006). Personalized services may not necessarily mean isolation from communities. In a study of the workings of direct payments in Norfolk, Dawson (2000) found that one consequence of directly employing a personal assistant was that stronger local links were forged, as families and friends of the paid worker tended to form a network of support around the person being cared for. This may mean that, rather than isolating individuals, personal budgets may enable people to buy into local life more directly.

Neighbourhood working

Below the level of community, there exists the neighbourhood as a grouping of residents in a close geographical area. Within larger communities of place, the sense of 'neighbourhood' is particularly acutely experienced by older people. SCIE (2006b) refers to 'ageing in a place' by people who have been part of a neighbourhood in earlier years. Pierson (2008) defines neighbourhood as 'ecological', based on the interplay between social and economic factors, nested within larger communities.

Not all neighbourhoods are inclusive, of course. Warren (1963) divides neighbourhoods into 'parochial' and 'anomic': the former provide mutual aid, while the latter will refer problems to outside agencies – such as social services. Sources of help within communities also have different characteristics depending on their source. 'Natural' (that is, voluntary and established) helpers within neighbourhoods will respond to any problem, as and when required; their advantage over paid helpers is that paid helpers only help specific people with specific problems (Patterson, 1977). Older people (Pugh et al., 2007) are particularly vulnerable to changes in the neighbourhood, such as resident turnover, economic decline and antisocial behaviour. The interconnectedness of older people's needs with the quality of life of other local groups means that successful neighbourhoods must work with younger residents and youth services to develop an integrated approach to development.

In a study of the coping strategies that supported older people in their daily lives in a rural part of Wales, Wenger (1984) found that professionals tended to underestimate the prevalence and persistence of informal patterns of support. Older people who were well established in communities could call on neighbours as well as family for support. This was particularly so in working-class communities, the distinction between friends and neighbours being seen as a middle-class construct. The social integration that involvement in community life provides is indicative of overall morale and satisfaction with life, and is for older people a more protective network than reliance on family alone.

Neighbourhood work is thus social work with a collective rather than an individual focus, which requires mutual trust and cooperation to create and sustain alliances. Its purpose is to facilitate action both in informal groups and in more formal organizations (Henderson and Thomas, 2002). So the neighbourhood way of working would seek to develop, for example, a luncheon club in a village hall, rather than commission meals on wheels for individual older people living in the same village, or to obtain funding to employ an advice worker to undertake welfare benefits checks. Traditional social work skills in needs assessment thus converge with more entrepreneurial skills in securing resources and negotiation with service providers.

Virtual communities

Chambers (2006) reconsiders the meaning of community in the existence of new social ties arising out of the changes in traditional relationships and the rise of anonymous and fragmented individuals in modern society. She sees a shift away from territoriality and a functionally organized society towards more open networks which are culturally linked. Information technology has a vital role to play here, in enabling people to communicate over time and space. Such communications can provide personal support and the possibility of virtual communities of care, or computer-mediated intimacy, comprising other older people and those with common interests. Relationships thus formed move from the sphere of obligation to that of choice and reflect the contemporary value placed on self-definition, as well as new opportunities for spatial mobility and globalization. Older people who have access to technology can be part of such communities and can choose whether or not age is a relevant characteristic by which to define their status and interests.

As consumers of services based on personal budgets, older people in this category will use the internet to source their care. Care agencies may offer their services in this way and assistive technology will be directly available for domestic use. Increasingly, then, the role of the social worker will become that of 'care-navigator', or developer of community resources which are catalogued for older people to view.

Conclusion

Work with communities embeds the social capital of older people, and supports their collective strengths. Social workers have important alliances to face to support the citizenship of older people in their localities. Involvement on a number of levels is possible: in developing the wider community, in focusing on neighbourhoods and in enabling older people to participate in 'virtual' relationships.

Chapter summary

1 The awareness of community for older people enables the experience of ageing to be located in time and place.
2 'Well-being' agendas for older people acknowledge the importance of proactive ageing as well as an absence of ill-health or problem behaviours.
3 Involving older people in the development of policy and practice promotes citizenship, as well as ensuring that services are responsive to the expressed needs of older people.
4 Challenging poor or inadequate service provision is an important corollary to the giving of rights to older people.
5 New alliances between older people, their organizations and social workers are possible to focus on agendas for change.

Key lessons

1 Understanding communities is an important part of effective networking, to harness resources to support older people. Particular communities – for example, those in rural areas – may have particular needs which are different from the mainstream, and which require adaptation and innovation.
2 Measuring the impact of social work intervention includes maintenance and change outcomes for older people, in which they have a proactive role.
3 Working with service users is fundamental to contemporary statements of social work competence and key expectations of service users include the challenging of formal agencies which do not promote the best interests of older people.
4 Social work training and practice needs to adopt a stronger community focus to overcome the isolation and marginalization of older people.
5 Revisions of the role of social workers place greater emphasis on working for older people in personalizing care through direct payments and individual budgets. This must be achieved within the context of using community resources and networks.

Activity

1 How can social workers and organizations of older people work together to develop older people's involvement in communities?
2 What are the barriers to doing this?
3 To what extent are the changes in family structures likely to impact on the family as 'carers' for older people, and to what extent can communities provide such care?

Further reading

J. Pierson, *Going Local: Working in Communities and Neighbourhoods.* Abingdon: Routledge (in association with Community Care), 2008.
This book describes how 'community practice' in health and social care can be developed; it includes a chapter on dignity and well-being for older people.

C. Taylor, *Return to Akenfield.* Cambridge: Cambridge University Press, 2006.
Ronald Blythe's classic study of Suffolk country life, published in 1969, is updated to 2004 by Taylor to show how much of rural life has changed in a generation. Taylor's book, like Blythe's, has a poetic quality and is constructed from interviews with mainly older residents.

Conclusion

Demographic changes have focused attention on the growing number of older people who potentially would benefit from social work intervention. This has provided an opportunity to reassess the appropriateness of different theoretical approaches to ageing and their translation into service provision and direct practice. Increasingly, the participation of older people themselves is sought after in this debate, which has shifted the emphasis from welfare provision to a more proactive rights agenda.

Independency, choice and dignity have become key objectives for service provision for older people, and this includes older people who are in need of protection or longer-term support. There are, however, obstacles to pursuing this agenda. A long history of service neglect, compounded by ageist attitudes, has meant that services for older people have had to be developed from a low baseline. An unsympathetic legal framework has meant that older people have been seen as passive recipients of welfare, rather than as active in their enjoyment of citizenship rights. Rationing of services has meant that scarce resources have been targeted on those in greatest physical need, often disregarding emotional well-being or the therapeutic value of personal relationships. Though person-centred care has developed a rhetoric, its achievement in practice has been constrained by managerial imperatives to ration, to process and to survey on the basis of officially constructed measures of need. Interventions have become short term and task-centred. A multiplicity of care providers has grown, requiring extensive systems of quality assurance as free-market principles of competition are shown to be unable to protect the interests of vulnerable consumers. Enabling older people to receive individual or personal budgets will challenge existing assumptions of service providers about what older people want, but will also need careful monitoring to ensure that less confident consumers are properly supported.

Individual models of social work with older people have been examined in this book with a view to evaluating their appropriateness for dealing with the major agendas of older age, including the preservation of past strengths, as well as compensation for present difficulties arising from physical or mental frailty, isolation or loss. Yet many of these issues are not located simply within older age; they have a long gestation from previous experience of health inequality, discrimination, family discord and poverty. Social policy and social work interventions which tackle these issues at source will also benefit older people. Strategic alliances may also be framed with people who are users of mental health services and with disabled people, who have recognized the structural difficulties which have to be tackled in order to improve the daily experience of individuals. Working with older people in groups, in families and in residential contexts is a key skill of social work for which an understanding of group dynamics, both positive and negative, is crucial. Finally, older people must be seen in the context of the communities to which they belong, either geographically or as communities of interest linking older people together as a collective. The social work role in supporting such communities will often lead to challenges to traditionally formulated assumptions about the role of older people.

Understanding diversity in older age, across age cohorts, and recognizing the perspectives of older people as defined also by gender, race and sexuality, open up awareness of the interlocking nature of oppressions. A focus on equalities must break down the barriers within services that may discriminate against older people within, for example, mental health services and palliative care, where home-based 24-hour services may traditionally not have been available. There is a particular need to improve the numbers of older people who are referred for therapeutic services, routinely made available to younger people. The spiritual dimension of end-of-life care must also be acknowledged for its importance to older people. Satisfaction in relationships and social encounters can be used by older people to compensate for physical limitations, and social workers have a role to play in retaining or creating those links. Financial security is also important to older people and income maximization through knowledge of the pensions and benefits system is an area in which older people welcome support.

The tasks of social work are therefore many and varied, ranging from care planning, to counselling, to advocacy. Increasingly, social workers concerned with older people will become facilitators, signposting older people as autonomous budget-holders towards services or helping to generate services for which there is no established provision. Divisions between professions are likely to become less rigid as the focus moves from 'who does what', to 'what gets done', assisted by shared assessment tasks. The management of more complex needs will differentiate between those tasks that require a professional qualification and the tasks of steering a wider range of older people through the access process which will be delegated to differently qualified staff. The period post-qualification will become critical, as newly qualified social workers move from generic training to the consolidation of knowledge in a specialist area. Beyond that, post-qualifying training will enhance the skills of social workers to analyse complex situations and to engage in transformative practice.

So while there will be a continuation into future times of the key knowledge base of understanding different approaches to ageing, of skills in communication and of facility in service provision for people at home, in residential settings and in community groups, for social workers with older people there will also be an increased emphasis on developing a personal expertise, on supporting others within a team and in acting as an advocate directly accountable to older people themselves.

References

Adams, R. (2007) Reflective, critical and transformational practice. In W. Tovey (ed.) *The Post-Qualifying Handbook for Social Workers*. London: Jessica Kingsley.

ADSS/LGA (2003) *All Our Tomorrows: Inverting the Triangle of Care*. London: Association of Directors of Social Services/Local Government Association.

Age Concern (2002) *Human Rights Act Policy Position Paper*. London: Age Concern.

Age Concern (2005) *How Ageist is Britain?* London: Age Concern.

Allen, K. (2001) *Communication and Consultation, Exploring Ways for Staff to Involve People with Dementia in Developing Services*. Bristol: Policy Press.

Alzheimer's Society (2007a) *Dementia UK: A Report to the Alzheimer's Society on the Prevalence and Economic Cost of Dementia in the UK*. London: Alzheimer's Society.

Alzheimer's Society (2007b) *Home from Home: A Report Highlighting Opportunities for Improving Standards of Dementia Care in Care Homes*. London: Alzheimer's Society.

Aminzadeh, F., Byszewski, A., Molnor, F. and Eisner, M. (2007) Emotional impact of dementia diagnosis: Exploring persons with dementia and caregivers' perspectives. *Age and Mental Health* 117(3): 281–90.

Anderson, D. N. (2001) Treating depression in old age: The resources to be positive. *Age and Ageing* 30: 13–17.

Arber, S., Davidson, K. and Ginn, J. (2003) *Gender and Ageing: Changing Roles and Relationships*. Buckingham: Open University Press.

Archibald, C. (2004) Sexuality and dementia: Beyond the pale? In A. Innes, C. Archibald and C. Murphy (eds), *Dementia and Social Inclusion*. London: Jessica Kingsley.

Arksey, M. and Glendinning, C. (2007), Choice in the context of informal care giving. *Health and Social Care in the Community* 15(2): 165–75.

Arksey, H., Hepworth, D. and Quereshi, H. (2000) *Carers' Needs and the Carers Act*. University of York: Social Policy Research Unit.

Arksey, H., Jackson, K., Croucher, K., Weatherly, H., Golder, S., Hare, P., Newbronner, E. and Baldwin, S. (2004) *Review of Respite Services and Short-Term Breaks for Carers of People with Dementia*. University of York: Social Policy Research Unit.

Askham, J., Briggs, K., Norman, I. and Redfern, S. (2007) Care at home for people with dementia: As in total institution. *Age and Society* 27: 3–24.

Asquith, S., Clark, C. and Waterhouse, L. (2005) *The Role of the Social Worker in the 21st Century*. Edinburgh: Scottish Executive Education Department.

Audit Commission (1986) *Making a Reality of Community Care*. London: HMSO.

Audit Commission (2003) *Human Rights: Improving Public Service Delivery*. London: Audit Commission.

Audit Commission (2004a) *Older People – Independence and Well-Being, The Challenge for Public Services*. London: Audit Commission.

Audit Commission (2004b) *Social Capital for Health: Issues of Definition, Measurement and Links to Health*. London: Audit Commission.

Audit Commission (2008) *Don't Stop Me Now – Preparing for an Ageing Population*. London: Audit Commission.

174

Baldock, J. and Ungerson, C. (1994) *Becoming Consumers of Community Care: Households Within the Mixed Economy of Welfare.* York: Joseph Rowntree Foundation.

Baltes, M. and Carstensen, L. L. (1996) The process of successful ageing. *Ageing and Society* 16(4): 397–422.

Baltes, P. B. (1987) Theoretical propositions of life span developmental psychology: On the diagnosis between growth and decline. *Developmental Psychology* 23: 611–26.

Bamford, T. (2001) *Commissioning and Purchasing.* London: Routledge (in association with Community Care).

Banerjee, S. and Macdonald, A. (1996) Mental disorder in an elderly care home population: Associations with health and social service use. *British Journal of Psychology* 168: 750–6.

Banks, L., Haynes, P., Balloch, S. and Hill, M. (2006) *Changes in Communal Provision for Adult Social Care: 1991–2001.* York: Joseph Rowntree Foundation.

Barclay Report (1982) *Social Workers: Their Roles and Tasks.* London: Bedford Square Press.

Barnes, M., Harrison, S., Mort, M. and Shardlow, P. (1999) *Unequal Partners: User Groups and Community Care.* Bristol: Policy Press.

Barnett, E. (1997) Collaboration and interdependence: Care as a two-way street. In M. Marshall (ed.), *State of the Art in Dementia Care.* London: Centre for Policy on Ageing.

Bartholomew, K. and Horowitz, L .H. (1991) Attachment styles among young adults: A test of a four-category model. *Journal of Personality and Social Psychology* 6(2): 226–44.

Beattie, A. (1994) Healthy alliances or dangerous liaisons? The challenge of working in health promotion. In A. Learthard (ed.), *Going Inter-Professional: Working Together for Health and Welfare.* London: Routledge.

Beck, U. (1992) *Risk Society: Towards a New Modernity.* London: Sage.

Bell, D., Bowen, A. and Heitmueller, A. (2008) *Independent Review of Free Personal Care in Scotland.* Edinburgh: Scottish Executive.

Beresford, P. (2007) *The Changing Roles and Tasks of Social Work from Service Users' Perspectives: A Literature-Informed Discussion Paper.* London: Shaping Our Lives.

Biestek, F. (1957) *The Casework Relationship.* London: Unwin.

Bigby, C. (2004) *Ageing with a Lifelong Disability: A Guide to Practices, Progress and Policy Issues for Human Services Professionals.* London: Jessica Kingsley.

Biggs, S. (2004) In pursuit of successful identities and authentic ageing. In E. Tulle (ed.), *Old Age and Agency.* New York: Hauppauge.

BIHR (2004) *Something for Everyone: The Impact of the Human Rights Act and the Need for a Human Rights Commission.* London: British Institute of Human Rights.

Bland, R. (1999) Independence, privacy and risk: Two contrasting approaches to residential care for older people. *Ageing and Society* 19: 539–60.

Blaug, R. (1995) Distortion of the face to face: Communicative reason and social work practice. *British Journal of Social Work* 25: 423–39.

Blaug, R. (2002) Engineering democracy. *Political Studies* 50: 102–13.

Blewett, J., Lewis, J. and Tunstall, J. (2007) *The Changing Roles and Tasks of Social Work: A Literature Informed Discussion.* London: GSCC.

Bohlmeijer, E., Roemer, M., Cuipers, P. and Smit, F. (2007) The effects of reminiscence on psychological well-being in older adults: A meta-analysis. *Ageing and Mental Health* 11(3): 291–300,

Bond, J., Peace, S., Dittmann-Kohli, F. and Westerhof, G. (eds) (2007) *Ageing in Society*, 3rd edn. London: Sage.

Bornat, J. (2001) Reminiscence and oral history: Parallel universes or shared endeavour? *Ageing and Society* 21(2): 219–41.

Bourdieu, P. (1986) The forms of capital. In J. Richards (ed.), *Handbook of Theory and Research for the Society of Education*. New York: Greenwood.

Bowes, A. and Dar, N. (2000) *Pathways to Welfare for Pakistani Elderly People in Glasgow*. London: Stationery Office.

Bowling, A. and Ilife, S. (2006) Which model of successful ageing should be used? Baseline findings from a British longitudinal survey of ageing. *Age and Ageing* 35: 607–14.

Bowling, A., Banister, D., Sutton, S., Evans, O. and Windsor, J. (2002) A multidimensional model of the quality of life in older age. *Ageing and Mental Health* 6(4): 355–71.

Boyle, G. (2005) The role of autonomy in explaining mental ill-health and depression among older people in long-term care. *Ageing and Society* 25: 731–48.

Braye, S. and Preston-Shoot, M. (1995) *Empowering Practice in Social Care*. Buckingham: Open University Press.

Braye, S., Preston-Shoot, M., Cull, L.-A., Johns, R. and Roche, J. (2005) *Teaching, Learning and Assessment of Law in Social Work Education*. London: Social Care Institute for Excellence.

Bretherton, I. and Mulholland, K. A. (1999) Internal working models in attachment relationships: A construct revisited. In J. Cassidy and P. R. Shaver (eds), *Handbook of Attachment Theory, Research Clinical Application*. New York: Guilford Press.

Brown, A. (1992) *Groupwork*, 3rd edn. London: Community Press.

Bruce, E. (2004) Social exclusion (and inclusion) in care homes. In A. Innes, C. Archibald and C. Murphy (eds), *Dementia and Social Inclusion*. London: Jessica Kingsley.

Cancian, F. and Oliker, S. (2000) *Caring and Gender*. London: Pine Forge Press.

Care, Older People and Ethnicity Project (PALCOPE) (www.priae.org).

Carstensen, L. L. (1992). Social and emotional patterns in adulthood: Support for socioemotional selectivity theory. *Psychology and Aging* 7: 331–8.

Challis, D. and Hughes, J. (2002) Frail old people on the margins of care: Some recent research findings. *British Journal of Psychiatry* 180: 126–30.

Challis, D., Clarkson, P., Hughes, J., Abendstern, M., Sutcliffe, C. and Burns, A. S. (2004) *Systematic Evaluation of the Development and Impact of the Single Assessment Process in England*. London: PSSRU.

Challis, D., Clarkson, P., Williamson, J., Hughes, J., Venables, D., Burns, A. S. and Weinberg, A. (2004) The value of clinical assessment of older people prior to entry to care homes. *Age and Ageing* 33(1): 25–34.

Challis, D. Hughes, J., Jacobs, S., Stewart, K. and Weiner, K. (2007) Are different forms of care-management for older people in England associated with variations in case-mix, service use and care-managers use of time? *Age and Ageing* 27: 25–48.

Chambers, D. (2006) *New Social Ties: Contemporary Connections in a Fragmented Society*. Basingstoke: Palgrave.

Chanan, G, (2004) *Measures of Community*. London: Home Office and Community Development Foundation.

Chau, R. (2007) *The Involvement of Chinese Older People in Policy and Practice*. York: Joseph Rowntree Foundation.

Cheang, M. (2002) Older adults' frequent visits to a fast food restaurant. *Journal of Aging Studies* 16(3): 303–21.

Cheek, J., Ballantyne, A., Byers, L. and Quan, J. (2006) From retirement village to residential aged care: What older people and their families say. *Health and Social Care in the Community* 15(1): 8–17.

Chenoweth, L. and Jeon, Y.-H. (2007) Determining the efficacy of Dementia Care

Mapping as an outcome measure and a process for change: A pilot study. *Ageing and Mental Health* 11(3): 237–45.

Cheston, R. and Bender, M. (1999) *Understanding Dementia: The Man with Worried Eyes.* London: Jessica Kingsley.

Chevannes, M. (2002) Social construction of the managerialisation of needs assessment by health and social care professionals. *Health and Social Care in the Community* 10(3): 168–78.

Chilvers, D. (2003) The case for specialist home care for people with dementia. *Journal of Dementia Care* 1(1): 20–1.

Clark, C. (ed.) (2001) *Adult Day Care Services and Social Inclusion.* London: Jessica Kingsley.

Clark, H., Dyer, S. and Horwood, J. (1998) *'That Bit of Help': The High Value of Low Level Preventative Services for Older People.* Bristol: Policy Press.

Clark, H., Gough, H. and Macfarlane, A. (2004) *It Pays Dividends: Direct Payments and Other People.* Bristol: Policy Press.

Clarke, A. and Bright, L. (2006) *Moving Stories: The Impact of Admission into a Care Home on Residents' Partners.* London: The Relatives and Residents Association.

Clarke, J. and Newman, J. (1997) *The Managerial State: Power, Politics and Ideology in the Remaking of Social Welfare.* London: Sage.

Clarke, J., Gerwirtz, S. and McLaughlin, E. (eds) (2000) *New Managerialism New Welfare?* London: Sage.

Clough, R. (2000) *The Practice of Residential Work.* Basingstoke: Macmillan.

Clough, R., Manthorpe, J., OPRSI, Raymond, V., Sumner, K., Bright, L. and Hay, J. (2007) *The Support Older People Want and the Services They Need.* York: Joseph Rowntree Foundation.

Coleman, P. G. (1994) Reminiscence within the study of ageing: The social significance of story. In J. Barnet (ed.), *Reminiscence Reviewed: Evaluations, Achievements, Perspectives.* Buckingham: Open University Press.

Coleman, P. G. (1997) Personality, health and ageing. *Journal of the Royal Society of Medicine* 90: 27–33.

Coleman, P. and O'Hanlon, A. (2004) *Ageing and Development.* London: Hodder Education.

Coleman, N. and Harris, J. (2008) Calling social work. *British Journal of Social Work* 38: 580–99.

Coulshed, V. (1991) *Social Work Practice. An Introduction,* 2nd edn. London: Macmillan.

Counsel and Care (2006) *Single Assessment Process Research Project.* London: Counsel and Care.

Counsel and Care (2007) *Care Contradictions: Higher Charges and Fewer Services.* London: Counsel and Care.

Crisp, B. R., Anderson, M. R., Orme, J. and Green Lister, P. (2005) *Learning and Teaching in Social Work Education: Textbooks and Frameworks in Assessment.* London: Social Care Institute for Excellence.

CSCI (2004) *Leaving Hospital: The Price of Delays.* London: Commission for Social Care Inspection.

CSCI (2005) *Leaving Hospital Revisited: A Follow-Up Study of a Group of Older People who were Discharged from Hospital in March 2004.* London: Commission for Social Care Inspection.

CSCI (2006a) *Real Voices, Real Choices: The Qualities People Expect from Care Services.* London: Commission for Social Care Inspection.

CSCI (2006b) *Time to Care.* London: Commission for Social Care Inspection.

CSCI (2008a) *Guidance for Inspectors: Short Observational Framework for Inspectors.* London: Commission for Social Care Inspection.

CSCI (2008b) *Putting People First: Equality and Diversity Matters: Providing Appropriate Services for Lesbian, Gay, Bisexual and Transgender People*. London: Commission for Social Care Inspection.

CSCI (2008c) *The State of Social Care*. London: Commission for Social Care Inspection.

CSCI (2008d) *A Study of the Effectiveness of Arrangements to Safeguard Adults from Abuse*. London: Commission for Social Care Inspection.

Cumming, E. and Henry, W. (1961) *Growing Old: The Process of Disengagement*. New York: Basic Books.

Curtice, L. and Petch, A. (2002) *How Does the Community Care? Public Attitudes to Community Care in Scotland*. Edinburgh: Scottish Executive Social Research.

Curtis, E. A. and Dixon, M. S. (2005) Family therapy and systemic practice with older people: W to now? *Journal of Family Therapy* 27: 43–64.

Dalrymple, J. and Burke, B. (2006) *Anti-Oppressive Practice: Social Care and the Law*, 2nd edn. Maidenhead: Open University Press.

DASN International. (www.dasninternational.org)

Davey. J. (2007) Older people and transport: Coping without a car. *Ageing and Society* 27: 40–65.

Davidson, K., Daly, T. and Arber, S. (2003) Older men, social integration and organisational activities. *Social Policy and Society* 2(2): 81–9.

Davies, B. and Challis, D. (1986) *Matching Human Resources to Needs in Community Care*. Aldershot: Gower.

Davies, M. (1994) *The Essential Social Worker*, 3rd edn. Aldershot: Arena.

Davies, S. and Nolan, H. (2003) Making the best of things: Relatives' experience of decisions about care home entry. *Ageing and Society* 23: 429–50.

Dawson, C. (2000) *Independent Successes, Implementing Direct Payments*. York: Joseph Rowntree Foundation.

Dawson, C. (2007) *Mental Health and Mental Capacity*. Social Work Law File, Norwich: UEA Monographs.

Demos (2007) *Personal Budgets*. London: Demos.

Dennis, M. S., Wakefield, P., Molloy, C., Andrews, H. and Friedman, T. (2007) A study of self-harm in older people: Mental disorder, social factors and motives. *Ageing and Mental Health* 11(5): 520–5.

DH (1989) *Caring for People: Community Care in the Next Decade and Beyond* (Cm. 849). London: HMSO.

DH (1991) *Care Management and Assessment: Practitioners' Guide*. London: HMSO.

DH (1995) *The 'F' Factor: Reasons Why Some Older People Choose Residential Care*. London: Department of Health.

DH (1997) *Older People with Mental Health Problems Living Alone – Anybody's Priority?* London: Department of Health.

DH (1998) *Modernising Social Services*. London: Department of Health.

DH (2001) *The National Service Framework for Older People*. London: Department of Health.

DH (2002a) *Fair Access to Care Services: Guidance on Eligibility Criteria for Adult Social Care*. London: Department of Health.

DH (2002b) *Single Assessment Process for Older People*. HSC 2002/001.

DH (2005a) *The National Service Framework for Long-Term Conditions*. London: Department of Health.

DH (2005b) *Opportunity Age*. London: Department of Health.

DH (2006a) *A New Ambition for Old Age: The Next Steps in Implementing the National Service Framework for Older People*. London: Department of Health.

DH (2006b) *Options for Excellence: Building the Social Care Workforce of the Future*. London: Department of Health.

DH (2006c) *Our Health, Our Care, Our Say: A New Direction for Community Services.* London: Department of Health.

DH (2007a) *Independence, Choice and Risk: A Guide to Best Practice in Supported Decision-Making.* London: Department of Health.

DH (2007b) *Putting People First: A Shared Vision and Commitment to the Transformation of Adult Social Care.* London: Department of Health.

DH (2008a) *Carers Strategy.* London: Department of Health.

DH (2008b) Dignity in care campaign. www.dhcarenetworks.org.uk/dignityincare/DignityCareCampaign/.

DH (2008c) *End of Life Care Strategy: Promoting High-Quality Care For All Adults at the End of Life.* London: Department of Health.

DH (2008d) *National Dementia Strategy*, Department of Health, London.

DH (2009a) Care networks care services efficiency delivery: Homecare re-ablement approach. www.carenetwork.org.uk/csed/solutions/homecare.reablement.

DH (2009b) *Improving Access to Psychological Therapies. Older People: Positive Practice Guide.* London: Department of Health.

DH (2009c) *Living Well With Dementia: A National Dementia Strategy.* London: Department of Health.

DH and Home Office (2000) *No Secrets: Guidance on Developing and Implementing Multi-Agency Policies and Procedures to Protect Vulnerable Adults from Abuse.* London: Department of Health.

DH and DWP (2008) *Lifetime Homes, Lifetime Neighbourhoods.* London: Department of Health and Department for Work and Pensions.

Dobash, R. E. and Dobash, R. P. (1992) *Women, Violence and Social Change.* London: Routledge.

Dominelli, L. (1998) Anti-oppressive practice in context. In R. Adams, L. Dominelli and M. Payne (eds), *Social Work, Themes, Issues and Critical Debates.* Basingstoke: Macmillan.

Douglas, H., James, I. and Ballard, C. (2004) Non-pharmacological interventions in dementia. *Advances in Psychiatric Treatment* 10: 171–7.

Drakeford, M. (2006) Ownership, regulation and the public interest: The case of residential care for older people. *Critical Social Policy* 26: 932–44.

Dressel, P., Minkler, M. and Yen, I. (1997) Gender, race, class and aging: Advances and opportunities. *International Journal of Health Services* 27: 579–600.

Dunning, A. (1995) *Citizen Advocacy with Older People: A Code of Practice.* CPA: London.

DWP (2005) *A New Deal for Welfare: Empowering People to Work* (Cm 6730). London: Department for Work and Pensions.

Eastman, M. (1984) *Old Age Abuse.* London: Age Concern.

Eastman, M. and Harris, J. (2004) *Placing Elder Abuse Within the Context of Citizenship: A Policy Discussion Paper.* London: Action on Elder Abuse/Better Government for Older People.

Ellis, K. (2004) Promoting rights or avoiding litigation? The introduction of the Human Rights Act 1998 into adult social care in England. *European Journal of Social Work* 7(3): 321–40.

Ellis, K. (2007) Disability rights in practice: The relationship between human right and social rights in contemporary social care. *Disability and Society* 20(7): 693–706.

Erikson, E. (1980) *Identity and the Life Cycle: A Reissue.* New York: International University Press.

Estes, C. (1979) *The Ageing Enterprise.* San Francisco, CA: Jossey-Bass.

Estes, C. (2001) Political economy of ageing: A theoretical perspective. In C. Estes et al., *Social Policy and Ageing.* Thousand Oaks, CA: Sage.

Evandrou, M. (ed.) (1997) *Baby Boomers, Ageing in the 21st Century*. London: Age Concern.

Evandrou, M. and Falkingham, J. (2000) Looking back to looking forward: Lessons from four birth cohorts for ageing in the 21st Century. *Population Trends* 99: 27–36.

Featherstone, M. and Hepworth, M. (1989) Ageing and old age: Reflections on the post-modern life course. In W. Bytheway (ed.), *Becoming and Being Old: Sociological Approaches to Latter Life*. London: Sage.

Feil, N. (1992) *Validation: The Feil Method*. Ohio: Edward Feil Productions.

Fernandez, J.-L., Kendall, J., Davey, V. and Knapp, M. (2007) Direct payments in England: Factors linked to variations in local provision. *Journal of Social Policy* 36(1): 97–121.

Fook, J. (2002) *Social Work, Critical Theory and Practice*. London: Sage.

Ford, P., Jonston, B. and Mitchell, R. (2006) *Skills Development and Theorising Practice in Social Work Education*. University of Southampton, SWAP.

Foster, M., Harris, J. Jackson, K. and Glendinning, C. (2008) Practitioners' documentation of assessment and care planning in social care: The opportunities for organisational learning. *British Journal of Social Work* 38(3): 546–60.

Foucault, M. (1991) *Discipline and Punish: The Birth of the Prison*. Harmondsworth: Penguin.

Freeman, T. and Peck, E (2006) Evaluating partnerships: A case study of integrated specialist mental health services. *Health and Social Care in the Community* 14(5): 408–17.

Frogatt, K. (2007) The 'regulated death': A documentary analysis of the regulation and inspection of dying and death in English care homes for older people. *Ageing and Society* 27: 233–67.

Gibson, F. (2004) *The Past in the Present: Using Reminiscence in Health and Social Care*. Baltimore: Health Professions Press.

Giddens, A. (1991) *The Consequences of Modernity*. Stanford: Stanford University Press.

Gierveld, J. and Peeters, A. (2003) The interviewing of repartnered older adults' lives with their children and siblings. *Ageing and Society* 23: 187–205.

Gilbert, P. (2003) *The Value of Everything: Social Work and Its Importance in Mental Health*. Lyme Regis: Russell House.

Gilchrist, A. (2004) *The Well-Connected Community: A Networking Approach to Community Development*. Bristol: Policy Press.

Gilleard, C. and Higgs, P. (2006), *Contexts of Ageing: Class, Cohort and Community*. Cambridge: Polity.

Glendinning, C., Challis, D., Fernandez, J., Jacobs, S., Jones, K., Knapp, M., Manthorpe, J., Moran, N., Netten, A., Stevens, M. and Wilberforce, M. (2008) *Evaluation of the Individual Budgets Pilot Programme, Final Report*. University of York: Social Policy Research Unit.

Glendinning, C., Clarke, C., Hare, P., Kotchetkova, I., Maddison, I. and Newbronner, L. (2007) Outcomes focused services for older people (SCIE Knowledge Review 13). London: Social Care Institute for Excellence.

Godfrey, M., Townsend, J. and Denby, T. (2004) *Building a Good Life for Older People in Local Communities: The Experience of Ageing in Time and Place*. York: Joseph Rowntree Foundation.

Godlove, C., Sutcliffe, C. Bagley, H., Cordingley, L., Challis, D. and Huxley, P. (2004) *Towards Quality Care: Outcomes for Older People in Care Homes*. Aldershot: Ashgate.

Goffman, E. (1961) *Asylums*. Harmondsworth: Penguin.

Goldberg, E. H. and Warburton, R. W. (1979) *Ends and Means in Social Work*. London: George Allen and Unwin.

Gooberman-Hill, R. and Ebrahim, S. (2006) Informal care at times of change in health and mobility: A qualitative study. *Age and Ageing* 35: 261–6.

Gorman, H. and Postle, K. (2003) *Transforming Community Care: A Distorted Vision?* Birmingham: Venture Press.

Gott, M. (2006) Sexual health and the new ageing. *Age and Ageing* 35: 106–7.

Griffiths, P. (2005) Self-assessment of health and social care needs by older people: A review. *British Journal of Community Nursing* 10(11): 520, 522–7.

Griffiths, R. (1988) *Community Care: Agenda for Action.* London: HMSO.

Griffiths, S., (1995) *Supporting Community Care: The Contribution of Housing Benefit.* London: NISW.

Grundy, E. (2006) Ageing and vulnerable elderly people: European perspectives. *Ageing and Society* 26: 105–34.

GSCC (2002) *Code of Practice for Social Care Workers.* London: General Social Care Council.

GSCC (2006) *Specialist Standards for Social Work with Adults.* London: General Social Care Council.

Guberman, N. and Maheu, P. (1999) Combining employment and caregiving: An intricate juggling act. *Canadian Journal in Ageing* 18(1): 84–106.

Gubrium, J. (1993) Voice and context in a new gerontology. In T. Cole, P. Achenbaum, P. Jakobi and R. Kastenbaum (eds), *Voices and Visions of Ageing: Toward a Critical Gerontology.* New York: Springer.

Gubrium, J. and Holstein, J. A. (1999) The nursing home as a discursive anchor for the ageing body. *Ageing and Society* 19: 518–38.

Hancock, R. and Wright, F. (1999) Older couples and long-term care. *Ageing and Society* 19(2): 203–37.

Hargrave, T. D. and Anderson, W. T. (2007) *Finishing Well: Ageing and Reparation in the Intergenerational Family.* New York: Brunner/Mazel.

Harris, J. (2003) *The Social Work Business.* London: Routledge.

Harris, T., Cook, D. G., Victor, C., DeWilde, S. and Beughton, C. (2006) Onset and persistence of depression in older people: Results from a two-year community follow-up. *Age and Ageing* 35: 25–32.

Havighurst, R. J. (1963) Successful ageing. In R. M. Williams, C. Tibbitts and W. Donahue (eds), *Processes of Ageing*, vol. 1. New York: Atherton.

Hawtin, M. and Percy–Smith, J. (2007) *Community Profiling: A Practical Guide*, 2nd edn. Maidenhead: Open University Press.

Healthcare Commission, Commission for Social Care Inspection and Audit Commission (2006) *Living Well in Later Life.* London: Healthcare Commission.

Healy, K. (2005) *Social Work Theories in Context: Creating Frameworks in Practice.* Basingstoke: Penguin.

Henderson, P. and Thomas, D. N. (2002) *Skills in Neighbourhood Work*, 3rd edn. London: Routledge

Henderson, R. (2007) Defining non–instructed advocacy. *Planet Advocacy* 18: 5–7.

Henwood, M. (2006) Effective partnership working: A case study of hospital discharge, *Health and Social Care in the Community* 14(5): 400–7.

Henwood, M. and Hudson, B. (2007) *Independent Living Funds* (Report by independent consultants). London: Department for Work and Pensions.

Henwood, M. and Hudson, B. (2008) *Lost to the System: The Impact of Fair Access to Care.* London: CSCI.

Henwood, M. and Waddington, E. (2002) *Outcomes of Social Care for Adults, Message for Policy and Practice.* Leeds: Nuffield Institute for Health.

Hepple. J. (2004) Psychotherapies with older people: An overview. *Advances in Psychiatric Treatment* 10: 371–7.

Hepple, J. and Sutton, L. (eds) (2004) *Cognitive Analytic Therapy and Later Life: A New Perspective on Old Age.* Hove. Brunner Routledge.

Heywood, F., Oldman, C., and Means, R. (2002) *Housing and Home in Later Life.* Buckingham: Open University Press.

Higgs, P. (1997) Citizenship theory and old age: From social rights to surveillance. In A. Jamieson, S. Harper and C. Victor (eds), *Critical Approaches to Ageing and Later Life.* Buckingham: Open University Press.

Hird, M. and Pavlich, G. (eds) (2003) *Sociology for the Asking.* Oxford: Oxford University Press.

Hird, S. (2003) Community wellbeing. A discussion paper for the Scottish Executive and Scottish Neighbourhoods Statistics, NHS, Scotland.

Hockey, J. and James, A. (1993) *Growing Up and Growing Old: Ageing and Dependency in the Lifecourse.* London: Sage.

Hockey, J. and James, A. (2003) *Social Identities Across the Life Course.* Basingstoke: Palgrave.

Holloway, M. (2007) *Negotiating Death in Contemporary Health and Social Care.* Bristol: Policy Press.

Howe, D. (1987) *An Introduction to Social Work Theory: Making Sense in Practice.* Aldershot: Wildwood House.

Howe, D. (1996) Surface and depth in social work practice. In N. Parton (ed.), *Social Theory, Social Change and Social Work.* London: Routledge.

Hubbard, R. and Rossington, J. (1995) *As We Grow Older: A Study of the Housing and Support Needs of Older Lesbians and Gay Men.* London: Polari.

Ife, J. (2001) *Human Rights and Social Work: Towards Right Based Practice.* Cambridge: Cambridge University Press.

Innes, A. and Sherlock, K. (2004) Rural communities. In A. Innes, C. Archibald and C. Murphy (eds), *Dementia and Social Inclusion: Marginalised Groups and Marginalised Areas of Dementia Research, Care and Practice.* London: Jessica Kingsley.

International Association of Schools of Social Work (2001) *International Definition of Social Work.* www.iassw.soton.ac.uk.

Jack, R. (1998) *Residential versus Community Care.* Basingstoke: Macmillan.

Jerrome, D. and Wenger, C. G. (1999) Stability and change in late life friendships. *Ageing and Society* 19: 661–74.

Johnson, J. (2002) Taking care in later life: A matter of justice? *British Journal of Social Work* 32: 739–50.

Joint Committee on Human Rights (2007) *Government Response to the Committee's Eighteenth Report of the Session 2008–07: The Human Rights of Older People in Healthcare.* www.publications.parliament.uk/pa/jt200607/jtselect/jtrights/81/8102.htm.

Jordan, B. (1995) Are the New Right policies sustainable? 'Back to Basics' and public choice. *Journal of Social Policy* 24(3): 363–84.

Jordan, B. (2007) *Social Work and Well-Being.* Lyme Regis: Russell House.

Joseph Rowntree Foundation (2004) *From Welfare to Well-Being-Planning for an Ageing Society: Summary Conclusions of the Joseph Rowntree Foundation Task Group on Housing, Money and Care for Older People.* York: Joseph Rowntree Foundation.

Jung, C. G. (2009) *Collected Works of C. G. Jung.* Princeton: Princeton University Press.

Keating, N., Otfinowski, P., Wenger, G. C., Fast, J. and Derksen, L. (2003) Understanding and caring capacity of informal networks of frail seniors: The case for care networks. *Ageing and Society* 23(1): 115–27.

Kellaher, L., with Hockey, J. and Prendergast, D. (2007) Of grief and well-being:

Competing conceptions of restorative ritualization. *Journal of Anthropology and Medicine* 14(1): 1–14.

Kemshall, H. (2001) *Risk, Social Policy and Welfare*. Buckingham: Open University Press.

Kerr, B., Gordon, J., MacDonald, C. and Stalker, K. (2005) Effective social work with older people. Scottish Executive Social Research. www.Scotland.gov.uk/Publications/2005/12/16104017/40208.

Killick, J. (1994) *'Please Give Me Back my Personality!' Writing and Dementia*. Stirling Dementia Services Development Centre.

King's Fund (2005) *The Business of Caring: King's Fund Inquiry into Care Services for Older People in London*: London: King's Fund Publications.

Kitwood, T., (1997) *Dementia Reconsidered: The Person Comes First*. Buckingham: Open University Press.

Knocker, S. (2006) *Helping Care Homes to Come Out*. London: Age Concern.

Kuhn, T. (1962) *The Structure of Scientific Revolutions*. Chicago: University of Chicago Press.

Laslett, P. (1972) *Household and Family in Past Time*. Cambridge: Cambridge University Press.

Law Commission (2008) *Adult Social Care: A Scoping Report*. London: Law Commission.

Lawrence, V., Murray, J., Samsi, K., and Banerjee, S. (2008) Attitudes and support needs of Black Caribbean, South Asian and White British carers of people with dementia in the UK. *British Journal of Psychiatry* 193(3): 240–6.

Lazarus, P. S. and Folkman, S. (1984) *Stress, Appraisal and Coping*. New York: Springer.

Leece, J. and Bornat, J. (eds) (2006) *Developments in Direct Payments*. Bristol: Policy Press.

Le Grand, J. and Bartlett, W. (eds) (1993) *Quasi-Markets and Social Policy*. Basingstoke: Macmillan.

Levin, E. Sinclair, I. and Gorbach, P. (1989) *Families, Service and Confusion in Old Age*. Aldershot: Gower.

Levine, C. and Murray, T. H. (2004) *The Cultures of Caregiving: Conflict and Common Ground among Families, Health Professionals and Policy Makers*. Baltimore, MD: Johns Hopkins University Press.

Levinson, D. J. (1986) A conception of adult development. *American Psychologist* 42: 3–13.

Levy, B. R. (2003) Mind matters: Cognitive and physical effects of ageing self–stereotypes. *Journal of Gerontology* 58B(4): 203–11.

Lieberman, M.A. and Tobin, S.S. (1983) *The Experience of Old Age: Stress, Coping and Survival*. New York: Basic Books.

Lipsky, M. (1980) *Street-level Bureaucracy: Dilemmas of the Individual in Public Services*. New York: Sage.

Lymbery, M. (1998) Care management and professional autonomy: The impact of community care legislation on social work with older people. *British Journal of Social Work* 28(6): 863–78.

Lymbery, M. (2005) *Social Work with Older People: Context, Policy and Practice*. London: Sage.

Lymbery, M. (2006) United we stand? Partnership working in health and social care and the role of social work in services for older people. *British Journal of Social Work*, 36: 1119–34.

Lyne, K. J., Moxon, S., Sinclair, I., Young, P., Kirk, C. and Ellison, S. (2006) Analysis of a care planning intervention for reducing depression on older people in residential care. *Ageing and Mental Health* 10(4): 394–403.

Manthorpe, J. and Illife, S. (2005) *Depression in Later Life*. London: Jessica Kingsley.

Manthorpe, J., Moriarty, J., Rapaport, J., Clough, R., Cornes, M., Bright, L., Iliffe, S. and OPRSI (2008) 'There are wonderful social workers but it's a lottery': Older people's views about social workers. *British Journal of Social Work* 38(6): 1132–50.

Marmot, M. (2004) *Status Syndrome: How Your Social Standing Directly Affects Your Health and Life Expectancy*. London: Bloomsbury.

McCrae, N., Murray, J., Banerjee, S., Huxley, P., Bhugra, D., Tylee, A. and Macdonald, A. (2005) 'They're all depressed aren't they?' A qualitative study of social care workers and depression in older adults. *Age and Mental Health* 9(6): 508–16.

McCreadie, C. (1995) *Elder Abuse, Update on Research*. London: Age Concern.

McCreadie, C., Wright, F. and Tinker, A. (2007) Improving the information about assistive technology for older people. *Journal of Assistive Technologies* 1(1): 33–41.

McDonald, A. (2006) *Understanding Community Care: A Guide for Social Workers*, 2nd edn. Basingstoke: Macmillan.

McDonald, A. (2007) The impact of the Human Rights Act 1998 on decision-making in adult social care. *Journal of Ethics and Social Welfare* 1(1): 76–94.

McDonald, A. and Taylor, M. (2006) *Older People and the Law*. Bristol: Policy Press.

McDonald, A., Postle, K. and Dawson, C. (2008) Barriers to retaining and using professional knowledge in local authority social work practice with adults in the UK. *British Journal of Social Work* 38(7): 1370–87.

McLeod, E. and Bywaters, P. (1996) Tackling inequalities in physical health: A new objective for social work. *British Journal of Social Work* 29(4): 547–65.

McLeod, E., Bywaters, P. and Cooke, M. (2003) Social work in accident and emergency departments: A better deal for older patients' health? *British Journal of Social Work* 33(6): 787–802.

McLeod, E., Bywaters, P. and Hirsch, M. (2008) For the sake of their health: Older service users requirements for social care to facilitate access to social networks following hospital discharge. *British Journal of Social Work* 38(1): 73–90.

McLeod, I. (2003) *Legal Theory*, 2nd edn. Basingstoke: Macmillan.

Mead, G. H. (1934) *Mind, Self and Society*. Chicago: University of Chicago Press.

Means, R. and Smith, R. (1994) *Community Care, Policy and Practice*. Basingstoke: Macmillan.

Miesen, B. (1992) Attachment theory and dementia. In G. M. M. Jones and B. M. L. Miesen (eds), *Care-Giving in Dementia: Research and Applications*. London: Routledge.

Miesen, B. L. and Jones, G. M. M. (2004) The Alzheimer Café concept: A response to the trauma, drama and tragedy of dementia. In G. M. M. Jones and B. L. Miesen (eds), *Care-Giving in Dementia: Research and Application*. London: Routledge.

Miller, E. and Gwynne, G. (1972) *A Life Apart*. London: Tavistock.

Milner, J. and O'Byrne, P. (2002) *Assessment in Social Work*, 2nd edn. Basingstoke: Palgrave.

Moriarty, J. and Butt, J. (2004) Inequalities in quality of life among older people from different ethnic groups. *Age and Ageing* 24 (5): 729–53.

Moriarty, J. and Webb, S. (2000) *Part of their lives: Community care for older people with dementia*. Bristol: Policy Press.

Morris, J. (1993) *Independent Lives? Community Care and Disabled People*. Basingstoke: Macmillan.

Morris, K. (2008) *Social Work and Multi-Agency Working: Making a Difference*. Bristol: Policy Press.

Mullender, A. (1996) *Rethinking Domestic Violence: The Social Work and Probation Response*. London: Routledge.

Müller-Hergl, C. (2004) Faecal incontinence. In A. Innes, C. Archibald and C. Murphy, *Dementia and Social Inclusion*. London: Jessica Kingsley.

Murphy, E. (1982) Social origins of depression in old age. *British Journal of Psychiatry*, 141: 135–42.

Murphy, J. (2004) Enabling frail older people with a communication difficulty to express their views: The use of talking mats as an interview tool. *Health and Social Care in the Community* 13(2): 95–107.

Neysmith, S. (ed.) (1999) *Critical Issues for the Future of Social Work Practice with Ageing Persons*. New York: Columbia University Press.

Norman, A. (1985) *Triple Jeopardy: Growing Older in a Second Homeland*. London: Centre for Policy on Ageing.

O'Connor, B. P. and Vallerand, R. J. (1994) The relative effects of actual and experienced autonomy on motivation in nursing home residents. *Canadian Journal of Aging* 13: 528–38.

O'Connor, J., Ruddle, H., Gallagher, M. and Murphy, E. (1988) *Caring for the Elderly. Part II: The caring process: A Study of Carers in the Home*. Dublin: National Council for the Aged.

ODPM (2006) *A Sure Start to Later Life: Ending Inequalities for Older People*. London: Office of the Deputy Prime Minister.

Office of Fair Trading (2003) Guidance on Unfair Terms in Care Home Contracts. www.oft.gov.uk/shared_oft/reports/unfair_contract_terms/oft635.pdf.

Ogg, J. (2003) *Living Alone in Later Life*. London: ICS.

O'Keeffe, M., Hills, A., Doyle, M., McCreadie, C., Scholes, S., Constantine, R., Tinker, A., Manthorpe, J., Biggs, S. and Evans, B. (2007) *UK Study of Abuse and Neglect of Older People: Prevalence Survey Report*. London: NatCen.

Older People's Steering Group (2004) *Older People Shaping Policy and Practice*. York: Joseph Rowntree Foundation.

Oldman, C. (2000) *Blurring the Boundaries: A Fresh Look at Housing and Care Provision for Older People*. Brighton: Pavilion.

ONS (2003) *The Census in England and Wales*. London: Office of National Statistics.

Óvretveit, J. (1997) How to describe interprofessional working. In J. Óvretveit, P. Mathias and T. Thompson (eds), *Interprofessional Working for Health and Social Care*. London: Macmillan.

Parker, G. (1993) *With This Body: Caring and Disability in Marriage*. Buckingham: Open University Press.

Parkes, C. M., Stevenson-Hind, J. and Marris, P. (eds) (1991) *Attachment Across the Life Cycle*. London: Tavistock.

Parsons, T. (1991) *The Social System*. London: Routledge.

Patmore, C. (2002) *Towards Flexible, Person-Centred Home Care Services: A Guide to Some Useful Literature for Planning Managing or Evaluating Services for Older People*. University of York: Social Policy Research Unit.

Patmore, C. (2004) Quality in home care for older people: Factors to pay heed to. *Quality in Ageing* 5(1): 32–40.

Patterson, J. L. (1977) Towards a conceptualisation of natural helping. *Arete* 4(3): 161–71.

Payne, M. (2005) *Modern Social Work Theory*, 3rd edn. Basingstoke: Palgrave.

Petch, A. (2003) *Intermediate Care: What Do We Know About Older People's Experiences?* York: Joseph Rowntree Foundation.

Phillips, J. and Waterson, J. (2002) Care management and social work: A case study of the role of social work in hospital discharge to residential or nursing care. *European Journal of Social Work*. 5(2): 171–86.

Phillips, J., Bernard, M., Phillipson, C. and Ogg, J. (2002) Social support in later life: A study of three areas. *British Journal of Social Work* 30(6): 837–54.

Phillips, J., Ray, M. and Marshall, M. (2006) *Social Work with Older People*, 4th edn. Basingstoke: Palgrave.

Phillipson, C. (1998) *Reconstructing Old Age: New Agendas in Social Theory and Practice*. London: Sage.

Phillipson, C., Bernard, M., Phillips, J. and Ogg. J. (1998) The family and community life of older people: Household composition and social networks in three urban areas. *Ageing and Society* 18: 259–89.

Philp, I. (2001) (ed.) *Family Care of Older People in Europe*. Oxford: IOS Press.

Philp, I. (2004) *Better Health in Old Age*. London: Department of Health.

Pierson, J. (2008) *Going Local: Working in Communities and Neighbourhoods*. London: Routledge.

Pilling, D. (1992) *Approaches to Community Care for People with Disabilities*. London: Jessica Kingsley.

Popple, K. (2006) Community development in the 21st century: A case of conditional development. *British Journal of Social Work* 36: 333–40.

Postle, K. and Beresford, P. (2007) Capacity building and the reconception of political participation: A role for social care workers? *British Journal of Social Work* 37: 143–58.

Powell, J., Robinson, J., Roberts, H. and Thomas, G. (2007) The single assessment process in primary care: Older people's account of the process. *British Journal of Social Work* 37: 1043–58.

Preston-Shoot, M. (2007) *Effective Groupwork*. Basingstoke: Macmillan.

Priestly, M. and Rabiee, P. (2002) Same difference? Older people's organisations and disability issue. *Disability and Society* 17(6): 597–611.

Price, E. (2008) Pride or prejudice? Gay men, lesbians and dementia. *British Journal of Social Work* 38(7): 1137–52.

Pritchard, J. (1999) *Elder Abuse Work: Best Practice in Britain and Canada*. London: Jessica Kingsley.

Pritchard, J. (2002) *Male Victims of Elder Abuse: Their Experiences and Needs*. York: Joseph Rowntree Foundation.

Pugh, R. (2000) *Rural Social Work*. Lyme Regis; Russell House.

Pugh, R., Scharf, T., Williams, C. and Roberts, D. (2007) *SCIE Research Briefing 22: Obstacles to Using and Providing Rural Social Care*. London: Social Care Institute for Excellence.

Putnam, R. D. (2000) *Bowling Alone: The Collapse and Revival of American Community*. New York: Simon and Schuster.

Quereshi, H., Challis, D. J. and Davies, B. P. (1983) Motivation and reward of helpers in the Kent community care scheme. In S. Hatch (ed.), *Volunteers, Patterns, Meaning and Motives*. Berkhamsted: The Volunteer Centre.

Quinn, A., Snowing, A. and Denicolo, P. (2003) *Older People's Perspectives: Devising Information Advice and Advocacy Services*. York: Joseph Rowntree Foundation.

Rapaport, J., Bellringer, S., Pinfold, V. and Huxley, P. (2006) Carers and confidentiality in mental health care. *Health and Social Care in the Community* 14(4): 357–65.

Rapoport, L. (1962) The state of crisis: Some theoretical considerations. *Social Services Review* 36(2): 211–17.

Rapoport, R. and Rapoport, R. (1980) *Growing Through Life*. London: Harper and Rowe.

Reed, J., Stanley, D. and Clarke, C. (2004) *Health, Well-Being and Older People*. Bristol: Policy Press.

Reid, W. J. and Shyne, A. (1969) *Brief and Extended Casework*. New York: Columbia University Press.

Reilly, S., Abendstern, M., Hughes, J., Challis, D., Venables, D. and Pedersen, I. (2006) Quality in long-term care homes for people with dementia: an assessment of specialist provision. *Ageing and Society* 24: 449–68

Richards, S. (2000) Bridging the divide: Elders and the assessment process. *British Journal of Social Work* 30: 37–49.

Roberts, H., Hemsley, Z., Thomas, G., Meakins, P., Robinson, J., Gove, I., Turner, G. and Sayer, A. (2006) Nurse-led implementation of the single assessment process in primary care: A descriptive feasibility study. *Age and Ageing* 35: 394–98.

Rosenmayr, L. and Köckeis, E. (1963) Essai d'une théorie sociologique de la vieillesse et de la famille. *Revue Internationale des Sciences Sociales* 3: 423–48.

Rosenthal, C., Martin-Matthews, A. and Keefe, J. M. (2007) Care management and care provision for older relatives amongst employed informal care-givers. *Ageing and Society* 27: 755–78.

Roth, A. and Fonagy, P. (2005) (with contributions from G. Parry, M. Target and R. Woods), *What Works With Whom? A Critical Review of Psychotherapy Research*, 2nd edn. New York: Guilford Press.

Rummery, K. (2002) *Disability, Citizenship and Community Care: A Case For Welfare Rights?* Aldershot: Ashgate.

Ryle, A. (2000) Origins of CAT. www.acat.me.uk/catorigihs.php.

Savishinsky, J. S. (1991) *The Ends of Time: Life and Work in a Nursing Home.* London: Bergin and Garvey.

Scharf, T., Phillipson, C. Smith, A. E. and Kingston, P. (2003) Older people in deprived neighbourhoods: Social exclusion and quality of life in old age. Research findings from the Growing Older Programme, 19. www.Shef.ac.uk/uni/projects/gap/Go Findings.

Schön. D. (1993) *The Reflective Practitioner.* New York: Basic Books.

SCIE (2006a) *Practice Guide 3: Assessing the Mental Health Needs of Older People.* London: Social Care Institute for Excellence.

SCIE (2006b) *Practice Guide 08: Improving Outcomes for Service Users in Adult Placement: Commissioning and Care Management.* London: Social Care Institute for Excellence.

SCIE (2007) *Knowledge Review 13: Outcome-Focused Services for Older People.* London: Social Care Institute for Excellence.

Scourfield, P. (2006) Helping older people in residential care remain full citizens. *British Journal of Social Work* 37: 1135–52.

Scrutton, S. (1999) *Counselling Older People: A Creative Response to Ageing*, 2nd edn. London: Edward Arnold.

Seddon, D., Robinson, C., Reeves, C., Tommis, Y., Woods, B. and Russell, I. (2006) In their own right: Translating the policy of carer assessment into practice. *British Journal of Social Work* 37: 1335–52.

Seed, P. (1988) *Day Care at the Crossroads.* Tunbridge Wells: Costello.

Sevenhuijsen, S. (2004) Caring in the hard way: The relation between obligation, responsibility and care in Third Way discourse. *Critical Social Policy* 20(1): 5–37.

Shemmings, D. (2005) *Adult Attachment Theory.* Norwich: UEA Monographs.

Shucksmith. M. (2000) *Exclusive Countryside? Social Inclusion and Regeneration in Rural Areas.* York: Joseph Rowntree Foundation.

Smale, G. and Tuson, G., with Biehal, N. and Marsh, P. (1993) *Empowerment, Assessment, Care Management and the Skilled Worker.* London: NISW/HMSO.

Smale, G., Tuson, G. and Statham, D. (2000) *Social Work and Social Problems: Working Towards Social Inclusion and Social Change.* Basingstoke: Palgrave Macmillan.

Solomon, A. and Haaga, D. (2003) Cognitive theory and therapy of depression. In M. A. Reinecke, D. A. Clark and A. T. Beck, *Cognitive Therapy Across the Lifespan.* Cambridge: Cambridge University Press.

Specht, H. and Vickery, A. (eds) (1977) *Integrating Social Work Methods.* London: Allen & Unwin.

Sperling, N. and Berman, W. (eds) (1994) *Attachment in Adults: Clinical and Developmental Perspectives*. London: Guilford Press.

Stalker, K. (2003) (ed.) *Reconceptualising Work with 'Carers': New Directions for Policy and Practice*. London: Jessica Kingsley.

Steele, J. (2004) *Risks and Legal Theory*. London: Hart Publishing.

Stevenson. O. (1996a) *Elder Protection in the Community: What Can We Learn From Child Protection?* London: Department of Health.

Stevenson, O. (1996b) Changing practice: Professionalism, consumerism and empowerment. In R. Bland (ed.), *Developing Services for Older People and Their Families*. Research Highlights in Social Work 29. London: Jessica Kingsley.

Stevenson, O. (1999) Old people at risk. In P. Parsloe (ed.), *Risk Assessment in Social Care and Social Work*. London: Jessica Kingsley.

Stewart, A. (2005) Choosing care: Dilemmas of a social market. *Journal of Social Welfare and Family Law* 27(3–4): 299–314.

Stewart, A., Harvey, I., Poland, F., Lloyd-Smith, W., Mugford, M. and Flood, C. (2005) Are occupational therapists more effective than social workers when assessing frail older people? Results of CAMELOT, a randomised controlled trial. *Age and Ageing* 34(1): 41–6.

Tanner, D. (2003) Older people and access to care. *British Journal of Social Work* 33: 499–515.

Tanner, D. and Harris, J. (2007) *Working with Older People*. London: Routledge.

Taulbee, L. R. and Folsom, J. C. (1966) Reality orientation for geriatric patients. *Hospital & Community Psychiatry* 17: 133–5.

Taylor, B. J. and Donnelly, M. (2006) Professional perspectives in decision-making about the long-term care of older people. *British Journal of Social Work* 36: 807–26.

Taylor, D. and White, S. (2000) *Practising Reflexivity in Health and Welfare: Making Knowledge*. Buckingham: Open University Press.

Thane, P. (2000) *Old Age in English History: Past Experiences, Present Issues*. Oxford: Oxford University Press.

Thompson, N. (1995) *Age and Dignity: Working with Older People*. Aldershot: Arena.

Thompson, N. (1997) *Anti-Discriminatory Practice*. Basingstoke: Macmillan.

Thompson, N. (2005) *Understanding Social Work: Preparing for Practice*, 2nd edn. Basingstoke: Palgrave.

Thompson, N. and Thompson, S. (2001). Empowering older people: Beyond the care model. *Journal of Social Work* 1: 61–76.

Timonen, V., Convery, J. and Cahill, S. (2006) Care revolutions in the making? A comparison of cash-for-care programmes in four countries. *Ageing and Society* 26: 455–74.

TOPSS (2002) *The National Occupational Standards for Social Work*. London: TOPSS.

Tornstam, L. (1996) Gerotranscendence: A theory about maturing in old age. *Journal of Ageing and Identity* 1: 37–50.

Towers, A.-M. (2006) *Control, Well–Being and the Meaning of Home in Care Homes and Extra Care Housing*. PSSRU Research Summary 38. Canterbury: PSSRU.

Townsend, J., Godfrey, M., and Denby, T. (2006) Heroines, villains and victims: Older people's perceptions of others. *Ageing and Society* 26: 883–900.

Townsend, P. (1981) The structured dependency of the elderly: A creation in the twentieth century. *Ageing and Society* 1(1): 5–28.

Townsend, P. (2004) Policies for the aged in the 21st century: More 'structured dependency' or the realisation of human rights? *Ageing and Society* 26, 161–79.

Turnbull, A. (2002) *Opening Doors: The Needs of Older Lesbians and Gay Men. A Literature Review*. London: Age Concern.

Twigg, J. and Atkin, K. (1994) *Carers Perceived: Policy and Practice in Informal Care*. Buckingham: Open University Press.

Van den Berg, F. (2006) A palliative perspective of caring for people with dementia. In B. M. Miesen and G. M. Jones (eds), *Care-Giving in Dementia: Research and Applications*, vol. 4. London: Routledge.

Van Sonderen, E., Ormel, J., Brilman, E. and van Linden van den Heuvell, C. (1990) Personal network delineation: A comparison of the exchange, affective and role relation approach. In C. P. M. Knipscheer and T. C. Antonucci (eds), *Social Network Research: Substantive Issues and Methodological Questions*. Amsterdam: Swets and Zeitlinger.

Victor, C. R. (2005) *The Social Context of Ageing*. London: Routledge.

Vincent, J. (1999) *Politics, Powers and Old Age*. Buckingham: Open University Press.

Wallin, M., Talvitie, U., Cotton, M. and Karppi, S.-L. (2006) The meanings of older people give to their rehabilitation experience. *Ageing and Society* 27: 147–64.

Walsh, C. C., Ploeg, J., Lohfeld, L., Horne, J., Machillan, H. and Lai, D. (2007) Violence across the lifespan: Interconnections among forms of abuse as described by marginalised Canadian elders and their caregivers. *British Journal of Social Work* 37: 491–514.

Wanless, D. (2006) *Securing Good Care for Older People: Taking a Long-Term View*. London: King's Fund.

Ward, A. (2007) *Working in Group Care*, 2nd edn. Bristol: Policy Press.

Ware, T., Matosevic, T., Hardy, B., Knapp, M., Kendall, J. and Forder, J. (2003) Commissioning care services for older people in England: The view from care managers, users and carers. *Age and Society* 23: 422–8.

Warren, R. (1963) *The Community in America*. Chicago: Rand McNally.

Webster, J. D. (1993) Construction and validation of the Reminiscence Functions Scale. *Journal of Gerontology* 48(5): 256–62.

Wenger, G. C. (1984) *The Supportive Network: Coping with Old Age*. London: Allen and Unwin.

Willcocks, D., Peace, S. and Kellaher, L. (1987) *Private Lives in Public Places: A Research-Based Critique of Residential Life in Local Authority Old People's Homes*. London: Routledge.

Williams, J. and Netten, A. (2005) English local authority powers, responsibilities and guidelines for managing the care home closure process. *British Journal of Social Work* 35: 921–36.

Wong, P. T. and Watt, L. M. (1991) What types of reminiscing are associated with successful ageing? *Psychology and Ageing* 6: 272–9.

Woods, B., Portnoy, S., Head, D. and Jones, G. (1992) Reminiscence and life-review with persons with dementia: Which way forward? In B. M. Miesen and G. M. Jones (eds), *Care-Giving in Dementia*. London: Routledge.

Woolhead, K., Calnan, M., Dieppe, P. and Tadd, W. (2004) Dignity in older age: What do older people in the United Kingdom think? *Age and Ageing* 33: 165–70.

Worden, J. W. (2008) *Grief Counseling and Grief Therapy: A Handbook for the Mental Health Practitioner*, 4th edn. New York: Springer.

Young, H., Grundy, E. and Jitlal, M. (2006) *Care Providers, Care Receivers: A Longitudinal Perspective*. York: Joseph Rowntree Foundation.

Young, J. and Stevenson, J. (2006) Intermediate care in England: Where next? *Age and Ageing* 35(4): 339–41.

Index